To Ann + Bernier
Two Who have always
   been a part of my life
You knew me when...
                Love,
                Lisa
                September 1990

Your people, my people

by *Lena Romanoff*
with Lisa Hostein

The Jewish Publication Society
Philadelphia · New York
5750 / 1990

Your people, my people

Finding acceptance and fulfillment as a Jew by choice

For

wherever

you go,

I will go;

wherever

you lodge,

I will lodge;

your people

shall be

my people,

and your God

my God.

(Ruth 1:16)

Library of Congress Cataloging-in-Publication Data

Romanoff, Lena, 1950-
Your people, my people : finding acceptance and fulfillment as a Jew by
choice / by Lena Romanoff with Lisa Hostein.
p.   cm.
Includes bibliographical references.
ISBN 0-8276-0360-6
1. Proselytes and proselyting, Jewish—Converts from Christiantiy.
2. Judaism—20th century. I. Hostein, Lisa. II. Title.
BM729.P7R65   1990
296.7'1—dc20   90-34693
                                                                    CIP

Designed by Adrianne Onderdonk Dudden

The names in this book have been changed, and the identities of the persons
whose stories are told in this work have been fully disguised in order to
protect the confidentiality and sacredness of friendship and of the counseling
relationship.

To my husband, David,
    loving partner in all that I am and do

And to our sons, Harris and Marc,
    who are a joy and a blessing to us.

Contents

Acknowledgments

Creating this book has been a challenging, meaningful, and fulfilling endeavor. It is not a solitary effort but a record of conversations and inspirations received from countless people.

My deepest gratitude is to my husband, David, and our sons, Harris and Marc, for their love and support. They have often provided the first forum of discussion and reflection about many of the ideas and questions surrounding conversion. I missed many Shabbat meals with them because I was a guest speaker elsewhere, but they understood. My appreciative audiences also understood why I urged them to spend Shabbat with their families.

I am especially indebted to Lisa Hostein, who assisted me in writing this book, for her perceptive editorial input, calm assurance, sharp judgment, and valued friendship. I am also grateful to Lisa's husband, Joel Oshtry, for his steadfast support for her work and to her mother, Rollie Hostein, who read this manuscript from the perspective of a Jewish mother; her penchant for detail and accuracy proved invaluable.

To Sheila Segal, my editor, a special kind of tribute is due. For Sheila—always tactful, always professional—exerted an important and beneficial influence upon the ultimate shape of the book. Working with her has been a decidedly educational and deeply gratifying experience. I am also grateful to Chaim Potok, chairman of the Jewish Publication Society's Publication Committee, for his enthusiastic support of this project and his critical reading of the manuscript.

My sincerest appreciation goes to Murray Friedman, director of the Philadelphia chapter of the American Jewish Committee. As a co-chair of the American Jewish Committee's Task Force on Intermarriage, I could always count on his support for my many conferences and workshops on conversion and mixed marriage.

As I review the individuals directly relevant to my life while working on this book, I am overwhelmed with my good fortune.

Rabbi Shalom Novoseller, my teacher, friend, and mentor, was the first to provide me with the opportunity to write for converts in his *Beth Tovim* bulletin, years before this book was even conceived. I am grateful for his confidence.

I am also most appreciative of my two friends who served as typists, Elaine Kravitz and Vincent Small. Their patience and diligence was most important to me.

A special thank you is extended to the following persons who have been helpful in one way or another, perhaps in ways they themselves may not recognize. To those whose work on the subject of intermarriage preceded mine: Paul Cowan of blessed memory, Rachel Cowan, Lydia Kukoff, Julius Lester, Egon Mayer, Rela Monson, and Devorah Wigoder. I hope they feel that this book is a worthwhile addition to their own work.

And to my family and friends who were always there for me: May Bonime, of blessed memory, Rabbi Mark Diamond, Samuel Diamond, Carol Edwards, Rabbi Dov Elkins, Neil and Joanne Hurowitz, Steven Jacobs, Hadassah Linfield, Lorraine Meyer, Patrick and Maria Payne, Helen Romanoff, Hyman Romanoff, of blessed memory, Rabbi Harold Romirowsky, Joseph and Silvana Salerno, Joseph and Nancy Santoleri, Rabbi Mayer Selekman, Robert Seltzer, Rabbi Joshua Toledano, Rabbi Gerald Wolpe, and Robert and Barbara Zimet.

Finally, I owe a special debt to the members of the Jewish Converts Network and the many others I interviewed. They gave of their time, energy, and trust, willingly opening up their lives and hearts to me, revealing their hopes, dreams, and the some-

times painful realities that are part of their lives. I am mindful of
the great privilege they bestowed upon me, and it is what I
learned from them, most of all, that appears in these pages.

L.R.

January 1990

Preface

One day before Thanksgiving I was in the supermarket buying some last-minute items for myself and my 87-year-old neighbor. As I turned the corner aisle I bumped into an acquaintance, the sister of my friend Rena. Rena and I had first met when our children were in the same class at Jewish day school.

Her sister and I were exchanging banal pleasantries, when she suddenly caught sight of the contents of my shopping cart. There, in plain view, was a package of porkchops, clearly labelled, two boxes of shiny silver tree tinsel, and a huge red box of Christmas cards. *Ho, ho, ho!* What was not clearly visible among the fruits and vegetables were my frozen Empire turkey, the frozen potato blintzes, and the Kosher corned beef that had been sliced on a separate slicer!

Rena's sister was clearly horrified, lost her composure, and blurted out, "Well, I'll make sure my sister doesn't send her son to your house anymore. Imagine—*tref* food! I've always had my doubts about converts." She turned away quickly and disappeared down a crowded aisle.

Ten years ago I would have run after her with my explanation, but not today. My response was little more than a deep sigh and another look at my neighbor's shopping list. I had forgotten the applesauce for the porkchops.

My supermarket experience would certainly leave many converts disheartened, if not devastated. It is a sad fact that incidents like this sometimes have to be faced by converts—even when, like me, they have been Jewish longer than they have known Christianity.

It is no wonder that there have been two consistent threads running through all of my interviews with converts: one, their desire to be accepted as "real Jews" and, two, their search for guidance on how to turn that hope into reality.

Twenty years ago, when I became a Jew, there was very little information on conversion. Conversions were handled as quietly as possible. Socially, intermarriage was considered a gross offense, and it was vehemently discouraged. However, if the impending union could not be stopped, then conversion was coerced as a last resort, with skepticism and misgivings on the part of the Jewish parents. Christian parents felt left out and their beliefs negated. The convert made the decision to convert with few resources other than academic information provided by books. There were no support groups and few, if any, role models; the likelihood of meeting other converts was small because conversion was such a shrouded affair. Community workshops, newsletters, and conferences on intermarriage and conversion, all commonplace today, were unthinkable at the time of my conversion.

My personal journey to Judaism probably began when I was five years old and was nearly expelled from Catholic catechism classes. "A bright girl," the nuns would tell my mother, "but does she have to ask so many questions? She makes it so difficult for us to get on with our teaching." It was more than the nuns could handle. Even at that young age, I felt that Catholicism did not belong to me, nor I to it. By the age of twelve I knew I did not want to be Catholic. I also knew that I believed in God and had a need for religion in my life. However, as a twelve-year-old child, I did not know that one could convert or change one's faith. Every night I prayed to God, confident that he could hear me without a priest as an intermediary.

Many years later, after a long and arduous quest for a religion I could embrace, I found that Judaism spoke to me. I remember many revelatory moments, but one of the most outstanding was when I discovered—to my great surprise and delight—that Judaism not only permits questions, it sometimes even requires them. It happened during a study session with my rabbi, a pious and solemn soul. I was answering question after question that he posed to me, as I had done each week for nearly a year. Suddenly he posed a problem to which I could not respond.

"Don't you know the answer?" he asked.

"I know the answer," I finally replied, "but I do not agree with it."

This ever stern rabbi underwent a total transformation. Elated, he rose from his desk and, with his eyes shining and his voice booming, banged his fist upon the table. "Baruch Hashem!" he shouted. "Bless the Lord! You are finally thinking like a Jew!" The text that day was Maimonides, but the lesson had nothing to do with Jewish law or philosophy. That day I learned that an educated Jew does more than answer questions; questioning the answers can be just as important. If I'd had any doubts before, I knew then that Judaism was mine. I was ready to cast my lot with the Jewish people.

Twenty years later, my inquisitiveness persists, and many of my questions of today still revolve around conversion, albeit with a different twist. After years of working with converts, including the founding of a nationwide network of support groups known as the Jewish Converts Network, I believe that it is time to question the answers given and assumptions still commonly held regarding the estimated 10,000 people a year who choose to become Jews.

In the wide-open marketplace of ideas in which we live, where choices of lifestyle, identification, and affiliation abound, every Jew who embraces Judaism is a Jew by choice: For the first time in Jewish history, Jews have the freedom not to identify as Jews.

The tide of intermarriage, certainly not a new phenomenon, is growing stronger and potentially more threatening to the Jewish community than ever before. At least one out of every three Jews chooses a non-Jew as a lifetime partner. There are an estimated 350,000 intermarried couples in America. In less than one half of these marriages, the non-Jewish spouse has converted to Judaism, sometimes out of coercion but more often out of a commitment to share all aspects of life with a partner. Nearly one third of these conversions occur after marriage, often prior to the birth of children, precipitated by a desire for family cohesiveness.

There is also the more curious phenomenon of the hundreds of Americans each year who choose Judaism not as an act of love or for the sake of marriage but, rather, because of a personal conviction that Judaism provides the most meaningful way of life. From a convicted felon in California who was deeply inspired by a Jewish friend while serving time in prison to a prominent Massachusetts academician who discovered that no degree of professional achievement could fill the spiritual vacuum gnawing at his life, the people who choose Judaism represent a myriad of lifestyles and defy simple categorization.

This book is a response to the overwhelming number of inquiries I receive from converts and their families, from rabbis and other Jewish community professionals, and from scores of other concerned Jews who seek a straightforward, pluralistic approach to the multitude of issues surrounding conversion—from developing self-confidence as a Jew, to interacting with Jewish and non-Jewish family, to finding acceptance within the broader Jewish community.

An exploration of conversion is as essential for the Jewish community as it is for converts and potential converts. Their relationship is, ideally, symbiotic: Without acceptance by the community, Jews by choice can never fully feel a part of the Jewish people, nor can the community benefit from their energy and commitment. By not welcoming converts, especially as their numbers increase dramatically, the community is not only causing pain to individuals and their children but is also rejecting a potential source of strength and commitment, a voice of the Jewish future.

We often hear the lament that we are losing our Jewish children to intermarriage. The flip side of this valid concern is to consider whom we might be gaining when non-Jewish partners consider and often embrace Judaism. Only with an understanding of the questions, the conflicts, and the emotional struggles of converts can born Jews even begin to appreciate the conversion experience. With that knowledge and sensitivity, a greater penchant for acceptance will, hopefully, follow.

If the Jewish community chooses to be unwelcoming or despairing, it will be turning its head toward the past. I am pleading for the future. If converts are courageous enough to seek out Judaism and become a part of the Jewish people, then born Jews must be courageous enough to meet the challenge and welcome them in.

Your people, my people

1

Considering a new identity

Some Jews might find it surprising that a man with the good Irish name of Tom McHale serves as president of a large, thriving Conservative synagogue in Washington, D.C. But members of his congregation do not. In fact, they find it hard to believe that just five years ago, Tom, then a potential convert, was so frustrated and discouraged that he nearly gave up his quest to become Jewish. If not for his persistence, they might never have known the dedication and commitment that this Harvard Medical School graduate and former Irish Catholic brings to their community.

Tom left the Church behind when he left his parents' home. During his early adult years, he concentrated on pursuing a medical career. Religion—or lack of it—was not a matter of priority for him, yet his increasing contact with Jewish students made him begin to wonder what it was about Judaism that inspired so much loyalty and pride among many of his friends. "I envied them when the Jewish holidays came around. They really looked forward to going home for Passover and Rosh Hashannah. I guess they detected my envy, because I was often invited along. I liked what I experienced."

The more he experienced, the more Tom felt that Judaism could fill a spiritual and cultural void in his life. Eventually, Tom decided that he wanted to become Jewish, but he had no idea how to proceed. "Here I was, a smart Harvard student, but I didn't have the slightest idea how to go about converting to Judaism. My Jewish friends, who were both amused and stupefied by my decision, were unable to help me—they had never even given the issue of conversion any thought."

Tom turned to books but quickly became confused by the conflicting information he found. He knew there were different branches of Judaism, but he needed clarification and explanations about what the differences meant. He consulted the phone book for the names of rabbis. The first two he called were Orthodox and told him they did not perform conversions. Tom did not mention to them that he was seeking to convert out of personal conviction. In retrospect, he says, "They may have been more receptive if I had told them I was not seeking to convert for the sake of marriage. But I didn't think of it at the time, and they didn't ask me my reasons. Their coldness and abruptness did not invite further dialogue. How was I to know?"

Tom next called a Conservative rabbi, who told him he was leaving for Israel the next day and would get back to him in six weeks. He never did. Two Reform rabbis agreed to speak to Tom. One told him he did not have to convert in order to join a synagogue; the other referred him to a sixteen-week course held in another town. He contacted a few more Conservative rabbis, all of whom said they did not have time to provide instruction.

By this time Tom was feeling weary and unwelcome. It seemed that his only realistic option was to enroll in the Reform course in the next town. The class was a disappointment. Tom felt frustrated by both the attitude of the other students—most of whom were there primarily for the sake of marriage—and by the student rabbi who taught the course. "She seemed more interested in obtaining data from us for her dissertation than she did in teaching us basic Judaism."

Despite his reservations about Reform Judaism, Tom went ahead with the conversion, confident that once he was Jewish he would find his proper niche.

He was in for a shock. After moving to New York City and shopping extensively for a synagogue, Tom found a Conservative congregation where he felt stimulated and comfortable, but the rabbi did not consider him a Jew because his conversion had not

Tom felt cheated and confused. Why had he not been informed that this might happen? How was he supposed to have known what to do if he had not even known what to ask? Luckily, the Conservative rabbi provided some reasonable and sensitive explanations and told Tom that he would arrange for these rituals to be performed after some further private instruction. For the first time, Tom felt that he understood the differences and similarities among the various branches of Judaism. In the process, Tom was also able to clarify his own inclination, leading him to the conclusion that Conservative Judaism best met his personal needs.

A few years later Tom moved back to Washington and, ironically, joined the synagogue whose former rabbi was one of those who did not have the time to help him convert. That rabbi had been replaced by a warm, welcoming individual. After a few years, expending tremendous amounts of time and energy working for the community, Tom was elected president of his synagogue.

Tom's story, like each convert's story, is unique, filled with its own special twists. But Tom's conversion experience is also woven with a thread common to many stories of conversion—the thread of confusion. For serious converts, a seemingly endless stream of questions keep popping up from the moment the idea of conversion emerges, throughout the entire conversion process, and for years beyond.

This chapter attempts to unravel that thread so that future converts to Judaism can avoid some of the unexpected knots and loops that characterized Tom's conversion and many others like his.

GETTING THE BASICS

- What does the conversion process entail?
- What are the options for preparing to convert?

• Under which branch of Judaism should I convert?

• Where do I begin?

It is not surprising that anyone who is considering conversion to Judaism would start off with these basic questions. Yet finding the answers can often be frustrating for the prospective convert.

Jewish tradition regarding conversion is actually straightforward. According to the Talmud, conversion to Judaism entails three things:

• *Kabbalat mitzvot*—acceptance of the Torah's commandments.

• *Brit milah*—circumcision (for men only, naturally), the physical sign of acceptance of the Covenant of Abraham. (If a man has already been circumcised, a drop of blood is drawn from the penis, a process known as *hatafat dam brit*.)

• *Tevilah*—immersion in the *mikvah*, a pool of water designated for ritual purification.

Many Jews, however, do not accept traditional Jewish law as their ultimate religious authority. Others accept the law in principle but interpret it in ways that differ from the strict tradition. Thus, conversions performed by some non-Orthodox rabbis may not require all of these traditional elements.

Prospective converts with Jewish partners can try to seek information from them, but many Jews are not familiar with the ins and outs of conversion either. So the couple asks their friends or parents, and the parents often turn to their rabbis for answers. If they consult a rabbi who is sensitive and positive about conversion, there is little problem and the process can begin smoothly. Unfortunately, many rabbis are unresponsive or even discouraging. Whereas some potential converts, like Tom, persist despite initial discouragement and obstacles, others find it difficult to look beyond what is perceived as initial rejection and their motivation to convert is diminished.

However, a prospective convert should know that, traditionally, a rabbi is required to turn down a conversion request three times to determine if the petition is sincere. Since many rabbis still abide by that tradition, it is possible that what is interpreted as rejection is in fact the rabbi's desire to make a serious, responsible evaluation.

My own experience in approaching a rabbi about conversion provides a case in point. I was full of confidence the day I entered the rabbi's office and brazenly stated, "Rabbi, I know all about Judaism, and I want to become Jewish."

The rabbi stood up and responded in a booming voice, "You have the audacity to stand before me and claim you know all about Judaism. My father and his father before him of blessed memory were rabbis, and they did not profess to know everything about Judaism. How dare you be so foolish!"

My confidence was shattered, but I managed to calmly persist. "Rabbi, I want to convert." I was thunderstruck by the answer. It was a loud, emphatic "No! I do not do conversions." I was pained. I ached to be Jewish. My Italian bravado gave way to Jewish chutzpah, and I persisted once more. "Rabbi, can we study together?" I held my breath. The black-garbed, fully bearded rabbi answered in a kind voice. "Be here at four o'clock next Tuesday," he said, with a slight warning: "And don't come into this synagogue dressed like that again." It was a hot July day, and I was wearing a bright red, sleeveless dress. What did I know?

In advising people who are beginning a search for information about conversion courses and programs, I usually suggest they call the local Board of Rabbis. The Jewish Federation, Jewish Family Service, Jewish student groups at local colleges and universities, and other Jewish communal organizations may also be helpful. In large cities, the options usually are more varied and the information more readily accessible. In small towns, only a few rabbis, or perhaps only one, may perform conversions, usually following a personalized learning program.

There is, of course, always the telephone directory with listings of individual synagogues and rabbis. Let Tom's experience serve as a reminder that sometimes it is necessary to call more than one. Patience and persistence usually pay off. However, if local numbers fail to provide the information needed, one should write to the central headquarters of each branch of Judaism to find out what's available in that community. (See the list provided at the end of this book.)

Once the potential convert has identified the available options, the next step is to evaluate each one and to make the choice that seems to fit best. Many questions immediately arise, especially for those who live in areas where there are several options: Is a private course with an individual rabbi better than a classroom setting with other students? What are the differences between Reform, Conservative, Reconstructionist, and Orthodox conversions? Why do some courses cost as much as $300, whereas others are free? Why do some programs last eighteen weeks, others last one year, and still others require just a few lessons over one week's time?

PRIVATE INSTRUCTION OR GROUP LESSONS?

Although certain standards and guidelines govern conversion within each branch of Judaism (see subsequent discussion and Appendix), some flexibility is allowed individual rabbis, the result often being a variety of options available. From the convert's perspective, these options can appear confusing. But a thorough investigation can lead to participation in a conversion program best suited to each individual personality and situation and, it is hoped, to a more meaningful experience.

For instance, a medical student with erratic hours might find private lessons with a rabbi more manageable than a group course. Likewise, a religious studies major, or anyone familiar with the basic teachings of Judaism, might find it more satisfying to learn with an individual rabbi. The rabbi in the one-to-one situation is better able to evaluate the level of Jewish knowledge and tailor the lessons to the individual.

Some potential converts, however, may feel intimidated by

the prospect of such a close relationship with a rabbi. They also may prefer a class situation in which they have the opportunity to meet other prospective converts. For couples, a conversion class provides an opportunity not only for converts to find each other but also for their Jewish partners to share feelings and ideas.

One drawback of a class setting is that the rabbi or instructor must try to meet the different needs of a variety of students—singles and couples of all ages, persons in first and second marriages, those converting out of conviction and those for the sake of marriage—all of whom come with different levels of knowledge and familiarity with Jewish terms and customs.

Imagine Joseph Mason, a 27-year-old journalist from Boston who grew up in a Jewish neighborhood and celebrated Jewish holidays with Jewish friends, in the same conversion course as Melissa Kimberly, a 21-year-old court stenographer from Tennessee whose fiancé was the first Jew she ever met; each would bring very different questions and concerns to the group. To some, such diversity would be viewed as exciting; to others it could be very frustrating.

Whatever one's perspective, the conversion class does tend to be the most common approach, particularly in large cities. Some rabbis believe that courses filled with diverse students can be more beneficial for everyone involved. One rabbi, who has taught converts at the University of Judaism in Los Angeles, remarked, "I prefer classes of students from many religious, cultural, and ethnic backgrounds. They tend to be livelier and more tolerant of each other's differences. They also tend to be more compassionate and empathetic toward each other's needs."

Sometimes, after beginning a course, a convert discovers that it is not meeting his or her particular needs. If that happens, it is best to seek another option without hesitation or delay. Mark Finkelstein, son of an Orthodox rabbi in Chicago, and his fiancée, Sherry, found their initial course choice to be a mistake when all of the attention seemed to be focusing on Mark rather than on Sherry and the other converts in the class. "How can such a thing happen to the son of a rabbi?" the others asked repeatedly. "Is your father angry and upset? How is the community responding?"

With each expression of fascination at Mark's impending intermarriage, Mark and Sherry felt increasingly frustrated in their attempt to explore Judaism together. "I'm sure that no ill will was intended, but we were tired of hearing, 'Even rabbis' children intermarry,'" recalls Mark. After a few weeks, the couple transferred to another program in the next county, where their family ties were not recognized, and both Mark and Sherry found much greater satisfaction.

For completely different reasons, the program in which Geoffrey Windhammer enrolled did not work out either. Geoffrey, a 34-year-old theology major from Montreal, moved to Philadelphia to pursue his studies and to begin the process of becoming Jewish. It took just one session of a Conservative-sponsored conversion class for him to see that he was much more academically advanced than the others and that the course seemed to be designed especially for couples.

"I realized immediately, as an older, single male that a basic conversion course would not meet my personal needs," Geoffrey explains. Instead, he made arrangements with a local Conservative rabbi to receive private instruction.

WHICH BRANCH OF JUDAISM?

Few issues epitomize the tensions among the different branches of Judaism as much as conversion. The question, commonly known as "Who is a Jew?" swirls beneath the surface of every debate among the branches like the lava of a volcano waiting to erupt. That eruption often occurs when the topic of conversion arises.

Traditional Judaism holds that a Jew is anyone born to a Jewish mother or converted to Judaism in a halakhic manner. Complicating this seemingly simple formula are two relatively modern phenomena: (1) changes in the conversion process itself as performed by some rabbis and (2) recognition by the Reform and Reconstructionist movements of "patrilineal descent," which considers as Jewish anyone who is born of a Jewish parent (mother or father) and raised as a Jew.

Although each branch maintains its own official policies regarding conversion and recognition of conversions performed by other branches, rabbis have considerable leeway to adjust the official stance to fit individual circumstances. Interviews with thousands of converts around the country indicate that there is in fact more flexibility within all the branches than is readily discernible at first glance. There are even extreme situations such as the one in which a rebellious son, trying to strike back at a mother who disapproved of his impending intermarriage, arranged for his fiancée to complete an Orthodox conversion in Boro Park, New York, in a matter of days for $700. This is mentioned only to warn converts of certain pitfalls and unethical behavior that can be encountered. Such stories, however, are clearly the exception rather than the rule.

The Reform Approach

Reform Judaism takes a liberal approach to Jewish law, maintaining that it is no longer binding but must be changed or developed to meet the needs of the modern Jew. Rooted in an ethical approach, the practices associated with the Reform movement vary from place to place depending on the particular rabbi and synagogue. Many traditional observances and rituals were eliminated or modified in keeping with Reform philosophy. In recent years, however, some Reform Jews have attempted to bring back certain rituals and traditions in a number of areas.

Given the liberal nature of the Reform movement, it is not surprising that the movement has taken a liberal approach to conversion. This branch of Judaism was the first to institute an outreach program for people considering conversion. Although the movement strongly encourages conversion of a non-Jewish spouse, its synagogues do accept as full members those non-Jews who have not undergone formal conversion but agree to maintain a Jewish home and provide their children with a Jewish education. Reform conversion programs are usually called "Introduction to Judaism" classes. Jewish partners are encouraged to participate along with the potential convert. The course of study usually lasts about eighteen weeks.

Completion of this course does not obligate conversion. In fact, I often urge non-Jews who have Jewish mates but feel they cannot convert, or are not ready to convert, to take this course as a first step toward understanding the ethnic and religious background of their Jewish partners. Since it is not billed as a conversion class per se, the enrollment often includes some born Jews who are taking the class purely for self-edification.

As for the conversion itself, the individual rabbi must decide whether the *mikvah* (for men and women) and the *brit milah* (for men) will be required, strongly encouraged, or presented as optional. A convert who has undergone a Reform conversion will be welcome as a member in any Reform or Reconstructionist congregation, but perhaps not in an Orthodox or a Conservative one. However, religious services in all synagogues are open to anyone who wishes to attend.

The Reform policy of admitting non-Jews to synagogue membership has been widely criticized, even within the Reform movement itself. Critics believe that acceptance without conversion diminishes the individual's motivation to convert. Why bother if they can enjoy the same status as the born Jews in their synagogue? This argument is compounded by the Reform movement's controversial decision on patrilineal descent, which negates the traditional rule that only a child born of a Jewish mother is considered Jewish. In the past, the desire to have Jewish children may have motivated many women to convert. Now that their children can be considered Jewish anyway, they themselves may be less likely to ever decide to convert.

Others respond to the criticism with the argument that lack of pressure to convert, combined with a warm welcome and the opportunity to become familiar with Judaism at a slower pace, leads to more and better committed converts. Those who have

worked closely in programming for Reform converts report this
to be the case.

The Conservative Approach

Conservative Judaism, sometimes described as a middle
ground between Reform and Orthodox Judaism, accepts the authority of the Written and Oral Law of the Torah and the Talmud
and believes that adherence to these laws strengthens the Jewish
community both socially and spiritually. But the movement also
maintains that modern-day realities necessitate certain modifica-
tion in the laws, as long as the decisions are made by authorized
scholars and rabbis and supported by halakhic arguments.
Among the changes over the years have been granting equal
status to women as members of a minyan and in the practice of
rituals; permitting Jews to drive a car on the Sabbath or holidays
in order to attend services; allowing men and women to sit together in synagogue; and altering the text of the prayerbook.

Non-Jews are not accepted as members of Conservative synagogues, nor are the children of non-Jewish mothers considered
Jewish. Although Conservative rabbis understand that the majority of their converts choose Judaism for the sake of marriage
rather than out of deep personal conviction, they maintain that
Conservative converts emerge from the conversion process with
a basic understanding of Judaism and usually go on to become
sincere Jews.

The Conservative movement requires a specific course of
study for the prospective convert, usually about eighteen weeks,
conducted in a private or classroom setting. If a Jewish mate is
involved, he or she is expected to attend the course as well. The
conversion requires *mikvah* for men and women, and *brit milah*
for men, or *hatafat dam brit* for men already circumcised. The
convert-to-be then appears before a *beth din* (a tribunal of three
rabbis—in this case, Conservative rabbis), whose members ask
questions to determine the emotional, spiritual, and academic
readiness of the potential convert.

As we saw in Tom's case, some Conservative rabbis do not

accept conversions performed by Reform rabbis if the *mikvah* or *brit milah* was not required or if a certain level of Jewish knowledge was not attained. This can also become significant if a couple wants to be married by a Conservative rabbi, but the non-Jewish partner was converted by a Reform rabbi who did not require the traditional rituals. In such cases, the Conservative rabbi may accept the conversion if the convert completes the rituals that were omitted. In some instances, Conservative rabbis have not recognized conversions done under Orthodox auspices because the rabbis believed the convert failed to attain a sufficient level of Jewish knowledge. The fact is that there are few absolutes in determining what is acceptable and what isn't. Much depends on the rabbi, the convert, and the individual situation.

Reconstructionist Guidelines

The Reconstructionist movement, Judaism's smallest and newest branch, defines Judaism as an evolving religious civilization whose essential unity derives from its peoplehood, not from its laws and theology. Founded by Rabbi Mordecai Kaplan, who was a professor at the Conservative movement's Jewish Theological Seminary before he established the Reconstructionist Rabbinical College, Reconstructionism holds that traditional laws guiding practice and rituals should be observed but are not binding.

Reconstructionist rabbis report a certain degree of flexibility in performing conversions and in accepting conversions by rabbis from other branches of Judaism. For the most part, Reconstructionist synagogues accept non-Jews as members if they are committed to Jewish living and to raising their children as Jews. In most congregations, the non-Jew can have voting privileges, but some rabbis do not permit a non-Jew to be called for an *aliyah* to the Torah.

With regard to conversion, the official movement policy requires a course of study—often conducted on an individual basis because of the movement's small size—as well as a *beth din*, *mikvah*, and *hatafat dam brit*. In actuality, however, many Recon-

structionist converts I counsel do not undergo all of the requirements. Some say that the *mikvah* was an option, and others say
there was no *beth din* present.

The majority of Reconstructionist synagogues and rabbis recognize and accept conversions performed by rabbis outside of
their own movement. Likewise, Reform and Conservative rabbis
generally accept Reconstructionist conversions, although there
have been cases in which Conservative rabbis did not accept
them as valid.

Orthodox Policy

Orthodox Jews, believing that the Torah was given by God,
maintain strict adherence to the laws of the Torah as they were
interpreted by the rabbis in the Talmud and in other works of
Jewish law. Both Written and Oral Law are immutable in the
Orthodox view. Many Orthodox Jews strongly oppose the practices of all other branches of Judaism, viewing them as violations
of the Torah that God revealed to the Jewish people.

Under Orthodox Judaism, the only acceptable reason for a
person to convert is personal conviction. The vast majority of
those who seek Orthodox conversions are serious people who
genuinely want to commit themselves to a traditional Jewish life.
Conversion simply for the sake of marriage is, at least according
to official policy, neither condoned nor permitted among the Orthodox. The Orthodox movement does not provide courses that
are designed, much less advertised, as leading to conversion. To
do so would be seen as condoning the existence of the kind of
interfaith relationships that are unacceptable in the Orthodox
community. But in some communities one may find, through
word of mouth, one or two rabbis who will conduct small organized classes for prospective converts or provide individual instruction.

The Orthodox conversion process always requires *mikvah*
and *brit milah* or *hatafat dam brit*. Acceptance of all the applicable mitzvot, the commandments of Jewish law, is expected.

The *beth din* must consist of three Orthodox legal authorities, usu- ally rabbis. However, a few converts have told me that they ob- tained their Orthodox conversions under less than ideal circum- stances, having undergone what they considered to be quick and superficial conversions that seemed to them little more than for- malities. Others, who converted for less than ideal motives— such as to appease family members or to be accepted as Jews in Israel—later confessed to me that they felt compelled to tell the rabbis what they wanted to hear regarding their intentions to practice traditional Judaism rather than to be honest about the less-than-traditional life-style that they felt they could more real- istically commit to.

Although it might be expected that Orthodox rabbis are more stringent and scrupulous than rabbis of other branches in their screening of converts, they often tend to appear more leni- ent, believing that what the convert does or does not do is be- tween the convert and God. As one Orthodox rabbi who super- vises conversions put it, "It is not for the rabbi to delve into the heart to determine if the convert is sincere. I must accept what he is telling me. The rest is between him and God."

Orthodox Jews do not accept or recognize conversions per- formed under the auspices of any other branch of Judaism, even if the traditional rituals were performed.

WHY ALL THE DIFFERENCES?

With regard to intermarriage and conversion—inevitable outgrowths of an increasingly open society—the various branches have each developed their own approaches to grappling with these issues, sometimes using their own arguments to dele- gitimize the other branches. From the Orthodox perspective, the more liberal movements of Judaism are not only violating basic Jewish law but also threatening the very existence of the Jewish community when they reach out to non-Jewish partners in inter- marriages, when they perform mixed marriages (something that all branches officially discourage but a minority of Reform and Reconstructionist rabbis do), when they perform conversions without satisfying the traditional requirements, when they pass edicts recognizing the children of non-Jews as Jews (the result of patrilineal descent discussed earlier), when they permit second marriages without a *get* (religious divorce), or when they ordain women as rabbis. The Orthodox accuse the liberal movements of catering to the needs of their constituents, thereby encouraging intermarriage and sacrificing religious authenticity.

The non-Orthodox, on the other hand, walk a tightrope. Although they do not want to encourage intermarriage, they also do not want to alienate young Jews, who, with or without approval from their rabbis or parents, are increasingly likely to become involved in intermarriages. Nor do they wish to alienate the non-Jewish spouses, who are seen as prospective converts. With some discrepancy even within each movement, the Reform, Conservative, and Reconstructionist response to Orthodoxy is premised on the underlying assertion that halakhah itself has evolved over many centuries and that even in the Talmud the rabbis disagreed on issues of conversion and intermarriage, as they did on most issues. The non-Orthodox firmly believe not only that it is unrealistic to expect traditional standards to be the sole basis for Jewish unity in modern society, but also that to take such an unaccommodating stance is certain to increase alienation and further assimilation among the majority of American Jews.

Yet, despite these significant differences, the proponents of the various movements do share some common bonds. Among these are a common history and identity, mutual support of many Jewish causes, and overlapping affiliation in various Jewish organizations. They all employ Hebrew in their worship services and share many common prayers and songs. They advocate Jewish education and affirm their belief in one God and God's covenant with the Jewish people.

Attempts have already been made and, it is hoped, will continue to be made to institute a standard of conversion that rabbis from all the branches of Judaism will be able to accept. With varying degrees of success, some cities have established programs in which the *beth din* is composed of rabbis representing the different branches. Although the attempt to have Orthodox participation has not yet been successful, many still see this as a desirable, even a viable, goal.

MAKING THE CHOICE

Imagine the bewilderment of a potential convert who, for any number of reasons, is considering casting his or her lot with the Jewish people but has no idea that the people are divided into at least four different groups! For the prospective convert, deciding under which branch to convert can be perplexing. When someone comes to me and says, with tremendous enthusiasm and confidence, "I want to become Jewish!" I often find it difficult, albeit necessary, to ask, "What kind of Jew do you want to be—Reform, Reconstructionist, Conservative, or Orthodox?" More often than not, the response is one puzzled, "Huh?" For the person who wants to convert out of conviction, there is usually some prior understanding about Judaism in general and perhaps even an affinity for a particular branch. But most prospective converts tell me that they want "just to be Jewish" in the ideal sense that they have been reading and learning about.

For the prospective convert involved in a relationship with a Jew, chances are that the only Judaism he or she has encountered is the type practiced by the partner and/or the partner's family. It usually, but not always, makes sense for this person, especially if he or she is seeking conversion prior to marriage, to convert under the auspices of the partner's movement. At the same time, I often encourage these people, once they have converted, to explore other synagogues and communities—with or without their partners—to familiarize themselves with the diversities in Jewish living and to ultimately choose the combination that feels right to them. That advice applies to single converts as well. (For more on finding a comfortable community, see Chapter 7.)

Sometimes selecting the movement under which to convert

can be a source of conflict between mates or between the prospective convert and his or her in-laws-to-be. Brenda Allan, a 28-year-old nursing supervisor in New York City, encountered such a problem when, after thoroughly exploring her options, she decided on a Conservative conversion. Her future in-laws, however, pushed for a Reform conversion because, she says, "They didn't want me to become too religious." For the sake of family harmony, Brenda relented and had a Reform conversion. One year later, however, she also had a Conservative conversion. "I finally realized that it was my decision, not my in-laws'," she says. "I chose to be a Conservative Jew even though my husband and his family are Reform."

Martin Fitzwater also chose the conversion course that his future in-laws lobbied for in order to avoid a conflict with his fiancée's family. "My in-laws, who were very concerned about what their relatives and friends might think, insisted I have an Orthodox conversion," says Martin, a 33-year-old CPA from St. Louis. Martin, like Brenda, relented but found the whole experience very distasteful. "The truth is that it was all a sham, and I was not courageous enough to be honest with myself and the rabbi. I have a piece of paper that says I had an Orthodox conversion, but my thinking and practices are actually best described by Reconstructionism. I urge others to follow their minds and hearts."

For Margaret Morrison, a 27-year-old dancer from Maryland, the conflict over conversion courses was with her fiancé, not his parents. Margaret met her Israeli fiancé, Yehuda, at a concert in Greenwich Village. After living together for four years, they decided to accept a job offer in Israel for a year. Once back in the United States, they decided to get married and return to Israel. Yehuda told Margaret she had to convert; otherwise she and their future children would not be accepted in Israel as Jews.

"When Yehuda insisted I have an Orthodox conversion so that we and our children would be fully accepted in Israel, I was shocked. Yehuda was an ardent Zionist, yet anything but a religious Jew. My only perceptions of the Orthodox came from my experiences in Israel, where I found them to be extremist in their positions, the antithesis of what Yehuda and I believed. Despite her misgivings and her resentment of Yehuda for his insistence, Margaret went ahead with the conversion. "Here I was, promising to keep a kosher home, while on the way home from my conversion sessions we would stop off to eat a cheesesteak and milkshake. Yehuda joined me without the slightest hesitation. I began to deeply resent the system that forced me to be dishonest in order to be able to go to Israel as a Jew." (For more about Israel and converts, see Chapter 9.)

As this chapter indicates, a person contemplating conversion has a tremendous number of issues to consider. Although that first step—deciding and proclaiming "I want to be Jewish!"—is both an important and a thrilling one, it must also be recognized as just that—the first of many significant decisions that must be made. The selection of the conversion course, the rabbi, and the branch of Judaism should be given careful consideration. Although it can be helpful to discuss questions with a friend, rabbi, spouse, or future in-laws, ultimately the decision should rest with the prospective convert, and no one else. My plea to prospective converts is the following: If you feel uncomfortable, pressured, or confused—stop! You may need more time for introspection. Conversion is too monumental a decision to be made under pressures of time, or even of love.

2

The emotional stages

When Rita Frank came to see me for the first time, she was five weeks into her conversion course and couldn't understand what was happening to her. "I have never taken anything seriously in my life," she told me. "I didn't even take the decision to convert seriously. I was only appeasing my fiancé's grandparents. I thought it would be fun to do something drastic. I even chuckled in anticipation of people seeing me, a blue-eyed blond, and saying, 'But you don't look Jewish!'

"Then I began my conversion class, and I was astounded at my own feelings. I don't understand where they are coming from. I suddenly began to think of my own Polish heritage and the Catholic religion I was born into but never explored. I became obsessed with the seriousness of my decision, what it would mean for me and my family. Am I the only one feeling this way?"

To Rita and the hundreds like her who wonder whether they are alone in experiencing a myriad of emotions—excitement and anxiety, guilt and loneliness, joy and sorrow—I can say without hesitation: you are not alone.

Once the initial decision to convert is made and the most suitable program chosen, converts-to-be often experience a sense of relief, a readiness to put the past behind them and devote themselves exclusively to becoming Jewish. But for some that relief may be short-lived once the learning process begins. Many are often unprepared for the depths of feeling, the internal conflicts that can emerge once the door to Judaism is opened. No two converts are alike. Each convert has his or her own personal story, an individual path that has led to this momentous undertaking. It is nearly impossible to predict how any one individual will respond at the initial port of entry—the conversion process itself. Yet from my experience in counseling hundreds of people involved in the conversion process from all over the country, I have noticed the emergence of a certain pattern of feelings that often accompanies this first big step. By recognizing these feelings as common to many converts, by grappling with them instead of suppressing them, each convert will, it is hoped, find it easier to develop an individual Jewish identity.

INTROSPECTION

Some converts explode with questions as the conversion proceeds: "Who am I? Where did I come from? Where am I going?" These existential issues tend to take on tremendous significance at times when transition forces an acute reevaluation of past beliefs and future goals. Beverly Grist, a 24-year-old nurse from Lincoln, Nebraska, wrote to me to share her feelings of wonder:

"I had never thought about my ethnic background until my Jewish spouse told me about his relatives from Russia who were forced to flee the pogroms. There is tremendous pride and a real sense of history in his family. When I began to explore Judaism, I realized that I was quite ignorant about my own family background. I discussed my heritage with my parents for the first time, and now I know I will be a Jew with English and Scottish ancestors. My spouse says I will be a WASP Jew. Only when I could feel good about who I am and what my family is was I able to feel proud about becoming Jewish."

Some prospective converts spend a great deal of time pondering their past, others very little. There are even times when deep introspection leads people to reverse their decision to convert. Roger Hamstead, a 39-year-old production manager at an auto parts company, is one such person who thought he was committed to converting to Judaism after marrying his Jewish wife and raising his young children as Jews. But after completing his conversion course, Roger felt he was unable to go through with it.

"I kept thinking about my parents, both of whom are dead. My father was a Methodist minister, like his father before him. Religion was a strong force in our household, but I continually longed for a richer tradition. I explored Judaism when I decided that Christ did not fit into my life. I thought that marrying a Jewish woman and raising Jewish children would give me the additional impetus to convert. But I realized that I couldn't go through with it at this time. It still troubles me. I know that my children are Jews according to halakhah, but there's still something missing that troubles me."

Roger is not alone in his struggle to reconcile conflicting emotions that often emerge only after one is fully engaged in a conversion program. I usually urge anyone who harbors such doubts to consider continuing with the instruction—whether class or private—and leave the ultimate decision of whether or not to convert until much later. At the very least, the instruction will provide a basic knowledge of Judaism, which will always be helpful, especially in a mixed marriage. More often than not, those with initial reservations do go on to convert because they find Judaism so meaningful. A small number are deterred by the realization that the conversion would be halfhearted and insincere. These people should be commended for abiding by their convictions. As one such woman once commented, "It is difficult enough deciding whether to continue on the course to becoming Jewish, but it would be even more difficult for me to live with my decision if it's not the right one."

INTELLECTUALIZATION

Concurrent with this internal exploration comes the intense process of learning what Judaism is all about. The history of the

Jewish people spans some four thousand years during which they have developed a rich religious and cultural heritage. An encapsulated view of this remarkable history, along with an introduction to Jewish holidays, laws, and customs, is among the subjects addressed in conversion courses.

For some, learning about Judaism requires a simultaneous unlearning of myths and misconceptions gathered over the years. Some of the misguided notions people have about Jews are pathetic; others are downright humorous.

Mabel Davis, a 23-year-old teacher from Iowa, recalls what she knew about Judaism as a child: "In the small town where I grew up, there was only one grocery store. The grocer sold two kinds of pickles—one sweet and the other kind we called 'Jewish.' Someone had tasted them and found they were sour, so we concluded that 'kosher' on the label was a spice. Did I have a lot to learn!"

Herbert Grover, a machinist from Kentucky, says: "I didn't know much about Jews and their ways. But I never did believe, as they sometimes taught us, that matzoh was made from the blood of Christian children. I was also taught that just like the Hindus didn't eat cows because they were sacred animals, Jews worshiped pigs and that's why they never ate pork. It may sound dumb, but in the foothills of Kentucky, it still holds true as far as I know."

The questions about Judaism are endless: What is the difference between a circumcision (the medical procedure) and a *bris* (the religious ritual)? Why is a glass broken during the wedding ceremony? What are the purpose and meaning behind a bar and bat mitzvah? Why are flowers not usually permitted at funerals? Many of the questions revolve around life-cycle events or keeping kosher, others around anti-Semitism, the Holocaust, and Israel. Some of the questions are theological.

Mary O'Hara from Syracuse writes: "I used to worry that my Jewish friends would die with original sin on their souls. It wasn't until conversion that I discovered that the concept of original sin does not exist in Judaism. I really like the Jewish idea that a person is born morally clean. He makes his own moral choice to sin or not to sin."

Another issue that frequently troubles converts is the concept of Jews as the "chosen people." April Katz believes that her childhood dislike of Jews stemmed from an encounter about chosenness with a classmate in sixth grade. "A Jewish girl told me that she was chosen by God. Since I was jealous of her anyway, I thought she was just being a snob. I suppose the stereotype stayed with me. In conversion class, I was the first one to ask about the 'chosen people.' While I loved David [her fiancé] and everything else I was learning about Judaism, I did not want my Christian friends to think of me as a snob. My rabbi made it all make sense when he explained that the concept does not mean superiority or rejection of other people, because everyone has a role to play on God's earth. It means the demands upon Jews are greater because, in the Torah, Jews are singled out to serve God and all humanity. I felt wonderful knowing that because I had chosen Judaism, I was chosen too."

DRIFTING BETWIXT AND BETWEEN

While in the midst of the conversion process, converts-to-be often feel themselves in a state of limbo. One convert expressed the view of hundreds when she said, "I'm no longer Episcopalian, but I'm not yet Jewish. What do I call myself? Where do I belong?" The prospective Jew may have intellectually terminated ties with a former faith, but he or she still has a long way to go before attaining the emotional readiness to label himself or herself Jewish. This unsettled feeling is usually exacerbated by the onset of a Jewish holiday. Does one who is in the middle of conversion celebrate one last Christmas? Is it okay to celebrate Hanukkah? How does one celebrate a holiday that is still so unfamiliar?

As one confused student put it in the midst of the fall holidays, "I can observe Rosh Hashannah, but I can't celebrate Sukkot. We didn't get to that chapter yet."

It is unrealistic for rabbis, families, or prospective converts themselves to expect Jews by choice to be able to suddenly abandon the familiar and fully thrust themselves into the unfamiliar by celebrating all Jewish holidays and events as soon as they decide to convert. I advise people in such a state of limbo to participate in Jewish celebrations as much as possible, depending on their intellectual and emotional readiness. If, at the beginning, they cannot become active participants because of inhibitions or lack of knowledge, they should become active observers. By this I mean taking advantage of every possible experiential opportunity to practice, observe, or learn about Jewish ritual, culture, or life-cycle events. Friends and family can be invaluable at such times to provide much-needed encouragement, nurturance, and knowledge.

The more religious a person is, the more difficult it can be to convert. Unlike those who formerly had religion in name only and feel they are only gaining by adopting Judaism, the religious person may feel he or she is sacrificing a great deal for the sake of a spouse. It is also sometimes difficult to understand, especially for one who was previously active in another religion, that converting to Judaism is more than just swapping one set of beliefs and practices for another.

Kathy James, a devout Catholic, was always looking for parallels between Catholicism and Judaism. Her marriage to Steve was delayed four years while she wrestled with the religious issues that divided them. She had relatively little difficulty substituting Chanukkah and Passover for Christmas and Easter. Unhealthy and inappropriate as these associations were, she even found in her own mind a connection between matzoh and the host and between Easter baskets and Purim's *mishloach manot,* portions of food sent to friends. She even equated the rabbinic sages with Christian saints. But Jesus created more of a problem.

"Do I really have to give up Jesus?" she asked me. She even had the notion that a Reform conversion meant she could still believe in Jesus. So I gave her the book *We Jews and Jesus,* by Samuel Sandmel, which has helped many converts with its straightforward explanation of the Jewish view of Jesus. It helped Kathy, but secretly she told me she hoped she could keep Jesus on the inside and still convert.

FEAR OF THE UNKNOWN

Fear of the unknown is a common theme sounded by prospective converts. This is uncharted territory, and converts, like anyone about to embark on the unfamiliar, often feel threatened by the unknown. They want to know what their lives will be like as Jews. "Who will be my Jewish role models?" wonder Rosalie Kowchik and many like her. Rosalie, a Polish Catholic museum curator, knew she didn't want to emulate her mother or grandmother; but understanding them had helped her understand herself and where she was going. That was before she decided to convert. As a Jew, she worried that she had no built-in network, no family pillar to accept or reject as she saw fit. "I felt very alone and fearful of the unknown future," she recalls of her preconversion days.

George Hart, a prominent biophysicist from Australia, was equally fearful of the future, but for different reasons. "Why am I, an author and respected scientist, fearful of my life as a new Jew?" he wrote to me, offering his own explanation: "I guess it is because I am an infant Jew. As an adult, it is difficult to start all over again. I learn the Hebrew alphabet like a first-grade child. I feel embarrassed when people expect so much of me as a new Jew. I have to remind them—and myself—that I don't have a Ph.D. in Judaism."

FEELING OVERWHELMED

Comes the middle or latter part of the conversion process, it is not unusual to begin feeling overwhelmed by the enormous amount of information that needs to be learned, understood, and assimilated. Paul Smolens, a 62-year-old Wall Street analyst, spoke for many when he said, "I had read several books on different aspects of Judaism and I had seen a few Woody Allen films, so I thought I knew something about Judaism. Was I ever wrong! How does one absorb four thousand years of rich history without becoming overwhelmed?"

Marilyn Patrice, a pianist from Wisconsin, had a different concern. At the age of 45, and with two small children, she was worried about being able to explain Judaism to her children. "There is too much to know, too much to read," she lamented. "When will I feel comfortable with Hebrew? Above all, how will I be able to impart Judaism, a faith still new to me, to my children? Do I know enough to answer my children's questions? Will they think I'm stupid or, worse, not a good Jew?"

Looking back on my own conversion experience, I remember a constant gnawing feeling that maybe this was too much for me. Part of those feelings stemmed from my concern that I was not fulfilling my rabbi's expectations and part from the sheer amount of information I wanted to learn and absorb. The vast numbers of Jewish texts and literature that detail Jewish history, philosophy, laws, and prayers are overwhelming. And that doesn't even include the experiential components of being Jewish that cannot be learned from books. My rabbi would assign several chapters of reading before each of our sessions. If I read only as far as assigned, he would berate me for not having the enthusiasm to read ahead. If, however, for the next session I had read ahead, he would scold me for having the audacity to presume that I knew enough to go on! His strategy may have been designed to keep me on my toes, but it also made me realize that one can spend a lifetime involved in Jewish learning, and there will always be more to know.

Two subjects unique to the Jewish people—Israel and the Holocaust—can be deeply perplexing and intimidating to a new or prospective Jew. Both of these subjects are dealt with in greater detail later in the book, but they are relevant here because the intensity of emotion and identification that the Holocaust and Israel evoke in Jews can often be quite puzzling to a convert.

A convert entering a family with Holocaust survivors most probably will confront the subject even before entering a conversion course. But for others the course may provide the first opportunity, no matter how brief, to learn and think about these issues—and to do so in a Jewish framework.

Margaret Riley, a former nun, said she had always thought of the Holocaust as "a dreadful act perpetuated by man's inhumanity toward man. It pained me to see television documentaries and to read about it. But still, it had always been something that had happened to others. It was not really part of me. I had compassion but no empathy." During her conversion course which included intense discussions about the Holocaust, Margaret found her feelings of sympathy for the Jews transformed to feelings of anger against those who had perpetrated such inhuman acts. "I found myself crying not for those who perished in the ravages of the concentration camps but for myself—my past ignorance and lack of empathy. The hurt is such that I have to remind myself that it wasn't even my own ancestors who were destroyed."

Brenda Joyce, a 31-year-old paralegal, confessed: "I am ashamed to say that I knew nothing about the Holocaust. After an emotional discussion in class, my fiancé and I discussed it for the first time. I began to feel shame, guilt, and disgust because the majority of people did so little to help the Jewish people in their time of need."

Although the Holocaust stirs up feelings of guilt and horror, it is still a subject that, after initial emotional discussions, is often put aside until a television program, an article, or a Holocaust remembrance day sparks the memory and revives the sentiments. Israel, on the other hand, is constantly in the news and therefore harder to set aside. And for many Jews, it is just as emotional a subject as the Holocaust, for Israel represents a triumphant Jewish people, a people who rose from the ashes of Hitler's camps to forge a new destiny in their homeland.

For a convert, a lack of history and information about the State of Israel often makes it difficult to comprehend its significance for the Jewish people. Many converts tell me that the introduction of Israel into their lives was as if a mate had said, "By the way, I forgot to tell you—I have a child I want you to adopt and love."

Frances Alpan, a former Mormon from Utah, said Israel became a sensitive subject between her and her husband in the early stages of their marriage. "My husband Saul expected me to hate the PLO [Palestine Liberation Organization] and love Israel. Actually, I abhor all fighting and resented having to take sides. His relatives could criticize Israel, but if I expressed a negative attitude, he would be concerned that people would not consider me a good Jew because I was a convert."

So how does a convert cope with this awesome amount of information being thrust out all at once? Some of these feelings of inadequacy and anxiety can be reduced if the convert is able to concentrate on the conversion process without simultaneous stress-inducing distractions such as wedding plans or job hunting. It is important to remember that becoming a Jew requires time, conscious effort, and a sincere commitment. The course merely provides a beginning, a basic foundation of Jewish knowledge on which to build throughout a lifetime. Take one step at a time, moving on to the next book or taking on a new ritual only when it feels right. Trying to learn or do too much at once will exacerbate feelings of anxiety that in turn may lead a potential convert to feelings of inadequacy. This chain reaction could impede the entire learning process.

CONVERSION DAY: APPREHENSION AND RELIEF

Toward the end of the conversion program, most converts experience a mixed reaction—a true commingling of apprehension and relief. Happiness about ending the program and reaching the goal of conversion itself is often tempered by apprehension about the conversion ceremony, especially if it includes—as it always will in Conservative and Orthodox and sometimes in the other branches as well—appearing before a *beth din* where one's knowledge and commitment will be tested. Although these feelings of anxiety are perfectly normal, it is important to remember that the rabbis on the *beth din* are not out to "get" anyone. Their job is to determine the intellectual and emotional readiness of the candidate. It is often helpful to talk to other converts to find out what their experiences were like.

Cynthia Lovenworth, a 22-year-old medical student, looks back with fondness and amusement at her *beth din* experience: "I stayed up the whole night before studying Jewish history and rituals, and I memorized all the blessings. My husband, Jeffrey, had accompanied me to every class and every session with the rabbis. He would even have come with me to the *mikvah* if they would have let him in. But I knew I was on my own. I was so nervous, I could not even eat breakfast. So there I was sitting before the rabbis, my stomach growling from hunger. The rabbis sensed that I was nervous, and they each tried very hard to make me feel more comfortable. The questions were easy: 'When do Jews fast? What is the blessing recited when kindling the Shabbat lights? Hanukkah lights? How does one prepare for Passover?' and so on. They also asked me my personal feelings about becoming Jewish and my plans for running a Jewish household. Toward the end, I began to relax. I had answered the questions satisfactorily. Then, when it was all over, I shook hands with the last rabbi and I blubbered, 'Thank you, Father, er, I mean, Rabbi!' He smiled and joked about it, but I was so upset that I turned white. Jeffrey took one look at me, emerging from the *beth din*, and he was convinced I had failed!"

Many who go to a *mikvah* as a part of their conversion find it to be a deeply meaningful experience—a spiritual cleansing and renewal; sometimes, even a mystical relief of tension. For Beth Ann Weiss, a sociology professor at New York University, the *mikvah* experience became the most meaningful part of her conversion process. "My rabbi had told me that a convert is actually a Jewish soul that happened to get caught in a gentile body, and immersion in the *mikvah* would change my status from gentile to Jew. I was a little apprehensive, but I really did feel Jewish when I came out. The '*mikvah* lady' helped because she was so sweet. She explained everything and made me feel welcome."

Leah Jacobs, a 26-year-old radiologist from Louisiana, provides this vivid description: "When I first walked into the *mikvah*,

I was a little taken aback because it appeared so old and gloomy. But in spite of its shabbiness, it was spotlessly clean. A very lovely older woman explained the basics of the ritual because she knew I was converting. (The *mikvah* is also used by Orthodox Jews on a regular basis.) She then led me to this Roman-like bath. I stepped in and immediately felt the warmth of the water. It was not hot and not cold, but just right. I went under the water three times and repeated the blessings that the woman told me to repeat. I remember feeling so pure, so feminine and clean—not physically clean but internally clean. When my fiancé came to pick me up, I kissed him and told him all about it. Later, when he wanted to have sex, I refused. He thought I was meshuga—a bit crazy—but I felt I wanted to remain in my undefiled state for at least 24 hours!"

Although immersion in the *mikvah* can provide a beautiful and positive experience, such is not always the case. Patricia Berman, a dancer from Wisconsin, relates her story: "My *mikvah* experience got off to a bad start when I was twenty minutes late for my appointment because I got lost on the way. The 'mikvah' lady' looked like a character out of an old Yiddish play, with her wig askew and dressed in an old housedress. She never smiled, and her directions were sharp and curt. When I recited the blessings, she had a hard time hearing me until I shouted them to her. When I got out, she was not there to hand me a towel. There I stood, a dripping wet new Jew. When she saw me padding around stark naked, she admonished me severely and handed me a towel. The experience had no special meaning for me. Later, at a meeting of a converts support group, eleven women related beautiful *mikvah* experiences. I felt cheated, but I'm glad to know that my experience was the exception and not the rule."

Conversion ceremonies vary from place to place and from rabbi to rabbi. Sometimes it is a private affair in which the conversion papers are signed in front of witnesses and simply handed over to the new Jew. Sometimes, particularly when large classes are involved, a special evening is set aside in the synagogue when speakers are invited, special readings are assigned, and each person's name is announced as they are called up to the *bimah* to receive their conversion papers. Friends, relatives, and spouses are invited. In other cases, the names of new converts are announced during a regular synagogue service. Some converts tell their fellow congregants their reasons for choosing Judaism. For these converts, that public expression is a wonderful experience. Others prefer to keep their stories to themselves. A public conversion may meet the needs of the rabbi or the synagogue, but it may not reflect the needs of the convert. Each convert's needs should be ascertained so that the ceremony is a comfortable and meaningful experience, one that provides a positive entry into Jewish life.

The completion of conversion is a time to celebrate. Perhaps a small gathering of friends and family is appropriate. Some in-laws, spouses, or friends mark the occasion by taking the new Jew out to lunch or dinner, or giving a gift of Judaica, flowers, books, or a donation to the synagogue.

ASSESSMENT

By the time the conversion process is complete, the Jew by choice should have begun to understand something about Jewish prayers, holidays, rituals, customs, history, and, it is hoped, a little Hebrew. However, converts discover very quickly that it is not enough to embrace Judaism by means of a conversion course. To become Jewish, one must not only accept the Jewish religion but also identify with the past, present, and future of the Jewish people. Jews feel pain when other Jews suffer, joy when Jews are triumphant. To acquire this identity requires time, patience, and commitment.

By this point, however, a Jew by choice should be beginning to understand that:

· Judaism is more than a religion; it includes ritual and ethical behavior for daily living.

· What a Jew does in his or her bedroom, kitchen, synagogue, and community to a large extent defines his or her Jewishness.

- The Jewish people are diverse, with separate branches of Judaism defining differing attitudes and levels of observance. But at the same time, the Jews are one people. The concept of Jewish peoplehood is as central to Judaism as the religion itself.

- Preparing for Jewish holidays and Jewish events is as important as the celebrations themselves.

- It takes time for a new Jew to incorporate Jewish values and celebrations into his or her total being. The convert, lacking a personal Jewish history and memory, must create his or her own, starting with the conversion process.

- Judaism grows and develops, sometimes waxing and sometimes waning, for new Jews as it does for many born Jews. But whereas it may or may not be okay for a born Jew to be a High Holiday Jew—remembering Judaism only on Rosh Hashannah and Yom Kippur—it is definitely not okay for a convert. Yes, the Jewish world expects something more from the convert. Even more important, as I tell every convert I meet, you should expect something more from yourself, lest you begin to feel hypocritical in your decision. The most successful converts are those who realize that Judaism provides not just cake for special occasions but bread for daily nourishment.

POSTCONVERSION HIGHS AND LOWS

The preeminent postconversion question asked by nearly every sincere convert is, "Okay, now I have my conversion papers in hand, I'm officially a Jew—but when do I begin to feel Jewish, I mean really Jewish, inside and out?"

The question always reminds me of the story about a visitor to Israel who asks an old man sitting at the foot of a mountain how long it will take him to climb the mountain. The old man does not answer. The man repeats the question several times but still is unable to elicit a response. Finally, the visitor starts up the mountain, and when he has gone just a little way, the old man shouts up to him, "It will take you three hours to climb that mountain!" The visitor is surprised and angry, for he has gone too far to turn back. "Why didn't you tell me this before?" he demands. The wise old man replies, "I could not tell you how long it would take you to climb the mountain until I saw how fast you could walk."

For the convert, too, the answer to "When do I feel Jewish?" depends on each individual's commitment and motivation. One cannot feel Jewish in synagogue without knowing the prayer service and how to sing along with other congregants. One cannot feel Jewish without ever having experienced Shabbat, participated in a Passover seder, dwelt in a sukkah, or lit candles on Hanukkah.

Terry Goldstine, a 27-year-old social worker in Philadelphia, had taken a fairly comprehensive conversion course, but very little time had been allotted for learning Hebrew. The few Hebrew blessings she did know had been memorized, and she was still relying on texts with transliterations. Her husband's family was Orthodox, and Terry longed to participate in their Shabbat services and Passover seders, which were conducted exclusively in Hebrew. A year after her conversion, Terry enrolled at Gratz College, where she took a course in conversational Hebrew and another one on understanding the prayers. Now Terry is exuberant that she can read Hebrew and chant the various parts of the service. "I can't believe how comfortable I feel in the synagogue now," she reports. "The most gratifying part is that I'll be able to help my sons with their Hebrew school lessons!"

The lesson here is clear: the more effort that goes into learning and involvement, the sooner the convert will feel comfortable. The challenge is not always easy to face. It takes determination, and even chutzpah, to immerse oneself in the thick of Jewish life. It takes courage to attend services, to observe rituals, and to recite prayers that do not yet feel totally comfortable or meaningful. It takes an inner resolve to explore Judaism and to devote time to creating a Jewish home that follows the Jewish calendar.

Practice is as crucial for developing confidence in being Jewish as it is for any new endeavor. Although conversion classes provide a vast amount of learning through books, generally very little time is devoted to the experiential component, to "hands-on" Judaism. It is not unusual for a recent convert to know in theory how to light Shabbat candles and to recite the blessings in both Hebrew and English but never to have actually lit them on a Friday night. Some male converts complain that they are not shown how to put on tefillin and wish they had been taught so that the task wouldn't seem so intimidating. The question is this: How does the convert translate what he or she has learned into everyday Judaism? As I often tell people in my support groups, don't only read about it, don't only talk about it—DO IT!

Converts who are fortunate enough to have spouses, in-laws, rabbis, friends, or other role models to guide them through the early stages of living Jewishly generally report less anxiety and feel less overwhelmed than those who are alone after conversion. For a single convert like myself, nearly twenty years ago, my rabbi in his infinite wisdom arranged for me to live with an older Orthodox couple who would be my adoptive Jewish family. While I provided them with a modest rent, they provided me with a loving Jewish environment. I was never an observer or a guest. Together we went to the *mikvah*, lit Shabbat candles, and rejoiced in Shabbat and holidays.

Although such an arrangement may be unusual, it would not be farfetched for congregations and communities to assign single converts or young conversionary couples with no extended family in the area to a local family for one year after conversion. That family would be responsible for helping the convert learn about and experience Shabbat and holidays and for providing general guidance through the first Jewish year.

START WITH SHABBAT

"But how and where should I start?" is the question posed by many a convert. The Jewish year, based on a lunar rather than a solar calendar, consists of twelve months (354 days) in ordinary years and thirteen months in leap years, which occur seven times every nineteen years. The numbering of the years is based on the calculation that Creation took place in 3761 B.C.E. The Jewish year begins with Rosh Hashannah on the first of the Jewish month of Tishrei. The Jewish week runs from Shabbat to Shabbat.

My advice to someone interested in creating an authentic link to Judaism is to begin with Shabbat. Shabbat, which we welcome each Friday at sundown, ends Saturday at sundown. With its observance as the day of rest comes a special opportunity to create a separation from the frenzy and hectic schedules that dominate the rest of the week.

Shabbat can mean different things to different people, but I will describe here a traditional Friday evening meal, a ritual that, once introduced on a regular basis, is certain to provide a meaningful bond to Judaism.

The Shabbat table should somehow be distinguished from the everyday table. That can mean using one's best china and linen or just adding fresh flowers. The table should be set with candlesticks, kiddush cup, kosher wine, and two challot covered with a cloth. The two challot symbolize the double portion of manna the Jews received each Friday while wandering in the desert so that they would not have to gather food on the Sabbath. Since no form of work or cooking is permitted on Shabbat, traditional Jews prepare for the Sabbath meals (Friday night and Saturday) before candle lighting. Once the candles are lit, eighteen minutes before sundown, Shabbat has begun. In many homes, it is the custom before the meal for the parents to bless their children.

Then the wine is poured and the kiddush (sanctification) is recited. After the washing of the hands, the blessing over the challah—*hamotzi*—is said, at which time the challah is broken and one piece is given to each person. The Sabbath meal—joyous, relaxed, and unhurried—is served. *Zemirot* (hymns) may be sung between courses or at the end of the meal, before concluding with the *birkat hamazon*, or grace after meals.

It is traditional to go to synagogue Friday evening or Saturday morning or both, although this may vary among the movements and in particular synagogues. In any case, Shabbat is a day to remove oneself from the daily pressures, the hectic pace of the rest of the week—which means no cooking, no shopping, no laundry. It is a time for prayer and study, for rest and reflection, for socializing, for spiritual growth.

The ending of Shabbat at sundown on Saturday is proclaimed with the brief but beautiful ceremony of Havdallah—meaning, literally, separation. Children especially love this ritual, which includes a blessing over wine and spices and a multi-wicked braided candle, which, at the conclusion of the ceremony, is extinguished in the wine.

For some, it is best to take Shabbat observance one step at a time. Try beginning with lighting candles, saying kiddush over wine and *hamotzi* over challah. When that feels comfortable, try adding some of the other blessings (over children, if applicable) or singing Sabbath songs. Remember, Shabbat should be a joy, not a chore. One should not first begin thinking about it after work on Friday. With practice, converts and their family and friends can establish a routine that will enable them to prepare for Shabbat before Friday so that, optimally, it is not a frantic rush just beforehand.

Those who are committed to a traditional observance of Shabbat should try to share the preparations and observance with other traditional Jews who are able to provide guidance until the convert develops his or her own self-confidence.

When beginning with Jewish ritual, the most important thing to remember is not to be afraid of making mistakes. Rita Margolies, who converted three years ago, recalls: "I was afraid I would sound funny or make a mistake, so I tried to avoid synagogues and religious rituals. I knew more about some aspects of Judaism than my husband did, but I was afraid of criticism. One Friday evening, we were at a friend's house for dinner and we decided to make a *motzi*, but no one knew how to do it but me! I did a fine job, and later that evening another friend, a born Jew, confided to me that she also had fears about doing certain Jewish rituals. At age 44, she had yet to make her own seder because she felt that Passover preparations were overwhelming. Her candid remarks helped me to feel less self-conscious and more confident about introducing certain rituals into our home. Only then did I truly start to feel Jewish."

Another convert, Sally Green, wrote that she never felt comfortable preparing for Shabbat and holidays because her mother-in-law always did so perfectly, and it was always assumed that Sally and her husband would go to their home for each Shabbat and holiday. "I know that she meant well, but I felt like a guest, not like an authentic Jew," recounts Sally. "Gradually, I began to insist on having my own Shabbat dinners. I invited my mother-in-law for a change. She rebelled at first but gradually accepted the transition. It was only after I was able to prepare and serve my own Shabbat dinners, make a seder, and build a sukkah—only then did I begin to feel Jewish."

Stephanie Fisher and her husband, Allen, moved back to Stephanie's home state of Alabama shortly after they were married. The first time Allen's parents came to visit them from New York, Stephanie was determined to make a "proper" Shabbat meal for her in-laws. She called me three times a week for three weeks prior to the visit, seeking advice and reassurance on how to do it just right. The day finally arrived, and as she recalls, it did not proceed exactly as she had planned.

"I was totally frazzled and very nervous. I had counted on Allen's help with the last-minute details, but he got tied up at work and had only a minute before he ran out to the airport to meet his parents. I asked him a question about the gefilte fish and soup, and all I remember him shouting back to me was, 'Just heat everything up!' Well, I did, and lo and behold, the first course was steaming hot gefilte fish! His parents were slightly shocked, and I was terribly embarrassed. Luckily, his father made a joke about it, and we ate it, cold, for lunch the next day!"

For Stephanie and others like her, repetition and persistence helped her to become more confident as time went by. I remember my own rabbi offering this advice when I was feeling overwhelmed. "Perfection," he said, "is impossible and not required. Constant improvement is all that is necessary."

It is important to remember that, although Jewish actions can lead to Jewish feelings, the transition is not automatic. Many Jews by choice can go through the motions of being Jewish without actually feeling the connection. This was my own experience. The first year after my conversion, I did everything I could to make myself Jewish. I went to synagogue every Shabbat, I baked my own challah, and joined every Jewish organization that I could, but still I did not feel Jewish. Now, eighteen years later, I go to services when I can, my family rejoices the few times a year when I bake challah, and I devote my energies to a chosen few organizations. But today I feel Jewish!

The point is, time cannot be rushed. Learning about Judaism, for born Jews as well as for converts, is a lifelong task. Whether it begins at birth or in a conversion class, Jewish learning never really ends until one's death. No matter how much knowledge can be learned from books, Jewish feelings must be developed and nurtured. No one can give a new Jew a sense of personal history or Jewish memories. For some, a few years is enough, but others need much longer. I can't emphasize this point enough: time, determination, and practice will make the Jew who has chosen Judaism fully Jewish.

For single converts this process requires a readiness to engage in self-education as well as the motivation to seek out Jewish role models, friends, and surrogate Jewish families. Loneliness will be diminished if the single convert becomes an active member of a synagogue or *havurah*, something that is not always easy because some synagogues do not provide enough opportunities for single Jews.

Married or engaged converts must face the challenge of integrating new feelings for Judaism with the beliefs and practices of a born Jewish spouse or fiancé. In some cases it means living up to their standards, but it is not uncommon for a convert to desire to live a more observant Jewish life than the spouse for whom he or she initially converted.

These differences sometimes provoke conflict with the Jewish partner and his or her family. Michael Greenspan, a moderately observant Jew, said of his wife: "I wanted Judy to be Jewish like me, not more or less, but I soon realized she had to find her own place. I did resent her imposing her stricter observances on me. After time, we found compromises; I became a better Jew, she became a lesser Jew."

Regardless of the level of observance, feeling Jewish depends not only on the actions of the convert but also on the attitude of friends, family, and the community. The drastically different experiences of Sheila Brown and Joseph Sherman reflect to some degree the relative ease each had in feeling Jewish. Even after Sheila converted, she says, "My husband continued to refer to me as his shiksa wife. I was hurt and insulted." Joseph, on the other hand, said, "I was made part of my wife's *mishpacha* [family] before I even considered conversion. After I converted, I knew I was a natural." Only with constant support and encouragement from family, friends, and the community at large will a convert ever truly feel Jewish.

3

Partners in conversion

"Both of us were so afraid to raise the issue, afraid to tred on shaky ground that might endanger our relationship." Paul and Marilyn Weiss speak for hundreds of couples as they reflect on the uncertainties and fears that the subjects of religion and conversion bring to a relationship.

Paul, a 29-year-old Jewish writer from the Bronx, and Marilyn, a 27-year-old health care worker from a strict church-going Midwestern family, knew from the outset of their relationship that "the religion issue was a very big problem." But rather than dealing with it directly, recalls Marilyn, "we decided just to sit on it."

Although Paul attended synagogue regularly and often spent his vacations in Israel, not until nearly a year into the relationship did he reveal to Marilyn that he felt so strongly about his Judaism that he would only marry a Jewish woman. It was a revelation that provoked more than a little resentment. "He never should have gone out with me in the first place, knowing that this was going to be a problem," Marilyn says. "But by the time I found out, it was too late; we were already too committed to each other."

Countless couples involved in interfaith relationships, particularly those in which at least one of the partners is committed to his or her tradition, tell me they never intended to fall in love with a person of a different religion. We all know, however, that love is rarely the result of rational decision making. Relationships begin as friendships and gradually develop in intensity and attraction, with shared interests, ambitions, and values overshadowing religious and ethnic differences. Difficult as the prospect may seem, it is imperative to the health and future of the relationship that interfaith couples initiate honest and open discussions about these differences as early as possible.

Marilyn remembers feeling angry with Paul when they finally did confront the issue for the first time, and she discovered that Paul had already done a lot of introspection on his own, leaving her in the dark. "He had discussed it with friends and family but had never talked about it with me. Here I had been agonizing about it and had no idea what was going on in his mind."

"I guess I was scared to mention it," recalls Paul in his own defense. "We had fallen in love rather quickly, and I guess I viewed our religious differences as a hurdle we would have to overcome in the future." Paul, inwardly hopeful that Marilyn would ultimately convert, also felt strongly that he didn't want her conversion to be "one of those forced things where one converts only to satisfy the other, without any spiritual commitment. I guess I hoped that Marilyn would come to the decision on her own."

Paul was lucky, for Marilyn did just that. When she began reading a few basic books about Judaism, her reaction was extremely positive. "I felt like I was coming home," she recalls. Despite her family's strong Catholic commitment, Marilyn says she had left the Catholic Church on her own several years earlier. "A lot of the problems I had had with Catholicism were not an issue with Judaism. Judaism emphasizes living in the here and now. It's not so important to question whether God exists or not; it's more important to live a moral life."

The more Marilyn read, "the more I felt very comfortable with the emphasis on action rather than faith, even though I still hadn't learned about Jewish rituals or history. I think it was especially easy because I wasn't divorcing myself from another religion. I had already done that on my own."

Paul and Marilyn, who would still encounter tremendous obstacles prior to their wedding—especially from her parents, who felt hurt and rejected—have a happy ending to report. Although they fully anticipate more hurdles as time passes, particularly when they have children, for now they look back on their prewedding year, during which time Marilyn converted, as an incredibly stressful but also tremendously rewarding period. They believe their experience helped to strengthen their relationship in unimagined ways as each step of the process was forged with love and support and a determined effort to understand each other.

Lest Paul and Marilyn's story make the ability to resolve religious differences sound too easy—because such a process, even if it has a happy ending, never is—we should also meet Rebecca Schwartz.

When Rebecca turned to me, she was a medical resident in Philadelphia and involved in a relationship with Edward Holden, a surgeon at a New York hospital. Rebecca had held on to a lifelong fantasy: "As a young girl, I would prance around in my mother's old lace slip, pretending it was my wedding gown. I just knew I was going to marry a Jewish doctor and have a big wedding in a large Conservative synagogue.

"Now I'm a doctor and I've found my doctor, but there's just one hitch. He's not Jewish. My childhood dream has been shattered. From the beginning of our relationship, I told Edward about my commitment to Judaism. At first he seemed indifferent. But when I tried to include him in my personal Jewish activities, his attitude turned downright negative. When I invited him to my parents' home for a Shabbat dinner, he made caustic remarks about Jews and Jewish food. He thinks the services at my synagogue are archaic. At my nephew's *bris*, he made it quite clear that he thinks circumcision is a primitive custom.

"Edward is almost every woman's dream come true. He is brilliant and handsome. But I cannot marry him because he does not respect my religion. Many of my friends think I am making a dreadful mistake. They argue that one difference should not be enough to end a relationship. What they don't understand is that the one difference is Judaism, and Judaism is an integral part of my everyday life. I feel deep, deep hurt because I really care about Edward, but I know our relationship would be doomed. I'm only glad that I learned about his feelings before we became even more attached."

There was little I could do for or say to Rebecca. She had not come seeking a solution; she had wanted to share her anguish and find out if others had experienced similar situations and how they had coped. Rebecca did not feel comfortable sharing her innermost feelings with her family, and most of her friends didn't understand. I was able to put Rebecca in touch with others who had experienced similar trauma to help her ease the pain.

The experiences of Paul and Marilyn and of Rebecca and Edward, though quite different, both illustrate the importance of confronting the issue of religious differences early in an interfaith relationship.

THE EARLIER THE BETTER

Whenever I am asked, "Isn't it risky to bring up religious differences too soon?" I answer with an unequivocal no! My work with hundreds of couples has confirmed my belief that it is never too early to begin an honest and open discussion about such crucial differences as religion and ethnic identification.

All too often I hear from couples, "Our differences do not pose a problem for us because we are not religious." This is the greatest myth harbored by interfaith couples. No matter how "unreligious" one may be, the fact is that a person's ethnic and cultural background, upbringing, family, and community are all factors that, consciously or not, inform his or her views on a variety of issues relating to life's central decisions. In addition, most interfaith couples should expect some degree of opposition to their involvement, usually from one family or both. Whether that opposition takes the form of temporary or permanent alien-

ation, lack of financial assistance for the wedding, or even a refusal to attend the wedding, couples need to be prepared to deal
with these possibilities.

For all these reasons, I can't emphasize enough the necessity
to open up and grapple with the issues at hand. Exactly when
and how the subject should be broached depends on each couple, but both partners should bear in mind that the earlier the
discussion, the less opportunity there is for lasting hurt and the
greater is the chance for reaching common understanding.

If Paul and Marilyn had raised the issue a little earlier in their
relationship, they might have averted some of the hurt and anger
Marilyn felt when she discovered that Paul had not been direct
with her about his feelings from the beginning. Still, once they
did grapple with the issues, they were able to develop solutions
that made both partners feel comfortable. And although Rebecca
and Edward ultimately were not able to resolve their deep-seated
differences, they recognized the unbridgeable gap early enough
that they avoided the even greater pain that would inevitably
have surfaced if the relationship had continued.

Such was the deep pain felt by William Sasloff and Eva Ben-
nett. Buoyed by the myth that "love conquers all," this couple
neither anticipated nor acknowledged the deep-rooted cultural
divisions that would ultimately lead to their separation after eight
years together. William, a 29-year-old engineer, and Eva, a sys-
tems design analyst of the same age, lived together for the last
three years of their lengthy relationship before they seriously confronted their religious differences. Prior to that, according to William, they had reasoned that "marriage is far off, so for now we
can each maintain our separate faiths. We go to Passover seders
and Easter dinners. She celebrates Christmas with her family, and
I celebrate Hanukkah with mine. Everyone seems happy."

As thoughts of marriage evolve, couples like William and
Eva often come to me looking for direction. Among the many
questions I ask them are, "Will you continue to celebrate both
holidays in your own home? What kind of wedding ceremony
will there be?" These questions just scratch the surface of a host
of issues that need to be addressed.

William had wanted to ask Eva about the possibility of conversion, but he was afraid to raise it while everything seemed to be going so smoothly. "As long as we were visitors in each other's family's home, everything was fine. But when we began to talk about marriage, it happened to be around Christmastime, and Eva wanted to get a tree for our apartment. I just knew I could not have a Christmas tree in my home. I had never specifically said so, but I assumed she would know how I felt because she hadn't questioned me when I told her I wanted to have a Jewish wedding and to raise our children as Jews."

As for the Christmas tree, Eva said, "We always went to Mom's for Christmas, and William always commented on how pretty the tree was. He knows I'm not religious. I don't understand why he doesn't want me to have a Christmas tree."

Despite eight years of sharing their life together, these important issues had never been broached in depth, let alone resolved. After several stormy and tearful sessions, William and Eva ended their relationship because neither one was willing or able to accommodate the other. William had mistakenly interpreted Eva's silence on his expressed desires for a Jewish wedding and Jewish children as tacit approval, and Eva had mistakenly interpreted William's aesthetic delight in her mother's Christmas tree as acceptance of having one in his own home.

Ironically, their worst fear—destroying what seemed to be a good relationship—may have been realized because of their procrastination. Not being religious people, both fully expected that they would be able to work out the issues as they arose in the future rather than confront them head on. That is not to say that William and Eva definitely would have been able to resolve their differences, but an earlier grappling with the issues could have reduced the pain and confusion.

Both Eva and William expressed dismay that they had "wasted" eight years of their lives. I would like to think that people like them view their relationships not merely as "wasted time," but, rather, as a learning and growing experience. I hope that the lessons learned will help them and others like them in their future relationships.

The importance of early discussions applies as much to those who consider themselves religiously observant as it does to those who think that religion doesn't matter. The problems that inevitably evolve in an interfaith relationship often have as much to do with ethnic identity and cultural upbringing as they do with religious issues. In other words, the potential difficulties in a relationship go much deeper than whether or not there should be a Christmas tree in the house.

Very often couples tell me that although they wanted to delve into discussions of religious differences early in their relationship, they had a hard time finding the words. Many couples say they feel more comfortable talking about sex than they do about religion. When partners encounter sexual difficulties, there are experts and books to consult; interfaith couples have few places to turn to resolve ethnic and religious disparities.

The fact is, the central issues raised by differences in faith and ethnic identity—questions of marriage, family, community, and world view—have no easy answers. No how-to book is going to erase the fundamental differences each partner brings to the relationship. Nonetheless, as a relationship develops, there is a process that partners can pursue to ensure honest and open discussions in order to determine each partner's feelings and flexibility as well as to ascertain the limits of love.

THE TESTING STAGE

Since open discussion during the very early stages of a relationship can be difficult for some people, partners often engage in a more subtle approach. I call it the "testing stage." This stage, sometimes carried out subconsciously, is an attempt to gauge reactions to divergences in religious as well as social, cultural, and ethical values.

Kevin Shapiro and Grace Johnson met at an anti-abortion rally in Washington, D.C. Although there was a spark of attraction, Kevin immediately noticed an ivory cross around Grace's neck and decided not to pursue it any further. A few weeks later, they met again at a conference on world hunger, where they discovered that they had many mutual interests. This time Grace noticed the Star of David around Kevin's neck but decided there was nothing to worry about. They were, after all, just becoming friends.

Six months later, Kevin felt profoundly confused by what had rapidly evolved into an intense and loving relationship. "Coming from a traditional Jewish background, I knew our relationship would be problematic, yet I wondered how such a perfect relationship could be wrong. Our distinctly different religions seemed secondary to our political activism. Deep down, I felt we should stop seeing each other, but I just couldn't."

After nearly a year, Kevin and Grace were living together. Throughout their relationship they each brought up bits and pieces of their separate pasts, looking for cues and reactions from the other. As the Jewish High Holidays approached, Kevin briefly explained their importance to Grace and watched intently for her response. "Maybe you can join me," he said cautiously. Grace responded positively.

Grace's experience was mixed. Though Kevin had briefed her on the meaning of the High Holidays, he had neglected to clue her in to a few practicalities. "I thought a simple skirt and blouse would do," Grace recalls, "but I felt terribly underdressed as I compared myself to people sitting around us. To make things worse, my dress shoes have two-inch heels and were my feet aching by the end of the day after standing for many of the prayers!" As hard as it may be for born Jews to understand, it is sometimes the little details that can make the difference for a non-Jew or a potential convert between feelings of belonging and alienation.

As for the service, Grace remembers feeling rather bored because of all the Hebrew she did not understand. "All in all, I was not very comfortable, but neither was I totally turned off," she says. "In retrospect, Kevin probably should have asked me to a regular synagogue service before introducing me to something as overwhelming as the High Holidays."

"On the other hand, it gave us plenty to talk about. I also saw a spiritual dimension to Kevin that I had never seen before. Somehow I felt more respect for him because of his commitment to his faith, and I realized how much he wanted me to enter into this part of his life. It was scary, unknown territory for me, but my love for him seemed to override everything else, even while I wondered how I could ever fit into his Jewish life."

The testing stage is a time for general discussion about religion, ethics, and values in an effort to understand a partner's feelings and attitudes. It is a time to share a Jewish book, a childhood experience, a Passover seder, or a friend's Jewish wedding to elicit reaction and discussion.

Bringing a partner home for Passover is very often cited by Jewish partners as a critical test. As one man (whose advice could have benefited Kevin) put it, "I didn't want to subject her to the High Holidays, but the Passover seder is so much fun that I knew if she reacted positively to it, there was at least hope for us."

Depending on the reactions to such experiences, the testing stage can generally lead to one of two conclusions about the possibility of conversion: (1) there seems to be at least minimal genuine interest in Judaism to warrant continuing and deepening the discussion, or (2) there is such a strong identification with the non-Jewish partner's own religion, or such a strong antipathy toward Judaism, that the Jewish partner feels fairly certain that the possibility of conversion is out. It is then up to the Jewish partner to determine whether this should mean an end to the relationship or whether the love is so strong that it overrides any other consideration, even the possibility of intermarriage.

From the non-Jew's perspective, the realization that his or her partner's Jewishness means so much to the partner can generate a resolve to accommodate those strong attachments. Or it can lead to the conclusion that, as one woman said, "My attachment to my religion is just as strong as his. Maybe this is as far as we can go."

Such was the case with David Brown and Susan Allen, two religious people who realized fairly quickly that neither of them wanted to give up what they cherished in their own tradition for the sake of a relationship. They had dated several times before they began "testing" each other. One night out, Susan decided to wear a silver cross to see how David would respond. He noticed immediately but tried to appear casual, asking if the cross had been a gift. Susan immediately launched into the story about her first communion and how much the cross meant to her because it was a gift from her godmother. David immediately sensed that the depth of her feelings about religion could create some problems, but he had already become quite interested in Susan, so he decided to pursue the relationship. A few weeks later, he invited Susan to his parents' home for Shabbat dinner. Susan was polite, quiet, and noncommittal about her feelings. Soon after, she invited David to accompany her to Mass. In a sense, they were engaging in a power struggle to determine which commitment was stronger. As David sat in church for the first time in his life, he felt deeply uncomfortable. The huge cross and statues seemed threatening and alienating. He looked at Susan and saw her eyes closed; she appeared to be in deep prayer. The next day, he explained how he felt. Both Susan and David realized they respected and admired each other's personal commitment to their separate traditions. They remained friends, but the relationship never developed beyond that.

ENCOURAGING CONVERSION

As an interfaith relationship intensifies beyond the initial days and weeks, a straightforward discussion of religious differences becomes essential. It is difficult to set an exact timetable for discussing such important issues. The first date is obviously too soon, but after the engagement is announced is much too late. There is no definitive good or right time, but I generally advise that three to six months into a serious relationship is the time to raise the issues of religious differences and, when applicable, the possibility of conversion.

Often one partner will say to me, "How can I ask my boy-friend/girlfriend/lover to convert when I know that I would never convert for anyone? Wouldn't it be fairer if we both just held on to our own traditions?" The question is a good one—in theory. Reality, however, dictates another mode of thinking.

It is a fact that interfaith couples can and often do have good marriages, with each partner observing his or her own tradition while simultaneously accommodating the needs and feelings of the spouse. Difficulties will persist, but two mature adults, through sensitivity and understanding, can rationalize and consider each other's differences. My main concern arises when couples tell me they plan to have a family. Children, unlike adults, are ill equipped to absorb two conflicting religions and cultures into their lives. They often become confused and overwhelmed. Questions such as 9-year-old Brandon Perez's are telling—and not uncommon. "If I'm Jewish, then how can I believe in Jesus?" he asked his parents. "And if I'm Catholic, how can I not believe in Jesus? Do I believe in him on Sunday but not on Saturday?"

Conversion Only for the Sake of Marriage?

People involved in interfaith relationships sometimes feel insincere about considering conversion for the sake of marriage. I too used to wonder whether conversion for marriage alone was something the Jewish community should encourage. What I have come to realize, however, is that there is a vast and crucial difference between converting for the sake of marriage and converting for convenience. Converting for convenience is when John asks Sally to convert because he knows that if she doesn't, his wealthy grandfather will cut him out of his will, or when Jill asks Brian to convert because she knows her parents will not attend the wedding if he doesn't. Contrary to commonly held assumptions among Jews, the number of converts who enter the conversion process with such questionable motives is very small.

There is no question, however, that conversions for the sake of marriage do comprise the majority of conversions to Judaism. After talking to hundreds of converts who have done just that, I now find it easier to understand how one can convert out of love for a Jewish partner. The most common explanation given by converts is the desire to share every aspect of life with the person they love. In expressing that love, partners seek spheres that unite rather than divide them. To know a person fully is to understand his or her past, share a present, and forge a future together. In seeking this unity, partners desire to make each other happy, without losing their individual autonomy or self-worth. Often, the non-Jewish partner discovers within Judaism certain beliefs, values, and ethics that are personally meaningful. It is a world the non-Jew would probably never have had the opportunity to explore if he or she had not become involved with a Jew.

Lois Lederman, a 32-year-old greeting card designer, captured her feelings this way: "When I fell in love with Hershel, I wanted to know everything about him—his interests, ideas, beliefs, and hopes. I did not expect or want him to be a facsimile of me. For instance, he introduced me to the world of opera. Though I never before would have thought of going to the opera, I took an interest in it because it meant so much to Hershel and I wanted to please him. Now I too love opera, and I owe my newfound interest to Hershel.

"I came to Judaism in much the same way. It was Hershel's love for his heritage that influenced me to explore it for myself. Although it was my love and respect for him that sparked my initial desire to discover Judaism, in the end it was my decision. Although I have not adopted all of Hershel's interests—tennis, for instance, I just can't get into—I came to believe it vital that we share something as important as religion. My Judaism is forever, and I know the entire process has brought us closer to each other. It is a part of our life we will always share with each other and our future children."

Usually the partner with the stronger commitment to his or her tradition will prevail in influencing a conversion. However, the subject should never be used as the focus of a power struggle in a relationship. Conversion is far too serious a matter to be used as a test of dominance. Commitment, not endurance, is the crucial element.

Interestingly enough, it is very rare that the Jewish partner ever considers converting out of Judaism. Even though little or no religion may be practiced, many Jews harbor a deep-seated historical and cultural attachment to the Jewish people. Perhaps four thousand years of history, punctuated by persecutions, pogroms, and the Holocaust have left a searing mark. Frank Korngold, a law student at a Midwestern university, echoed the thoughts of countless other Jews when he observed: "I'm not a religious person, but I have a knee-jerk response to being Jewish. All around me there are constant reminders of what Jews have endured to be Jewish. I could not convert because I could not live with myself; it would be an act of betrayal. It would be like saying that my relatives and the six million who died in the Holocaust perished for nothing."

Another reason Jews rarely convert is that most Christian denominations do not require conversion in order to be married by the Church. Each denomination has its own rules and teachings that serve as guidelines for intermarriages. Although most I have encountered do not require conversion by the Jewish partner, some do require a pledge to raise the children in the Christian faith. Some Christian clergy will perform intermarriages only outside of a church, others may require baptism. Although Christian clergy are concerned about intermarriage, public discussion about the issue seems less widespread than in the Jewish community. Perhaps this is because intermarriage is not seen as a threat to the continuity and survival of Christianity in the same way that many Jews perceive it as a threat to the future of the Jewish people.

I have heard from hundreds of Jews about their reasons for not being able to convert from Judaism, or even to intermarry. One woman put it this way: "If enough people intermarry, there may not be any Jews left. That is frightening after we have endured so much and come so far. Other religions have so many adherents they are not threatened by the loss of a few hundred, or even a few thousand, through conversion."

Others find it more difficult to identify their feelings. Their words are simpler: "I just know that I am a Jew, I want to remain a Jew, and I must marry a Jew."

It is this commitment to the Jewish people that not only prevents the Jewish partner from converting out of Judaism but also serves as the basis for encouraging the non-Jewish partner to convert to Judaism.

Raising the Delicate Issue

When it comes to encouraging conversion, the Jewish partner is more instrumental than any other figure. Rabbis, future in-laws, or even marriage counselors can bolster the encouragement by being good Jewish role models and by being warm and welcoming, but it is still the Jewish partner—the one with the most influence on and intimacy with the potential convert—who has the greatest impact.

The manner in which the subject of conversion is raised is crucial. A Jew who says to his or her partner "I can love you and marry you only if you convert" is attaching conditions to that love and risks losing the partner if the condition is not met. On the other hand, a Jewish partner who has expressed his or her feelings about Judaism and has provided opportunities for the partner to become acquainted with Jewish tradition and thinking can sensitively say, "I love you, and I would love for you to consider conversion. I will be with you 100 percent of the way."

The two approaches are very different. In the latter, conversion is an extension, not a condition, of love. It gives the non-Jewish partner the freedom to evaluate his or her feelings. It doesn't require an immediate response. In the first scenario, the non-Jew is more apt to respond negatively in a quick and vehement manner to such absolute demands, taking a stance from which retreat is difficult.

In the second, more congenial, scenario, the Jewish partner must embark on a path of gentle, pervasive persuasion. The following discussion suggests ways to introduce Judaism to a partner in just such a manner.

Invitations to Judaism

Inclusion is very important. Toward the beginning of the relationship, invite the non-Jewish partner into your Jewish life, both past and present. Begin by talking about special memories: the first Passover seder you remember or the one at which you drank too much sweet red wine. Talk about what Hanukkah means to you and your family or how thrilled you have always been by the stirring sounds of the shofar on Rosh Hashannah. Or maybe even how you used to leave the synagogue sanctuary on cue with your friends when the rabbi began to deliver his sermon on Yom Kippur. Share both the negative and positive memories of your Jewish upbringing. Sharing traditions and memories is a way for both partners to explore the development of certain religious and ethnic feelings and to understand your current practices and spiritual beliefs.

When the non-Jewish partner does not come from a religious home or has moved away from religious roots, ideal opportunities exist for exploring whether that religion still has meaning and whether he or she is open to choosing a new religious identity.

Meg Johnson, a 28-year-old nurse, felt that Episcopalianism had lost much of its meaning for her. She accompanied her parents to church on the holidays but had a take-it-or-leave-it attitude. As she became involved with Steve Katz, she began to admire and understand his commitment to Judaism: "Steve really loved Judaism and was deeply committed to maintaining the lifeblood of his Jewishness through his children. He told me about his past and how horrendous Hebrew school was for him. He doesn't like the idea of having to buy tickets for the High Holidays. He thinks the price of kosher food shouldn't be so ridiculously high. I admired his honesty. I listened and I learned. Together we read books and explored. When he didn't have the answers to my questions, we sought help from others. By the time he asked me to consider conversion, I was ready. I had an idea what being Jewish would mean to me and how it would change my life."

Include your partner in as many holiday and life-cycle celebrations as possible. Perhaps you can bring your partner to a nephew's *bris*, a friend's *aufruf*, or a cousin's wedding. Give simple explanations. If a partner expresses interest in a particular aspect of ritual or holiday celebration, in Israel, or in Jewish history, explore the subject together and follow through with reading and discussions.

A wonderful gesture that invites participation is giving a gift of a Jewish ritual object to your partner. Pam Howarth chose a lovely kiddush cup as a birthday present for her boyfriend, Bob Barton. On it, she had inscribed the blessing over the wine in Hebrew and in English transliteration. They had not yet discussed conversion, but Bob had shown much interest in Jewish rituals. His reaction to the gift was joyous: "Everyone in Pam's family was so accomplished in Jewish matters. I often felt left out. I was always trying to learn and Pam picked up on my interest. I was delighted with the kiddush cup, especially because I could use it immediately. The transliteration gave it meaning until I could learn Hebrew. I saw the gift as a welcoming statement, an invitation to join the club. I was not yet ready to convert, but I knew that Pam and her family would stand by me."

Tom Gordon, a 25-year-old stock broker, had a very different experience, one that caused a great deal of confusion and hurt until he was able to cut through the surface to uncover what lay beneath.

"Barbara and I had been living together for two years. During the Jewish holidays she would visit her family and never invite me. She told me we could not get married because I was not Jewish. Every time I raised the subject, she became defensive and refused to talk. The few times I visited with her folks, they were either very cold toward me or ignored me altogether. I was totally confused and felt that Barbara's family was inordinately rude. I kept asking Barbara how I was so different from her and her family. They were not religious, did not belong to a synagogue, and absolutely relished barbecued pork sandwiches.

"Finally, after too much time, I confronted Barbara and insisted on an open, honest discussion. We talked about our cultural differences, about Jewish history, and about the Holocaust. Only then did I discover that Barbara's grandparents were Holocaust survivors who looked upon all non-Jews with disdain. I had thought her family disliked me as a person, but I was wrong. They just associated me with all the suffering that non-Jews had inflicted upon them. Their stereotypical thinking got in our way and had influenced Barbara. I loved her and would do anything for her. I offered to explore conversion. Her family seemed relieved but still somewhat concerned. Nonetheless, after learning more about Judaism, I felt comfortable with it and felt that conversion was but a small step on my part so that we could stay together."

Barbara, like all Jewish partners involved in an interfaith relationship, should have taken an inclusive rather than an exclusive approach from the start. Of course, sometimes the Jewish partner needs to come to terms with his or her own feelings before sharing them with the partner. Be alert to certain cues, both verbal and nonverbal, that the non-Jewish partner is open to the possibility of conversion. In this case, Tom's boldness and persistence finally enabled Barbara to face up to the issue. Someone with less determination than Tom might have ended the relationship, without either one of them realizing that conversion was an option.

Explore Together

Some Jews tell me they are embarrassed because they don't have the answers to their partners' questions. Don't be embarrassed, but be honest. So few of us really know enough about our religious traditions. We are born into a religious culture that we often take for granted unless we are motivated to learn and explore more, or unless we are challenged to reevaluate that which we have taken for granted, as someone involved in an interfaith relationship often is.

The best way to deal with a lack of knowledge is to explore together. In the long run, such a learning process will strengthen the relationship by bringing both partners not only closer to Judaism but closer to each other as well.

Be creative and imaginative in presenting Judaism as a way of life. Don't concentrate only on the serious holidays, but share the fun ones too. Aaron Cohen, a 23-year-old disc jockey, used his sense of humor to explain Purim to Fran, his non-Jewish girl-friend. He dressed up in a costume and concocted a huge *mish-loach manot*, which he delivered to her, calling it a Jewish Easter basket. He had put in the package his partner's favorite foods plus the traditional fruits, candy, and hamentaschen. Fran was thoroughly enchanted by his gesture, and he used the opportunity as a springboard to talk about what Purim and other holidays had meant to him when he was growing up.

Edna Jacobs, a 24-year-old reading specialist, took her boyfriend John to Brooklyn to visit her childhood synagogue for Simhat Torah. Edna had prepared John by explaining the holiday to him. But he was still totally surprised by the spirit and celebration he witnessed as throngs of people danced in the streets to celebrate the Torah. It was an unforgettable experience, especially for a Quaker from Vermont. Later, as the two of them munched on the apples given out during the service, they discussed John's reactions and Edna's childhood memories. She confided how she used to go back for a second apple when she thought no one was looking and her guilt over not being sure if taking a second apple was stealing. For Edna, taking John to her favorite Jewish places was an important way of expressing her commitment and involving him in her life. As she put it, "You can only talk so much about Simhat Torah, a Jewish wedding, or a Soviet Jewry rally. Only by experiencing them can John begin to feel what I feel."

Don't just focus on the religious aspects of Judaism. Visiting Jewish museums and bookstores, attending lectures on Jewish topics, and seeing films are always a good idea. One man introduced his partner to Judaism by taking her to a Hasidic song and dance festival. Since the woman was a singer and dancer, she was immediately attracted to this Jewish form of artistic expression.

A visit to New York City's Lower East Side on a Sunday morning can provide a good opportunity to explore a little history about earlier Jewish settlement in this country and at the same time enjoy a little old-world culture, great shops of Judaica, and, yes, even the food that is so often associated with Jews. Why eat in a hamburger joint when you can introduce your partner to matzah ball soup, hot knishes, sour pickles, and freshly baked bagels? "Do Jewish people eat these foods every day?" non-Jews often ask. The answer is that some people eat some of these foods some of the time. Explain to your friend what role, if any, these foods have played in your life. One young Jew said that these foods were as foreign to him as they were to his Methodist girlfriend.

The goal is to introduce your partner gradually and sensitively to as many sensory Jewish experiences—sights and sounds, flavors and smells—as possible. Use these opportunities to relate the Jewish beliefs and values you find most appealing and meaningful.

In opening the door to Judaism, do not be overbearing. Judaism should be introduced one step at a time. It is also important to be honest with yourself as well as with your partner. One should not expect more from the non-Jew than what you as a Jew are willing to practice and acknowledge on a personal level. Suddenly insisting on going to synagogue every Shabbat when that has not been your life-style will eventually cause resentment on your part and consternation in your partner. One of the most disillusioning discoveries for a potential convert is to find that the partner is pretending to be more observant than he or she really is, especially if he or she reverts to nonobservance after the conversion. There are many other ways to let someone know that Judaism is important.

Of course, if a genuine resurgence of interest in Judaism emerges as a result of your non-Jewish partner's presence, by all means pursue it. Jewish partners commonly find themselves rediscovering Judaism at the same time they are introducing it to their non-Jewish mates. As one Jewish partner observed, "Because of my intense discussions about religion with my fiancé, I now look at my Judaism not as something inherited, but as something to be discovered. It's not that I forgot my Jewish priorities, I just had never really clarified them in the first place." Indeed, many Jews who have ceased active involvement in Judaism, for whatever reason, find that introducing a non-Jewish partner to Judaism allows an evaluation of Judaism from an adult perspective, perhaps for the first time.

Ronald Maislin, a 37-year-old high school principal, believes he would have continued to be a "High Holiday Jew," attending synagogue and expressing his Judaism only on the High Holidays, had he not fallen in love with a non-Jew. During Ronald's first marriage to a Jewish woman, "certain things were assumed," he says. "There was never a question that a rabbi would officiate at our wedding and that our children would be Jewish. But that was about the extent of our Jewishness."

After his divorce, when Ronald became involved with Debbie, a non-Jewish woman, "all of the things I had taken for granted became major points of discussion: Could I get married in a church with a priest? Could I have children who were not considered Jewish? I could not honestly answer these questions until I seriously reevaluated my own Jewish feelings. I started going to synagogue again and exploring Judaism in a way I never before had as an adult. I realized my understanding of Judaism had not progressed one bit since my bar mitzvah. I shared my new discoveries with my fiancée so that by the time I asked her to convert, she knew my feelings were sincere."

Through his wife Margie's conversion, Ernest Green, 29, also was able to expand his own Jewish knowledge, which had stagnated at the level of a 13-year-old's. "I harbored wonderful Jewish memories from my childhood but had suppressed all my Jewish involvement and observance. Through Margie, I fell in love with Judaism all over again. I realized that I wanted to impart a warm, active Judaism to my future children. It was really through Margie that I, too, became a Jew by choice!"

THE HYPROCRITE PHENOMENON

The reawakening of Ronald's and Ernest's dormant Jewish feelings raises the problem faced by many uninvolved Jews who find themselves—not surprisingly owing to their disengagement from most things Jewish—locked in an interfaith relationship. I call it the "hypocrite phenomenon." It usually involves some variation on the following scenario.

Martha, a 28-year-old real estate broker raised as a Methodist, was totally confused about the newly professed Jewish commitment of her fiancé, Eric Goldberg. "Eric and I dated for two years, and the only thing Jewish I ever knew about him was his name. I never saw him go to synagogue. Later, I found out he went home to his parents for Passover seders and the High Holidays. Together, we ate all kinds of food—he was particularly fond of lobsters and ribs. There was not one Jewish book or article in his apartment, and we never discussed Jewish issues. Was I ever shocked during our first real discussion about marriage when he practically demanded that I convert to Judaism and insisted we be married in a synagogue by his rabbi. If I had had a clue about his feelings at the beginning of the relationship, I may not have been so confused."

Eric, however, saw things a little differently: "I'm Jewish. I'm proud of my people, but I don't feel that I have to advertise my Jewishness. Martha doesn't understand that even if I never set foot in a synagogue, I'm still a Jew."

Jewish partners often come to me wrestling with issues similar to Eric's. They say things like "I'm not a practicing Jew when it comes to ritual and attending synagogue, and I don't observe the holidays or keep kosher, but I want my partner to understand that Judaism is very important to me. I even want her to convert, but she thinks that's strange. How do I convey my feelings without coming across as a hyprocrite?"

Many Jews in modern America believe it is enough to *feel* Jewish, to be a gastronomic or cultural Jew, perhaps with the notion that, inexplicable as it is, they have little "J" cells in their blood. Sometimes, an awareness of Jewish history, of centuries of persecution, prompts an instinctual commitment to the survival of the Jewish people.

When it comes to encouraging conversion, these Jews understandably find it difficult to explain their seemingly inexplicable commitment to their partners. Even outwardly observant Jews often have difficulty expressing their feelings about Judaism, but they at least have their actions to illustrate the bond. Very often, the daily visible commitment to Judaism more than anything else sparks a non-Jewish partner to consider conversion seriously. But Jews who are not visibly engaged in a Jewish lifestyle have a more difficult time convincing their mates of their commitment to Judaism.

In such relationships, the testing stage often comes much later—sometimes too late—in the relationship, when questions surrounding marriage and weddings arise. If and when the subject of conversion comes up, the non-Jewish partner is often as surprised and confused as Martha was when Eric sprang his demand on her. Once again, I must stress the importance of addressing these issues at an earlier stage, no matter how difficult or irrelevant they may then seem.

For uninvolved Jews fearful of coming across as hypocrites, I suggest that honesty is the best path to pursue. As a relationship begins to intensify, be up-front about feelings in a way similar to that of Jacob Kramer, who told his non-Jewish girlfriend simply, "I'm not a particularly knowledgeable or religious Jew, but deep down I feel Jewish, and I want you to consider sharing that feeling with me. Let's explore together."

The techniques of introducing a non-Jewish partner to Judaism are the same for the uninvolved Jew as they are for the involved Jew. The major difference is that in the former case, introducing one's partner to Judaism may mean exploring the basics of Judaism together and enlisting outside help. One word of caution: it is unfair to ask someone to convert to something that the Jewish partner knows little about. Enroll in a basic Judaism course together. Consult the local Jewish Federation, community center, or synagogue for the courses available in a particular city or town. Also ask about community programs, organizations, and holiday celebrations that might provide avenues for exploration. Locate sources for Jewish books, records, and tapes that can facilitate learning about Judaism in the privacy of one's own home. Go beyond the realm of nominal Judaism and together explore concepts and practices of more observant Jews. Get in touch with a local synagogue to help arrange a Shabbat experience with a family. Go to a Jewish museum, a Jewish lecture, or a movie.

Of course, none of these will be effective unless the attitude of the Jewish partner is positive. The Jewish partner serves not only as a role model, but also as an ambassador for Judaism. If the Jewish partner does not demonstrate an interest in his or her heritage or concern for the future of the Jewish people, there is little reason to expect the non-Jewish partner to care either.

POPPING THE BIG QUESTION

I am amazed at the number of people who say to me, "I might have considered converting a long time ago, but [he/she] never asked me." One of the simplest and most overlooked ways to encourage conversion is to simply ask: "Would you consider sharing my Jewish life with me?" Of course, the question can be popped only after a substantive and meaningful introduction and exposure to Judaism. Although no steadfast rule can apply to all couples, I usually recommend that the non-Jewish partner be exposed to at least one Jewish year—replete with holiday celebrations, life-cycle events, and more—before being asked to consider conversion.

How the question is posed is very important. Every individual is different, and each person must find the approach that is best suited to his or her partner's needs. Interviews with hundreds of spouses who asked their partners to convert have generated a few standard pointers: be honest and open; find a quiet place and time when both partners are healthy and free from distractions or outside worries; do not combine it with any other event such as a birthday or holiday—it is unfair to ask someone to convert as a personal present; choose a romantic setting, but never before or after sexual intimacy.

The "romantic approach" is most often mentioned as both appreciated and successful. When Ronald Maislin asked his fiancée, Debbie, to convert, he chose a quiet atmospheric restaurant. His nervousness was evidenced by the fact that he had written out his thoughts ahead of time. His major, and not uncommon, dilemma was whether he should first ask Debbie to marry him, then to convert, or vice versa. "I didn't want her to think I was blackmailing her into an answer. But the fact was I probably would not have married her without conversion." During dessert, he recalls, "I took Debbie's hand and looked lovingly into her eyes and said, 'Debbie, you mean the world to me. I want to marry you. But my Judaism also means a great deal to me. I want to share my life and my religion with you. Will you consider becoming my Jewish wife?' When Debbie agreed, I was ecstatic. We ordered a bottle of champagne and toasted our good fortune!"

Madeline Plotnick, a 28-year-old music teacher from Phoenix, used her culinary talents to set the mood to pop the question. "I had been dating Al for eighteen months. He knew how deeply I felt about Judaism, but he didn't seem to think it would be a problem. Whenever he tried to speak about marriage, I changed the subject. Finally, I decided it was time to address the issue directly. I invited Al over for a candlelight gourmet dinner, complete with all his favorite Jewish foods. After dinner, we sat by the fire, and I took a deep breath and plunged in: 'Al, I know you've been thinking about marriage. I want to marry you. I love you very much. I look forward to raising beautiful children together. But I want our children to be Jewish, not just because I'm

Jewish but because they would share a common religion with both of us. I want you to become a Jew so that we can share everything together. I will help you in every possible way to obtain a proper conversion. And if you say no, I'll never cook like this for you again!" Al did say yes, but I suspect it had more to do with Madeline's approach and her promise to support him rather than her cooking talents. Today, Al is the president of a large Conservative synagogue in the Southwest.

The direct romantic approach, though a favorite, doesn't work for everyone. Some require a more indirect form of expression. Michael Horton, a 28-year-old doctor, was unable to face a possible rejection and so wrote a love poem to his girlfriend, Karen. In it he extolled her virtues as well as his commitment to Judaism and asked her to become his Jewish wife. "I asked her to consider my proposal seriously but ended by saying that if she could not convert or at least consider it as a future option, then I did not want her to respond to my letter—ever. I waited one very long week. The answer was encouraging. She agreed to marry me and explore the possibility of conversion."

Michael and Karen's story has an interesting twist. Karen took the Reform movement's "Introduction to Judaism" course but felt she was not ready to convert in time for their wedding. She did, however, want to please Michael by having a Jewish wedding. They managed to find one of the few Reform rabbis who perform mixed marriages, and Karen attributes her ultimate decision to convert two years later to the support of that rabbi. "I can tell you in all honesty that if our rabbi was not so helpful, I never would have converted. His attitude assured me that there would be a place for me in Judaism when I was ready. Two years later, before the birth of our first son, I decided that I was ready to be a Jewish wife and a Jewish mommy."

Some Jews involved in interfaith relationships think that the easiest way to persuade a partner to convert is to say that the pressure is coming from parents or a rabbi. This approach, however, often backfires because it is viewed by the potential convert as an unacceptable form of coercion and often inspires unhealthy resentment of both the partner and the partner's family. Although it is acceptable to indicate that most rabbis do not perform mixed marriages without conversion or that parents would be thrilled to know that conversion is being considered, it should be made clear that one should consider conversion for the sake of Judaism, because of what Judaism has to offer, and not solely as a favor to the Jewish partner. That is why I stress that the non-Jewish partner must make a decision while equipped with some basic knowledge of and experience with Judaism. Above all, the Jewish partner cannot command, threaten, or pressure someone to convert. He or she must be prepared to answer some frequently asked questions, such as "What does it mean to convert? What Jewish life-style am I expected to lead?"

Responses to the request to convert usually take one of three forms:

1. A DEFINITIVE YES marks the beginning of a very important process, one in which the non-Jew needs his or her partner's continuing support and encouragement. Converting is like going through major surgery. If someone leaves you at the hospital door, it is not nearly as comforting as having someone there to support you and share your experience. The most successful convert is one who never feels alone.

2. I NEED MORE TIME is probably the most common response, requiring patience and understanding on the part of the Jewish partner. The potential convert may need time to be alone to contemplate the idea; he or she may need support and encouragement without pressure. A few basic books about Judaism, if not already read, may help at this point. Find out if a support group for converts exists in the area so that the potential convert can talk to others who once faced the same questions.

3. A DEFINITIVE NO, meaning that the non-Jewish partner cannot or will not consider conversion as an option. The Jewish mate should listen carefully to the reasons and try to understand the feelings behind the words. If a strong commitment to another religion is the reason, an impasse may have been reached. However, other reasons may present the possibility of a future conversion. Such reasons may include not enough information about Judaism; fear of parental reprisals; or concern that the decision

would adversely affect the parents' emotional or physical well-being. Consider whether the relationship may still be secure if the partner is willing to raise the children as Jews or perhaps even have them convert. Remember also that nearly one-third of all conversions occur after marriage. One's circumstances or feelings might change. Increasing familiarity with Judaism, the desire to raise children in a one-religion, one-tradition household, and life-cycle events are all catalysts that have inspired other non-Jewish partners to reconsider conversion as an option long after the wedding ceremony.

If the disparities appear irreconcilable, a separation period might be helpful. Counseling from a rabbi, other clergy, or other professionals might help.

If, after a designated period, the obstacles appear insurmountable and a mixed marriage is not an acceptable option for the couple, the relationship will have to end. Although loving relationships are always difficult to end, those severed because of irreconcilable ethnic and religious life-styles seem particularly difficult. It may provide little consolation, but the fact is that hundreds of couples have made similar heart-rending decisions.

The poignant story of Betty Ann Thomas, the only daughter of an Episcopalian minister, and Alan Saltz, an Orthodox Jew who was named for his grandfather, a well-known Hasidic rabbi, provides a case in point. When Betty Ann, a nurse, and Alan, a doctor, met at the hospital where they both worked, they soon became keenly aware of their religious and cultural differences. They both came from religious families and also carried the commitment over into their own lives. They did not date because of their separate backgrounds, but they saw each other every day at work, where they discussed patients, shared meals, and, in time, fell in love. Each one tried desperately to convert the other, but neither of them considered it an option, both because of their own strong religious identification and because each one knew how distressed their families would be.

Betty Ann recalls, "I prayed and cried for days. I couldn't concentrate on my work. I lost my appetite. I couldn't run away from my feelings of utter despair and burning love. I raged inside and directed my wrath at God, myself, my parents, his parents, and fate itself. 'Why me?' I would plead. I didn't ask to fall in love with Alan. Was God testing me? I made myself emotionally and physically sick. I couldn't live with him or without him. But I realized how many lives we would destroy with our love and marriage. If we ended the relationship, only two people would suffer. It was the unselfish thing to do. The irony of it all is that I was attracted to Alan because of his religious zeal. Maybe we ended the relationship because we loved each other too much to hurt each other's religious convictions."

A SUMMARY OF GUIDELINES

Patience and endurance are critical.

Benjamin Franklin once said, "A man convinced against his will is of the same opinion still." Likewise, coerced conversion does not make for a willing or committed Jew. Here are some key points for the Jewish partner to remember:

1. Be clear in your own mind about what Judaism means to you.

2. Obtain as much information about intermarriage and conversion as possible so that you will be fully prepared to discuss in detail the questions and concerns raised by your partner.

3. Be persistent but patient. Do not expect your partner to love Judaism after just one encounter with a holiday celebration or Jewish program. Your goal is to start your partner seriously thinking about Judaism.

4. Present Judaism in a positive light in terms of personal needs. What does Judaism offer you as a couple? Discuss the advantages of a common religion and life-style.

5. Listen to the feelings behind the words spoken by your partner when discussing religious issues. Be alert to signals of acceptance or rejection.

6. Maintain a sense of humor! It comes in handy in many difficult situations, not just this one.

After a non-Jewish spouse or partner has agreed to convert, a sigh of joy and relief may be in order, but the Jewish partner's role as chief supporter and cheerleader has just begun. The attitude and approach of the Jewish partner is perhaps the single greatest factor that determines the successful acculturation and integration of the Jew by choice. Both through the conversion process and long after, the Jewish spouse must be there to provide encouragement and guidance.

To begin with, Jewish partners should make every effort to participate in the conversion course along with the prospective convert. Conversion can be a highly emotional experience. If it is being done primarily for the sake of marriage, it is essential that both partners engage in the process together as the first important step in building a Jewish future together.

The experience of Wendy Baines provides an example of insensitivity to a convert's needs, a situation to avoid at all costs. Wendy, a 33-year-old biologist from Princeton, had already left the Methodist church when she became engaged to Edward Polsky. He did not push for conversion, but she felt strongly that their children should be raised with only one religion. When Wendy decided to convert to Judaism, Edward was pleased but basically indifferent, believing that it was her decision—and therefore her responsibility—and absolving himself from all involvement. He refused to participate in the conversion classes, leaving Wendy feeling quite alone. "Whenever I saw other couples whispering to each other about a statement the rabbi made or squeezing each others' hands for reassurance, I ached for Edward to be there. I wanted to elicit his feelings and responses and compare them to mine. I tried to talk to him after the classes, but it was not the same. I could recapture the words, but the feelings were gone."

Edward's passivity toward his fiancée's conversion is not unique. It stems from ambivalence, ignorance, or the misguided notion that a conversion is not the Jewish partner's business. Particularly when the Jewish in-laws are the ones most adamant about conversion, the Jewish spouse may feel uncomfortable with the whole situation and go along with it just to keep the peace. The convert may go through the process and learn what is expected, but without ongoing support from the spouse, resentment and alienation can take hold. A full adjustment and integration into Jewish life will take longer if, in fact, it ever occurs. A couple of years later, the Jewish spouse may wonder why the convert still wants a Christmas tree, is fearful of holiday get-togethers at Rosh Hashannah and Passover, or even talks about having a child baptized "just to be safe."

My advice to Jewish partners who may, for whatever reason, feel ambivalent, is to set aside personal feelings and be as supportive and helpful as possible to the prospective convert. Use the experiences of Bob Martin and Paul Weiss as role models of support.

Bob's wife, Patricia, recalls Bob's encouragement prior to her first seder as a new Jew. "He knew I was scared and overwhelmed at the thought of my first seder. I was going to be meeting his extended family for the first time. I had just completed my conversion class, and I did not yet feel Jewish. I wanted Bob to be proud of me and was desperately afraid of making a mistake or saying something stupid. Bob was a real gem. He took the time to review my notes on Passover with me. During the seder, he explained things in a way that did not make me feel silly or left out. He even made sure I was clued in to the inside family jokes and stories. His caring attitude made my transition into Judaism much easier."

Marilyn Weiss is equally convinced that her conversion was facilitated by her husband, Paul, who was by her side every step of the way. One of the most memorable things Paul did to guide and encourage Marilyn was to make her tapes with the prayers said during Shabbat services. "Everday I listened to the tape on my way to work. It was a wonderful way to learn, and now I feel so much more comfortable at synagogue on Shabbat," she says.

As I have emphasized in previous chapters, a new Jew is an intellectual but not yet an emotional Jew. He or she cannot immediately share the feelings of a born Jew about Israel, the Holocaust or a special Jewish movie or event. Nostalgia, pride, and heartfelt emotions will only emerge with time and with constant exposure to a Jewish environment. It is here that a spouse can be invaluable in guiding a Jew by choice and nurturing those feelings.

A potential point of conflict can arise when the convert becomes more knowledgeable about Jewish history, rituals, or holiday celebrations than the Jewish partner or the partner's family. The Jewish partner should try to channel any feelings of resentment or intimidation into pride and happiness. The new Jew is not trying to outshine his or her spouse but, rather, to demonstrate new knowledge and make the partner proud. He or she is looking for affirmation for a new Jewish self. It is the Jewish partner's job to express pride and pleasure in that achievement and to encourage further study and commitment.

One thing is certain: The non-Jewish or recently converted partner will be watching the Jewish partner closely. A spouse will react positively to positive Jewish experiences and role models and react negatively to negative ones.

In preparing for Jewish holidays and life-cycle events, the new Jew will look to the veteran for guidance. The Jewish partner should explain what the celebration is about, who will be there, the special songs and prayers involved. In some cases, it may be advisable to remind people to be especially welcoming and helpful, though not too oversolicitous. At the celebration or event, do not abandon the new Jew, but continue the explanations. Afterward, discuss feelings on both sides. Remember to express pleasure that your partner was there to share it with you.

PROBLEMS ARE INEVITABLE

Conversionary couples may be right in thinking, as they often do, that their path through life will be easier than that of interfaith couples, for whom there exists a greater potential for rift and conflict in the attempt to incorporate into one home two separate religions and cultures. Nevertheless, conversionary couples are wrong to assume that certain problems unique to their situation will not arise. Whether those problems revolve around degree of observance, holiday celebrations, how to maintain close ties with the Christian side of the family, or how to validate and incorporate the convert's past into family life, it is virtually guaranteed that conflict will come knocking at the conversionary couple's door.

Before the Wedding

Areas of potential conflict among conversionary couples can span a broad spectrum, ranging from relatively trivial issues, such as what to serve at the wedding when people from two very different cultures marry, to more lasting decisions, such as whether to live in a predominantly Jewish neighborhood.

In the first instance, for example, Yuri and Harvey Seligman almost never made it to the *chuppah* (the canopy under which the bride and groom are married) when Yuri's desire to incorporate her Chinese heritage into the kosher menu exploded into a family battle. In the second, Claudia and Joel Herson struggled long and hard over whether to move into a predominantly Jewish neighborhood in their Texas city. Claudia, who had converted before their marriage, was shocked and hurt by Joel's accusation that she did not want to be "really Jewish" because she preferred to live in a heterogeneous community. There were many tears and nasty words before Claudia made Joel understand that, since she had never known any Jews before meeting Joel, she felt intimidated by the prospect of living in an exclusively Jewish neighborhood.

Another family misunderstanding, based solely on different cultural practices, threatened Emma Laslow's relationship with her sister-in-law when she failed to throw a baby shower during Emma's first pregnancy. Only several months after the birth did Emma learn that traditionally Jews do not have baby showers or give baby gifts prior to the birth because it is considered bad luck.

The Thwarted New Jew

It is not unusual for a new or potential convert to discover in Judaism a source of spiritual fulfillment, only to have his or her genuine desire to become a more observant Jew thwarted by the spouse. This unanticipated divergence of views spawns many an argument between disgruntled spouse and disillusioned convert, as illustrated by the case of Marty and Rena Goldman. Marty, a 38-year-old orthodontist from California, considers himself an ethnic but unobservant Jew. When his wife, Rena, a 35-year-old convert, began finding more and more meaning in the tradition and wanted to bring it home, he rebelled. "I could handle lighting candles on Shabbat, but I had no desire to revamp my entire kitchen to keep kosher. When I didn't give in, Rena's conversion rabbi spoke to me on her behalf, which made me really angry and resentful that the rabbi was interfering in my life. My wife kept screaming at me: 'Why won't you let me be Jewish?' "

After a few years of anguish and discussion with a local support group for converts, Marty came to realize that "Rena felt cheated. I had dampened her joy and love for Judaism. While I was so bent on not having her force her ideas on me, I became guilty of foisting my lack of commitment onto her." Together, they worked out a rather unusual arrangement whereby Rena keeps kosher and Marty doesn't. Says Marty, "We prepare foods on separate counters and use separate shelves. It's almost as much trouble as if I kept kosher, too. I guess when the children come along, I will keep kosher inside the house, but not outside."

Emily and Dan Rudd, on the other hand, were unable to reconcile their different ideas about Judaism. Says Emily, a 34-year-old history professor from New York: "My almost perfect marriage dissolved because my husband became too involved with Judaism. He started out with a Reform conversion and ended up becoming a Lubavitcher. He wanted to change my life in a radical way, while I was content to remain a Reform Jew. Finally, the pressures became so great, I gave him an ultimatum. He chose Hasidism over me. We divorced shortly thereafter."

Dan's version of the story is slightly different: "My wife wanted me to convert so that our future children would not be confused about their religious identity. But after I agreed, she felt her job had ended. She attended conversion classes with me only three times. She took no interest in my studies, and I had to coerce her to accompany me even to Reform services. What really upset me was that she knew so little about Judaism and cared even less that she knew so little. Maybe my knowledge threatened her and my enthusiasm overwhelmed her, but she refused to discuss the issue. All I heard from her was, 'I don't have to prove I'm a Jew.' "

Paradoxically, their two children, for whom Emily and Dan wanted to provide a secure religious identity, are growing up experiencing two extremes of Judaism, since the two parents share custody of the children. Says Emily: "As the children grow older, I try to provide explanations they can understand. All in all, they have adjusted better than I have, accommodating themselves to the rules and customs of each household. They most certainly never kiss the mezuzzah upon entering my door as they do at their father's home!"

The Christmas Tree Dilemma

The story of Aron and Lynn Rothstein, and their Christmas tree struggle, illustrates another difficulty conversionary couples may face. Aron explains:

"My wife wholeheartedly agreed to give up her Christmas tree after she converted. But after eight years of marriage, as the children grew older, they began to cry and beg for a Christmas tree and Christmas decorations. Part of their affinity for Christmas stemmed from the warm and joyous celebration they experienced with Lynn's large Irish family, with her dozens of cousins and aunts and uncles. 'Everyone is celebrating Christmas,' they would complain. My first reaction was to forbid my wife and children to visit her family on Christmas. I quickly abandoned that idea, which had made me into a first-class ogre. When the holidays finally ended, the turmoil subsided, but we knew it would resurface each year.

"At our support group, after some reluctance, we aired our problem and were stunned by the initial reaction. Other members wanted to know what we had done throughout the year that was Jewish, that had instilled in our kids a sense of belonging and pride in their Jewishness. One couple, speaking from experience, suggested that conversionary families sometimes have to work harder to inject a Jewish character into the family dynamic. I resented the implication that we were not good Jewish parents. I felt resentment toward my wife, feeling that it was because of her that I had to exert an extra effort to be Jewish. Why should I have to prove my Jewishness? Upon further discussion and later introspection, I gradually came to realize that if I wanted my family to *be* Jewish, then together we needed to *do* Jewish. My kids desired only what they saw, and, unfortunately, they had seen nothing really Jewish at all.

"It took us a long time to incorporate Judaism into our lives. Together, we explored and we learned, bringing meaningful Jewish activity into our home. The children continue to visit their Christian grandparents and cousins at Christmastime, but I no longer hear pleas for their own Christmas tree. Instead, the children proudly display their menorahs at the family Hanukkah party we have each year."

Convert's Non-Jewish Heritage

It is perfectly natural for conversionary couples to confront reminders of their disparate backgrounds continually, especially reminders about the convert's non-Jewish past. Either these differences can be used as an asset to encourage cultural exploration while rooted firmly on Jewish ground, or they can be divisive.

Patricia O'Neal and her husband, Steve Simon, chose the healthier route. They used Patricia's Irish Catholic ties to enhance the family's understanding about her past. When Patricia converted, she embraced Judaism wholeheartedly, becoming an active and knowledgeable member of her Jewish community. Patricia, still fiercely proud of her heritage, calls herself an Irish Jew and has taught their two children about Ireland and Irish folkways. Steve does not feel threatened by her continuing attachment to her Irish roots. Her Irish identity, in turn, does not diminish the family's commitment to Judaism and an active Jewish life-style. When the children were old enough, the family visited Ireland, where they met some of Patricia's relatives and explored "Mom's country." Their next overseas trip was to Israel, where their bonds to the Jewish people were enhanced.

Making a marriage work is difficult and complex enough without the added strain that stems from disparate ethnic and religious backgrounds. Patricia and Steve, like many conversionary couples, may have to work harder to make their marriage successful because they frequently are forced to confront unanticipated differences. Conversionary marriages can be just as successful as endogamous marriages and, in some cases, even more so. Marriage is not a battle. It is an opportunity for two people to mature together, to live common values, and to share common dreams. But more than love is required to make it work. Communication, mutual understanding, and respect are vital. For all couples, a successful and loving marriage requires imagination, foresight, and enough flexibility to fulfill the wishes and aspirations of each partner, while simultaneously aspiring to common goals.

4

The Jewish parents:
from oy to joy

There is a story told of a Jewish father who meets his neighbor in the lobby of his apartment building. The neighbor says to the father, "I hear your son is getting married."

"Yes," responds the father proudly. "He is marrying a nice Jewish girl."

"What? She's not a real Jew. I heard she's a convert! If it were my son, I would disown him!"

The father ponders this for a moment, then replies, "You are right. If he were your son I would disown him, too. It's always easy to disown another man's child. As for me, I'll keep my son—and his beautiful bride!"

Jewish parents are not always as level-headed as this father about their child marrying a convert to Judaism. I receive hundreds of letters from parents all across the country with scores of questions and concerns. Some of their comments go like this:

"Intellectually, I know that my daughter-in-law's conversion makes her a real Jew, but emotionally I cannot fully accept her as one of us."

"My future son-in-law has expressed a desire to convert. What do we say to him? How involved should we become?"

"We will be meeting our future daughter-in-law's parents for the first time. Should we talk about her conversion? What do we say?"

"My son-in-law is in the middle of his conversion course, and Hanukkah is in two weeks. Is it OK to buy him a menorah?"

"Now that Henry is one of us, how exactly should we treat him?"

"AT LEAST THERE WILL BE A CONVERSION"

Most Jewish parents react with alternating feelings of despair, hurt, and failure when a child informs them that he or she is seriously involved with a non-Jew. One daughter, anxious to avoid a family conflict she felt certain would erupt if her parents knew of her involvement with a non-Jew, decided not to tell her parents of her relationship until she was already engaged and her fiancé had decided to convert. This woman succeeded in averting a conflict—indeed her parents welcomed their future son-in-law wholeheartedly once they knew he was converting—but in doing so she virtually shut her parents out of an important part of her life for more than a year.

Some Jewish parents, especially those with older unmarried children, do not get upset at such news. They may feel that the happiness of their child, and the fact that their child has found *someone* to marry, overrides any other consideration. But, by and large, most Jewish parents, even those without much visible connection to Judaism or the Jewish community, experience a pang of loss, stemming from their own personal commitment to the survival of the Jewish people and, at the very least, to the continuity of their own Jewish family.

Among those most vehemently opposed to the prospect of intermarriage, some parents are initially inclined to go to any length to end the relationship. Through outbursts, threats, and pleadings, the first stage in the sabotage plan is directed at the son or daughter. When that fails, and it usually does, discouragement is aimed at the non-Jewish partner through displays of indifference, coldness, or downright hostility. When these tactics do not produce the intended result, namely a dissolution of the relationship, most parents eventually move on to a more accommodating approach: accepting the inevitable.

Though these parents may still oppose the impending marriage, they begin to hope for a conversion, reasoning that "at least my grandchildren will be Jewish" or "at least the rabbi can marry them in a Jewish ceremony." When conversion does become a reality, the initial sigh of "oy" turns to joy, along with a deep sigh of relief. But with this new phase comes another set of potential problems.

Explaining the Sudden Change in Behavior

One of the initial problems is one of embarrassment. Now that their child will be marrying a convert rather than a non-Jew, parents no longer display the same coldness and hostility and are ashamed of their earlier behavior. The prospective convert, baffled by this sudden turnaround, often becomes wary of these new welcoming signals. He or she is uncertain of the true feelings and intentions of the partner's parents.

Such was the confusion of Amy Cohen, a 26-year-old convert from Pittsburgh. "I thought my husband's parents were schizophrenic," she says. "For a whole year, they had screamed and shouted their displeasure at us. When I told them I was planning to convert, they suddenly took me in their arms and rejoiced. I did not know how to respond. How was I supposed to forget all the nasty words they had hurled at me and Michael? Was I to pretend that all of a sudden everything was fine between us? It took me a long time until I realized that their behavior had reflected their deep concern for Michael and for Judaism."

Amy's mother-in-law, Ruth, tries to explain: "I was totally unprepared for my son's involvement with a non-Jew because we have always led an observant Jewish life. I always thought that intermarriage happened only to assimilated Jewish families. My instinctive reaction was to do everything in my power to break up the relationship. My rabbi, my relatives, and my friends all supported me.

"I knew that Amy was a wonderful person in every way, but the fact that she was not Jewish negated everything else. I am terribly ashamed at what spilled out of my mouth. I threatened to disinherit Michael. I demanded repayment of old student loans, which I had previously told my son he should consider gifts from us. I told him we would not come to their wedding or contribute one penny. I was so desperate I would have said or tried anything. My son, of course, was furious with me.

"In a way I think I just needed to get it out of my system. I had to be able to feel that I had fulfilled my obligation as a Jewish parent. Deep down, I could understand why Michael loved Amy. I was truly relieved and happy when she decided to convert. I could accept her without guilt. Amy did not know what to make of me. I realized I owed her an explanation. It was painful, but we sat and talked about it."

As uncomfortable and embarrassing as such a direct encounter may be, I strongly recommend Ruth's approach. Unless an apology and explanation of such prior hostile behavior are attempted, the convert, or convert-to-be, and her spouse may continue to harbor resentment. The words, letters, or actions may be set aside for the sake of familial harmony, but they may never be forgotten. There may always be distance between the convert and the in-laws, precluding any chance of developing a truly close family relationship.

I strongly believe that it is the obligation of the parents to initiate such dialogue when warranted, but if they don't, and if the convert and/or spouse is feeling conflicted and uncomfortable with the situation, then either one of them should approach the parents with an invitation for an honest discussion.

Most parents truly want to say and do the right thing, but because of their lack of exposure to converts, they don't always know how to react to the idea of a convert joining the family. First and foremost, they should take their cues from the convert. From the moment that a child or his or her partner talks about the decision to convert, parents should respond with enthusiasm and warmth. They should indicate their support and willingness to assist in any way possible.

Words such as these are appropriate and helpful: "We are very happy to hear about your decision. We wholeheartedly welcome you into our family. We appreciate the tremendous amount of introspection it must have taken for you to reach this important decision. We are here to help in any way we can."

Later on, the parents should continue contact through calls or letters. It is acceptable for parents to inquire about the conversion program, to find out what their future child-in-law is learning and feeling in response to the material. Parents should be alert to areas in which they can be of assistance—locating books or a sponsoring rabbi, or providing opportunities to participate in Jewish activities and celebrations.

If Jewish parents cannot answer the questions the prospective convert is sure to ask, they should be honest about it and offer to help him or her find the answers. Whenever possible, invite the convert to join in holiday celebrations with the family.

Parents should feel free to go ahead and buy their future son-in-law a Hanukkah menorah even if his conversion is still a few weeks away. However, be careful not to be too pushy. He may welcome the gift but not yet feel psychologically ready to use it or to dispense with his Christmas celebration. If one is uncertain how the convert-to-be would react to such a gesture, let him make the final decision by extending him an offer such as: "I saw a lovely menorah in the synagogue gift shop and was thinking of buying it for you," or "The gift shop has some beautiful menorahs. I would like you to choose one as a gift from us." Both scenarios give the convert an opportunity to accept or decline graciously.

If the Jewish mother has established a good rapport with her future daughter-in-law, she might be asked—or she can offer—to accompany her to the *mikvah* if it is part of the conversion process. This can be a moving experience for both women, and it can also create a special bond in the relationship. If there is a conversion ceremony, the Jewish parents should attend if possible. Another lovely idea is to provide the new convert with a gift of Judaica, such as Shabbat candlesticks or a *tallit.* Celebrating with a quiet lunch or dinner at home or in a restaurant is another gesture that tells the convert he or she is welcome in the family.

Jewish parents should not distance themselves from one who has chosen Judaism. The convert or convert-to-be needs affirmation of his or her Judaism, especially from the Jewish family. Next to the Jewish partner, the partner's parents are generally the first role models the convert encounters. The new Jew closely listens to and observes what the parents-in-law say and do. The attitude is critical. Parents-in-law of a convert have the added obligation of being not only good in-laws but adoptive parents as well. Converts still have their own family, but it is to their new Jewish family that they will turn for guidance in their new lives as Jews.

Oversensitivity is also a potential problem. How should a disagreement or difference of opinion—be it about plans for the wedding or a specifically Jewish issue such as plans for a seder—be handled?

Sarah and Jack Kahn were horrified when Kathleen, their Irish daughter-in-law-to-be, announced one night at dinner that there was going to be a cash bar at the wedding, especially since they had planned to contribute to the costs. They were also upset that the wedding was going to be held at a hotel rather than in a synagogue. They didn't know what to say.

Some Jewish parents are afraid to confront the convert and instead ask their children to serve as go-betweens. Converts can take offense at this strategy, interpreting, however mistakenly, that the Jewish family lacks confidence in them as new Jews. Once again, direct communication is the best approach.

After the conversion has taken place, do not draw attention to the new Jew's non-Jewish past. The Torah teaches that the convert must be welcomed and treated with love and consideration. Again and again, the Torah says: "You shall love the stranger." The Hebrew word for "stranger," *ger*, is the same word used for "convert."

In practical terms for Jewish parents, as well as for all Jews, this means that one should not refer to the new Jew as a convert. Do not introduce her as "Alice, my daughter-in-law who converted" or him as "Jim, the new Jew in our household." The new Jew is a Jew. If explanations must be given to family members, they can be given quietly and privately.

Some relatives or friends may look at the convert with disdain or suspicion. It is up to the Jewish parents to set an example by showing total acceptance.

ACCEPTING THE CONVERT AS A REAL JEW

During my speaking engagements, workshops, and counseling sessions, as well as through the mail, hundreds of Jewish parents have asked me the same question about the conversion of their child's prospective spouse: "Will my son-in-law—or daughter-in-law—be a 'real Jew'?" For many members of the Jewish community who have had little contact with converts, this is a very real question. When the convert is about to enter one's own family, the question transcends the realm of theory and becomes more pressing and, at times, more confusing.

Let me state it as unequivocally as I can: If a person converts and sincerely accepts the basic principles of the Jewish tradition, commits to a Jewish life-style, and identifies with the Jewish people, that person should be regarded as a full-fledged, authentic Jew. Though the convert has a non-Jewish family and a different ethnic and cultural past, he or she is a Jew and the marriage should be seen as nothing less than a marriage between two Jews. A rabbi can marry this couple because there are no religious barriers to such a marriage. One exception, according to the Orthodox, applies to a Jewish male of priestly ancestry, a Kohen, who may not marry a convert. Only the Orthodox follow this law.

Intellectually, Jewish parents may understand all of this, but emotionally they don't always feel comfortable with the convert and therefore find it difficult to be warm and welcoming. My advice: Fake it! That's right. Though initially it may be difficult to fully accept the situation, make a conscious effort to be friendly and accepting anyway. After several forced attempts, one may be surprised to find the deliberate giving way to the natural. Parents will begin to feel more comfortable as they simultaneouly get to know their daughter- or son-in-law better and as they become more exposed to the reality of conversion.

The Question of Sincerity

The convert's sincerity and motivation are another frequent concern among Jewish parents. Most Jews by choice do convert for the sake of marriage. Some Jews view conversion in this context as the lesser of two evils, with the alternative being an intermarriage without conversion. Parents might disapprove of this so-called conversion of convenience.

Attaching this stigma to a convert without giving the new Jew a chance can prove to be self-defeating. If the convert feels that all efforts made will never be enough to compensate for not being born Jewish, he or she may just stop trying.

Conversion done for the sake of marriage does not automatically create an insincere convert. Among those involved with conversion courses in the Reform, Reconstructionist, and Conservative movements, it is generally believed that a person who comes to Judaism as an extension of love for a Jewish partner often finds personal fulfillment in Judaism after becoming familiar with the tradition. Even among the Orthodox, who generally do not condone conversion for the sake of marriage—insisting instead on a purely personal desire to become a Jew and to live a traditional Jewish life—I know of dozens of instances in which Orthodox rabbis have provided a conversion knowing full well that the primary motivation was to marry a Jew.

The fact is that it takes time, determination, and tremendous effort to become Jewish. Those who question a convert's sincerity should remember that it is far easier to remain a non-Jew than to convert. The convert deserves much more than suspicion and alienation.

As Robin Frank, a convert dismayed by her lack of acceptance, wrote: "It is true that I probably would never have converted if I had not met Nathan. He provided my initial exposure to Judaism. His love and enthusiasm for his Judaism were inspirations to me. However, I'm the one who decided to convert— not Nathan. I studied very hard to become Jewish. I went to the *mikvah* and before the *beth din*. If Nathan walks out on me tomorrow, I will still be a Jew. I have accepted Judaism wholeheartedly. Why can't Jews accept me wholeheartedly?"

Most converts are sincere in their preparations for becoming Jewish. Like Robin, they acknowledge that they probably would never have considered conversion if they had not met or been influenced by a Jewish partner, but most maintain that the decision to convert ultimately was their own.

Sadly enough, some born Jews disregard the level of commitment and sincerity of the convert. In their eyes, a convert is a convert and will always be a convert. These Jews forget or ignore the fact that Jewish tradition holds a very different view. The first Jewish convert, the Biblical Ruth, remained unswervingly committed to the Jewish people after her husband's death. Yet whereas she, the foremother of King David, is revered in the Jewish tradition for choosing Judaism, converts of today are not.

I especially find it ironic when I hear Jewish parents say that they would rather their child marry a secular, assimilated Jew than a convert. In these cases, the convert is greeted with hostility or suspicion, whereas those same parents would never pass such judgment on the uncommitted Jew. It is unfair to impose a double standard—to expect more from a convert than from a born

Jew—especially since the convert's level of commitment is often greater than that of the born Jew. Regardless of what brings the new Jew to Judaism, we should treat that person as a sincere Jew. No one has the ability or the right to look into another Jew's heart.

Despite the overwhelming majority of sincere converts, a minority do not become committed Jews. In all of my interviews and contact with converts, I have discovered so few of these cases that I felt compelled to understand why they had never assimilated into a Jewish world and, in some instances, why they had continued to observe Christian holidays instead of Jewish ones.

In every case, the convert lacked either a supportive rabbi, spouse, or Jewish family. They had not found warmth, encouragement, or acceptance from the Jewish people in their world. Some of these converts were actually ridiculed by their Jewish spouse or family for their desire to live an observant Jewish life. If a convert fails to become the type of Jew we desire, then maybe we need to look to ourselves for the cause. After all, *kol yisrael aravim ze bazeh*: all Jews are responsible for one another.

RELATING TO
THE CONVERT'S PARENTS

Developing good relations with your *machatanim* (the Yiddish word for a child's spouse's parents) can be a delicate issue even when both families are Jewish. Cultivating relations with this new extension of your family when they are not Jewish and may, in fact, be feeling hurt and rejected because their child has chosen Judaism requires special sensitivity and effort. From wedding plans to holiday celebrations, the dynamics of an interfaith extended family are very different from those in which both families come from the same tradition.

The first meeting should, naturally, be friendly and cordial whether it occurs at a restaurant, the home of the groom's parents, the home of the bride's parents, or the couple's home. Although it is important for the Jewish parents to try to make the Christian parents feel comfortable with their child's decision to convert, the subject should not be dwelled upon. A simple statement such as, "We are very happy to welcome your daughter to Judaism" is appropriate and sufficient. Specific details about the upcoming wedding or other concerns are best left for future meetings. Parents should concentrate instead on the attributes and plans of the couple, focusing on the positive aspects of the relationship rather than on negative concerns.

The Wedding Plans

Most couples today have greater input into their wedding plans than in years past. Some even share in or absorb the entire financial costs. Even when the couple takes full responsibility for the wedding, the new convert may eagerly welcome advice from the Jewish family, since he or she may not be familiar with Jewish wedding traditions. Jewish parents should offer their advice and support, but if they sense that the convert feels threatened by too much intrusion, it is probably best to step back a bit and refer the couple to books or to a rabbi.

Many Jewish parents make the mistake of assuming that because the convert is a Jew and the wedding is Jewish, they should take charge of the menu, the flowers, and all the other details. This is especially problematic when the bride is the convert and her family is paying for the wedding. A commonly accepted practice today among many families—and one that seems to lead to the most peaceful weddings among conversionary couples—is to divide the costs between both families, with the help of the couple when possible. Whatever the financial arrangement, Jewish parents should be careful not to be too domineering. They should take their cues from the couple.

It is the job of the Jewish parents as well as the couple to keep the Christian parents informed of the wedding plans. Many Christian parents have never been to a Jewish wedding and have no idea what to expect. Often, their child's conversion, coupled with an alien ceremony, makes them feel like strangers at their own child's wedding. They had envisioned a church wedding and an altar for their child, not a synagogue and a *chuppah!* Being sensitive to these feelings and explaining what they can expect prior to the wedding day might help ease their predicament.

Furthermore, couples and parents should remember that the only part of the Jewish wedding that has to be Jewish is the ceremony. The reception can reflect the backgrounds and wishes of both families. Although Christian parents can have little, if any, input into the ceremony, they can contribute ideas for the reception. I have attended lovely Jewish weddings where the French, Irish, and Japanese cultures of the respective spouses were clearly evident. If the food is kosher, what difference does it make if it is cooked Hungarian, Italian, or Jewish style?

At one particularly memorable wedding, the Chinese bride, a convert, wore a white wedding gown for the wedding ceremony and a red gown, in the Chinese tradition, for the reception. The music was a combination of Chinese and American, with a couple of horas thrown in. The food also skillfully combined the two cultures. The parents and the couple had clearly invested a great deal of time planning the wedding. As a result, they succeeded in making it a comfortable and joyous time for two families of different faiths and cultures.

The Jewish parents' relationship with their child's in-laws should not end with the wedding. The depth of the relationship may depend as much on personalities as it does on religious and cultural differences. In-laws need not be invited frequently but should be included in major family events. Jewish parents who feel comfortable doing so may send cards to the Christian family on Christian holidays. Some families see each other only at times of births, weddings, and deaths. Others have become close friends as well as relations and unite for Passover seders and Hanukkah parties. Each family must work things out in its own way, and, it is hoped, with the good of the entire family, especially the conversionary couple, in mind.

WILL MY GRANDCHILDREN BE REAL JEWS?

Many Jewish parents, having finally accepted the Jewishness of their daughter- or son-in-law, still worry about their grandchildren. I often hear such concerns expressed in the following ways: "I know they have a Jewish home and they are being raised as Jews, but they have Christian family. Will my grandchildren be influenced by their Christian relatives? What will be the reaction of other Jews to my grandchildren? Will they be different because their mother is a convert?"

As I have emphasized repeatedly, a convert is a full Jew and so too are his or her children. And just as Jewish parents are not obliged to explain or justify their children-in-law's conversions to friends, neither are they required to defend their grandchildren's Jewishness. If the grandparents view and treat their grandchildren as Jews, then others will follow suit.

There is no question that children of conversionary marriages are exposed to traditions other than Judaism early in their lives. Except in the most extreme cases, converts cannot—nor should they want to—sever relations with their family or deny their children contact with their family.

Some converts experience severe tensions and polarization over family loyalties. Loyalty to the Christian family is sometimes tested and strained as the convert tries to maintain family ties with the non-Jewish relatives while simultaneously leading a Jewish life.

CELEBRATING HOLIDAYS

Conflicting emotions are often exacerbated at holiday times. The Jewish family should be sensitive to the convert's predicament and try not to aggravate the situation by questioning the couple's decisions, or placing unnecessary strains on the couple at this time.

To avoid confronting Christian holidays, some converts limit contact with Christian family members to nonreligious times and settings. They prefer gatherings on religiously neutral occasions such as birthdays, anniversaries, and Thanksgiving, rather than during religious holidays such as Christmas and Easter. Of course, this method does not work for everyone, nor do most converts recommend or practice it. They usually cite the importance of family togetherness rather than the holiday itself as a reason to be with their families on Christmas and Easter. Avoiding a visit does not change the fact that some family members worship differently and celebrate separate holidays.

Among the holiday guidelines suggested by converts is that the conversionary family explain to the Christian family that, as Jews, they will be celebrating only Jewish holidays, but that they will, when possible, join them for Christmas to share the time of love and family closeness. The Jewish family should send Christmas gifts in Christmas or neutral wrapping paper to the Christian family at Christmastime. Likewise, the Christian family should be encouraged to send Hanukkah presents wrapped in Hanukkah paper at Hanukkah.

I encourage conversionary couples to make the most of Hanukkah even though it is a minor holiday on the Jewish calendar. It should be made fun and joyous so that children feel that their December holiday is fun and interesting, too.

Grandparents can play an active role in making sure their grandchildren learn about and enjoy Hanukkah. If they live close enough, such activities can include helping each child make his or her own menorah; planning a Hanukkah party; baking cookies in the shape of dreidels or menorahs, making *latkes* (potato pancakes), applesauce, and *sufganiyot* (doughnuts); buying books and tapes about Hanukkah; playing dreidel games.

For grandparents who live far away, a lot of pleasure can be derived—at both ends—from sending grandchildren surprise packages with eight small gifts, one for each night of Hanukkah, including dreidels and Hanukkah gelt.

Throughout the years, I have found that conversionary couples who run Jewish households, celebrate Shabbat and Jewish holidays, and educate their children about Judaism do not produce children who are confused about their identity. The children will identify as Jews if Jewish activities are practiced in their home throughout the year. It is usually only those children who have no continuous positive connection to Judaism who are confused when they see Christian members of the family celebrating different holidays.

If non-Jewish members of the extended family are saying or doing things that may be offensive to the children's Jewish sensibilities, the issue should be taken up by the convert, not by the Jewish family.

Finally, grandparents should strive to treat all their grandchildren equally, whether they are part of a conversionary family or not. They should avoid both coolness and overindulgence so as not to make any of the children feel different from their cousins.

One Jewish grandmother who lived far away from her son and daughter-in-law sent dozens of Jewish children's books, tapes, candles, menorahs, toys, and gelt each Hanukkah to the conversionary couple and their children. She sent a check for the children of her other daughter, who had married a born Jew.

After years of such practice, she wistfully observed she had been sending the gifts to the wrong home. The conversionary couple keeps a traditional Jewish home, observes Shabbat, keeps kosher, and enrolls their two daughters in a Jewish day school. The born Jewish daughter and her born Jewish husband, who also have two daughters, practice little in the way of Judaism, have never joined a synagogue, and are providing no Jewish education for their children.

This grandmother is now confident about the Jewish future of her conversionary grandchildren. It is her other grandchildren, born of two born Jews, whom she worries about most.

5

The non-Jewish parents: will I lose my child?

When Dorothy McGallan sent her oldest daughter off to an Ivy League college in the East from their rural Wisconsin town, her list of worries was long: "I worried Louise might get pregnant. I worried that she might get involved with drugs. And I worried about her academic success. The last thing in the world that ever entered my mind was the possibility that Louise would fall in love with a Jewish man."

When Louise came home for Christmas during her senior year and announced to her parents that she was engaged to a Jew and that she was planning to convert to Judaism, Dorothy and her husband were dumbfounded. "We just didn't know what to say to her. The thought of intermarriage and conversion had never even occurred to us. We weren't even exactly sure just what converting to Judaism meant!"

As Dorothy's experience indicates, the issues of intermarriage and conversion occupy relatively little, if any, space in the minds of most Christian parents, especially when compared with their Jewish counterparts. One reason for this is purely numerical: with so many more non-Jews than Jews in this world, the probability that a non-Jew will arrive home announcing an engagement to a Jew is far lower than the probability that the reverse might happen. Thus, for today's committed Jewish parent, such a scenario is an ever-present fear, whereas the non-Jewish parent rarely gives it a thought.

Even for non-Jewish parents who may have considered the possibility, the prospect of their child intermarrying or even converting may not seem as threatening as it does for Jewish parents. No one believes that the future of the Christian community is endangered as a result of a few, or even several thousand, conversions each year.

Because of the general absence of discussion about intermarriage and conversion in their communities or their churches, most Christian parents find themselves unprepared to deal with their feelings when a child informs them that he or she intends to become a Jew.

Regardless of the initial reaction—whether one is a devout Baptist who sees such a step as a betrayal of the family and the church or a lapsed Methodist who wholeheartedly accepts the impending conversion and marriage—nearly all Christian parents inevitably encounter certain issues. From the fear of alienation at the wedding ceremony of one's own child to the sudden cessation of shared holiday celebrations, parents encounter both religious and cultural differences that could threaten family relationships if not handled sensitively on both sides.

BREAKING THE NEWS

Many converts say that one of the most difficult aspects of their entire conversion experience was informing their family of the decision. Vicki Lynne Herman recalls: "I thought I could talk to my mom about anything at all. I had always told her about my sexual experiences and even about my first encounter with drugs. We both prided ourselves on our mother–daughter closeness. But I kept putting off telling her about my decision to convert. I loved her too much and felt sure it would deeply hurt her."

Arthur Wentzel says that telling his father, an Episcopalian minister, about his decision to convert was so difficult it marked a turning point in his life. He says that, at the age of 27, "I finally entered adulthood. When I confronted my father, he was as angry as I had imagined he would be. I had to be the one to remain calm and take control of the situation for the first time in my life."

Some find the prospect so frightening and the potential repercussions so threatening that they simply never tell their families. Their reasons are varied and very personal. Twenty-one-year-old Janice Murdoch of Chicago could not bring herself to tell her Catholic parents about her conversion to Judaism because she felt certain that her mother, afflicted with terminal cancer, and her father, distraught by his wife's illness and himself recovering from a second heart attack, would not be able to withstand the blow.

Others conceal their conversions for fear of familial reprisals, such as being cut off from an inheritance or ongoing financial support. Some are just too afraid to deal with the anticipated wrath or rejection of their parents.

Though such secrecy may seem a difficult feat, the fact is that with today's high level of mobility and geographic separation dividing families, it is indeed possible to become a Jew and to conceal it from one's family. I do not, however, recommend such an approach.

Except in some extreme situations, I believe it is healthier for all involved for the convert to confront his or her parents directly. But the decision must ultimately be made by the Jew by choice, for it is he or she who must live with the consequences. Janice, for instance, knew her own family's situation better than her rabbi, friends, and support group members, who had repeatedly urged her to tell her ailing parents of her new identity. But Janice had done what she considered to be the best thing for herself and her family.

For the overwhelming majority of converts who do tell their families, a few guidelines are in order. These are suggestions compiled by consensus from the hundreds of converts I have interviewed. Remember that they are recommendations that have worked well for many, but not all, converts. Each suggestion must be evaluated, tailored, and implemented according to each person's individual and familial circumstances.

1. Tell your parents in person, if at all possible. A telephone call or a letter is not a substitute for the personal interaction that is most effective in conveying such an important decision.

2. Use your own discretion to determine the appropriate timing, but remember that it shouldn't be too long after your decision. Hearing about a child's conversion through a third party, be it another relative or a friend, can be devastating.

3. Do not spring the news during major Christian holidays like Christmas or Easter, or even on special personal days such as birthdays or anniversaries.

4. Arrange a time when both parents will be present. It is unfair to ask one parent to tell the other one for you.

5. Leave your Jewish partner at home. The majority of converts agree that the presence of the Jewish partner is not a good idea, at least during the initial discussion. Parents should, however, have been given ample opportunity to meet your Jewish partner before being told. Subsequent discussions of issues and concerns relating to the conversion can certainly include your partner.

6. Understand your own motivation and be prepared to explain and defend it. Reactions to an announcement of conversion will vary, but you are almost certain to be asked, "Why do you want to be Jewish?" It is hoped that your decision to convert, whether for marriage or not, stems from your own personal conviction based on at least minimal knowledge of Judaism and Jewish life experiences. Share with your parents what you find appealing about Judaism, the richness and beauty of the religion and the tradition. In doing so, however, be careful not to denigrate your family's religion. You are the one converting, not your family, and you must continue to be respectful of their beliefs.

Although each convert emphasizes different aspects of Judaism to his or her individual family, many have indicated that their families responded most positively when they shared a desire to create a home with one religious tradition, to provide a coherent identity for future children, and to share that identity with both spouse and children. The better able you are to convince your parents that this is a decision you take very seriously, the more receptive and understanding they are apt to be.

7. Do not tell your parents you are being pressured to convert. (First of all, if you are being pressured from either your partner or your partner's family, *do not convert!*) Most parents want their children to be happy with their life's decisions. Many even want their children to have real spiritual fulfillment, even if it is derived from another tradition. Most of all, they want to feel confident about their child's decision to embrace Judaism. The sense that their child's decision is not a personal and genuine one weakens that confidence, making the decision more difficult to accept.

8. Provide reassurances to your family. Be sure to state clearly and explicitly that although religious ties will be broken, the social, familial, and emotional ties that have always bound you with your biological family can and will remain the same. Reaffirm your love for your parents and respect for your heritage. Express your understanding that your decision to convert may be difficult for your parents to accept. Indicate your willingness to exert the extra effort that may be required to ensure open communication and a positive relationship.

9. Be understanding, but firm. Although it is important to convey empathy with your parents' position, it is equally important to stand firm by your decision. If you cannot demonstrate to others your determination to convert, you should perhaps be rethinking your decision. At the very least, you should be proceeding slowly with the conversion process. Your parents, more than anyone else, will detect that uncertainty and find it most troubling. As one mother told me, "My daughter tried to convince us that she wanted to be Jewish, but when we became upset, she said she wasn't so sure anymore. Later she said she had decided to go ahead with it. My husband threatened to disinherit her, and she vacillated once again. If she really loved Judaism, nothing we say should change her mind. I think she is terribly confused, and that upsets me more than anything!"

Another father, on the other hand, felt reassured by the strength of his son's conviction. "At first I couldn't cope with the idea of a Jewish son," he says. "I did everything possible to dissuade him. When I saw there was nothing I could do or say to change his mind, I realized this was not a decision he had made lightly. I admired his power of conviction. Although I would have preferred that he had become a good Baptist, I'm proud that he is a good Jew and I'm happy for him."

One convert who had a particularly difficult time with her family's response says, "My Judaism became so important to me, I was willing to defend my decision at all times. Every time I fought for my right to choose Judaism, it made my Jewishness that much more valuable to me."

10. Follow up with a letter. Many converts have found that writing a letter to their parents, following their initial discussions, has helped a great deal. By restating your feelings about Judaism as well as your devotion to your family, such a letter can help clarify your position and ensure that your parents understand the message you are trying to convey.

HAVE I LOST A CHILD?

Reactions to the news that a child intends to convert to Judaism, not surprisingly, vary from family to family. Much depends on such factors as the general relationship between child and parents and the strength of the family's ties to its own religion. If a Jewish partner is involved, how long the relationship has been going on and how well the parents know and like that partner may further influence their reaction. If the relationship has continued for some time, the convert-to-be may find that his or her parents are not surprised when confronted with their child's decision to convert.

From the parents' perspective, it is important to understand that when children inform their parents of the intention to convert to Judaism, they are not asking for permission or approval. Rather, they are seeking acceptance and respect for the decision to become a Jew.

Whatever the circumstances, converts or prospective converts should not expect their parents to react to the news with wholehearted acceptance or instant happiness. Parents need time to get used to the idea. Ideally, parents will come to understand the decision, especially if they are convinced their child is sincere and that this will make him or her happy. As one Catholic mother put it, "I was surprised how much my daughter had learned about Judaism. She was convinced it would bring her happiness and fulfillment. It was not exactly what I'd planned for her future, but she is an adult. I respect her decision. As long as she is healthy and happy, everything else is secondary."

Other parents are less accepting. They may express concern, anger, or disapproval. They may feel an initial sense of grief that they are losing their child to another religion. They may feel guilt and remorse, blaming themselves and feeling that they failed to provide the groundwork for ongoing commitment to the family's faith. They may feel personal rejection as well. Some parents perceive conversion as a battle for power, with their side having lost. Some parents may also worry how their friends and other family members will react to the news.

Concerns are sometimes expressed in ways such as: "My son has never shown interest in religion before; why would he want to convert to Judaism?" or "My daughter has known very few Jews in her life; how can she become Jewish?" or "Our religion has always been good enough for him until now. Why is it no longer good enough?" or "It seems to me that my son is converting just to appease his fiancée and her family."

Above all, parents of prospective converts often express a sense of helplessness. As one mother put it, "I know my daughter is old enough to make her own decisions, but isn't there anything we can do?"

Annette Giacommucci, a mother from Canton, Massachusetts, was hurt and angry when her daughter, Nancy, decided to marry a Jewish man. She and her husband refused to attend the wedding. Four years later, Nancy rekindled that anger by informing her parents that she was considering conversion to Judaism. "I knew I could never approve of her decision," Annette recalls. "Deep down, I felt left out of her life. I felt that we had failed to transmit our Catholic faith to Nancy. I worried that she would not be able to meet me in the next life. I wrote her over sixty-five letters urging her to reconsider. I threatened and cajoled, but nothing worked."

Another parent, John Karkalous, a Greek Orthodox, was also pained by his son's decision. "Since my future grandchildren would not be baptized or raised as Greek Orthodox, I felt that my son had severed my lifeline of immortality."

John, having married a Lutheran, found it difficult to understand his son's desire to convert to his fiancée's religion. "My wife and I had never seen the need to convert to each other's faith, so I couldn't understand why Steve was so adamant. Why hadn't he taken his parents' feelings into consideration?"

It is up to the convert to try to assuage as many concerns and fears as possible. The parents of both Nancy and Steve had done everything possible to dissuade their children from converting. But once they realized their determination, they gradually began to accept their children's decisions. Most parents eventually feel that if the alternative to acceptance is permanent estrangement from both their child and their grandchildren, acceptance will prevail. In most cases, it takes more than a difference in faith and ethnic identity for parents to sacrifice their relationship with their children voluntarily.

After several years of counseling from both their priest and a therapist, John Karkalous and his wife realized just that—they did not want to lose their relationship with their son and his family. "Reluctantly, we resolved to live with the situation. It took us a few years to get over our feelings of personal loss and a deep sense of failure as good Christians. Even ten years later, we still feel pangs of hurt during Christmas. But we have four beautiful, healthy grandchildren, and the joy of being there to watch them grow now seems much more important than what they believe."

Like John, Annette says she still does not approve of her daughter's conversion, but she has come to accept it. "Nancy is very happy as a Jewish wife and mother of two sons. Our relationship has been wonderful since I realized there are some things I cannot control or change. My daughter laughs at me, but

I still pray for her. I know it won't change anything, but it makes me feel better."

Some parental reactions may lead to some shocking discoveries. That's what happened to Rose MacQuire, a 29-year-old single convert from Providence, Rhode Island. She says she honestly did not expect her nonpracticing Christian parents to be "too upset" by her decision to convert. But instead of finding acceptance, she discovered that her parents were anti-Semitic. "It was very painful for me to hear my parents using racial epithets and making derogatory, prejudicial remarks about Jews in an effort to convince me to change my mind," Rose recalls.

In other cases, some parents will be so outraged by a child's decision to convert that they refuse to talk about it. They may even become abusive and hostile. A dialogue may prove impossible. A convert whose parents react this way should not undermine his or her own efforts by returning the hostility. Try to arrange another meeting time. If this, too, is resisted, then the convert should try sending the parents a carefully worded letter explaining his or her decision. It may also help for the convert to elicit support from another sympathetic family member who is willing and able to intervene on his or her behalf. Such behavior is unlikely to continue forever. Even among those parents who continue to disapprove, the anger and disappointment usually dissipate over time. In my experiences with thousands of converts, I know of only a dozen or so cases in which all family ties have been severed as a result of conversion. In such extreme cases, the converts may ultimately have to ask themselves this question: "If my family disowns me, will I have the strength and support needed to continue to be a Jew?"

TIME HEALS

The experiences of Marilyn Weiss provide a good example of how persistence, patience, and accommodation can generate the hoped-for transition from resistance to acceptance.

"For a whole year between the time I told my parents I was going to convert until my wedding, it was a step-by-step process, filled with a great deal of uncertainty and anxiety," Marilyn recalls. "My parents are devout Catholics who attend church every day. I knew it was going to be tough on them, so I kept putting off telling them of my decision. Finally, Paul [then her fiancé] urged me to do it.

"My parents were very calm in their reaction. I was especially amazed at how good my mother was. She told me it was difficult for her but that she still loved me, and we would always be welcome in their house. My father just refused to talk about it. They told me they would always love me, but they couldn't come to our wedding because it would be setting a bad example for their grandchildren to show that they accepted us."

After many letters back and forth in which Marilyn wrote everything in her power to prove her sincerity and commitment to Judaism, as well as her love and respect for her family, Marilyn's parents decided they would come to the wedding. She continues:

"The next big issue erupted over my father's refusal to wear a yarmulke. We wanted to have the wedding at a Conservative synagogue, but I knew that wearing a yarmulke was going to be a problem for him. I talked to the rabbi, but he said a yarmulke must be worn. I talked to my father and tried to present it to him as something he should do out of respect for someone else's religion. He talked to his priest, who also happens to be one of his best friends. The priest encouraged him to stand firm. In the end, we decided to have the wedding at a hotel instead of a synagogue. I made it very clear to my parents that I felt we were making a sacrifice by not having the ceremony at a synagogue but that I felt it was more important that they be there.

"At last, I thought everything was going to be all right. In finalizing the details, I wrote and asked them both to walk down the aisle with me, in the Jewish tradition, but told them that if they felt more comfortable with just my father giving me away, that would be OK. Then I got a letter, a very nice letter, that ended by saying that they felt they couldn't give me away because, again, it would set a bad example. I was heartbroken.

"In the end, they backed down on that, too. Step by step, they let go. It was a very hard year, but I'm glad I stuck with it—and with them—because in the end, it was a beautiful wedding!"

Marilyn believes her parents are more accepting now, but she expects that their hurt will continue to resurface. "I know when my children are born, it will be difficult for them," she says. "Everyone in my family has been baptized in my mother's gown. The fact that the tradition will stop with my children will be a tremendous blow."

Marilyn's father still even hopes for her return to Catholicism. One day while playing pool with Marilyn's husband, Paul, her father turned to him right before he positioned his pool stick on the edge of the table and said, "I hope if Marilyn wants to come back to the Catholic faith someday, you won't stand in her way." Before Paul could even respond, his father-in-law's eye was back on the eight ball.

Ruth Lewis also went through a difficult transition with her family when, at the age of 24, she converted to Judaism out of personal conviction. Her parents, Fundamentalist Christians from North Carolina, were devastated by the news. They blamed themselves and insisted on knowing why she was "punishing them." Ruth, who legally changed her name from Christine, found no initial support from her family. They refused to acknowledge her new name. "My parents continue to make me feel guilty and won't let me be a Jew in peace," she wrote to me on one occasion. Finally Ruth confronted her parents, letting them know that although their relationship was very important to her, she would not let them succeed in making her feel guilty any longer. After more than a year of continual correspondence and many encounters filled with fights and tears, Ruth's parents now address her as "Ruth." Her mother's letter to her says it all: "Let's forget our differences and make the most of what we have in common. We can share love, happiness, and each other."

Another family found that time forced a change in their attitude, mostly because they were confronted with the issue more than once. Richard Tate, a Methodist from Hackensack, New Jersey, remembers being livid when his oldest daughter announced her decision to convert after being married to a Jew for several years. "We tried unsuccessfully to dissuade her. Deep down I guess I was happy she had found something to believe in, though I would have preferred she had stuck with Jesus. We survived the pain, but it took a few years. The wounds had not yet healed when our son announced that he, too, would be marrying a Jewish woman. He didn't intend to convert, but he wanted to be married by a rabbi and share his wife's religion. The hurt and anger were not new to us; they were as real as before. This time, however, the pain didn't last quite so long. When our youngest daughter, at 18, told us she wanted to convert to Judaism out of pure conviction, we gave her the name of a rabbi and then went to a movie. Who knows? Maybe my wife will be next!"

ACHIEVING HARMONY

The tune may be slightly different than it was before a Jew suddenly waltzed into the family, but the rhythm of the non-Jewish family can and should go on. The key elements to ensure that the family stays together are communication and sensitivity—on the part of all parties involved.

Parents of converts often express concern that they feel left out of their children's lives. Prior to conversion, parents are too often not told their child's reasons for converting and are not sufficiently informed about what conversion entails. They are usually among the last to find out that conversion is even being considered. Converts sometimes feel that the less they talk about it with their parents, the easier it will be for them. Parents, on the other hand, unless they are vehemently opposed to the conversion, often say they would feel better about their child's decision if they were included in the process.

When Beverly Hunt learned of her daughter's impending conversion, she felt "rejected and disillusioned." She wondered, "Will our grandchildren still love us? What role will we play in their lives? Luckily for us, Jane shared her experiences with us. We knew what she was reading and studying. Through her, we were better able to understand her, her husband, and her husband's family. We may not share everything, but we do feel part of their lives."

Explain the Changes and the Constants

Parents of converts often fear alienation and rejection because of a lack of knowledge about Judaism. They do not understand what will and will not change in their child's life. For this reason, constant communication and sharing of information are essential ingredients for a healthy relationship. A convert should explain to the family that he or she is the same person as before, with a different religious and cultural orientation. He or she should never criticize or ridicule the family's—and his or her former—faith.

Converts should provide details about the conversion process and describe how they intend to incorporate Judaism into their lives. If they plan to keep kosher and observe Shabbat, they should be sensitive in explaining how this will affect their ability to eat in the parents' home or drive to visit them on Saturday. Depending on the converts' level of observance, they may decide that they can no longer eat in the parents' home at all or that they just won't eat meat there. Parents should not be expected to change their life-style because their child decides to convert, but they may be willing to accommodate some new needs. They can do this, however, only if they are informed of those needs. For instance, if parents have traditionally begun each meal with grace that invokes the name of Jesus Christ, they may not think to refer instead to God unless the convert informs them if it is offensive.

These are issues that need to be worked out over time. But open discussion from the outset ensures a stronger relationship as the Jew by choice tries to forge a new identity and as the family simultaneously wrestles with the implications.

One Christian mother was concerned that she would lose her daughter as did her neighbor, whose daughter had married a very Orthodox Jewish man. "When my daughter told me she was going to convert, I was afraid she too was going to become very religious and I would never see her. I had no idea that there were different branches of Judaism. When she explained the differences to me, I felt much better. I knew what she expected of me and the changes I could expect from her as a Jew."

Celebrating the Holidays

Handling holiday celebrations can, particularly during the convert's initial years as a Jew, be a delicate subject among family members. Frank discussions between convert and family with points of clarification early in the process are essential. Christian families must be told straight out that a conversionary home is a Jewish home. No Christian holidays are celebrated in the home, nor is it appropriate to have Christian symbols such as Christmas trees or wreaths, or Easter baskets. It is up to the convert to keep his or her family informed about the Jewish holidays and their meaning so that Christian parents can, if they choose, respond with the appropriate greetings or gifts at the right time.

Some converts find it helpful to buy their families a Jewish calendar. Carolyn Reef found such a gesture indispensable when year after year her parents unwittingly planned family social events that coincided with the High Holidays or Passover. "At first they resented my gift, but later they realized it was a good solution," she recalls.

When it comes to the December holidays, non-Jewish parents should be asked to send Hanukkah presents wrapped in Hanukkah or neutral paper. At no time of the year are rosaries or necklaces with crosses appropriate gifts for any member of a Jewish family. The convert, in turn, should send Christmas presents. It is entirely appropriate for the convert to invite his or her family to share Jewish holidays. Likewise, the convert and his or her immediate family can visit the Christian family while they celebrate their holidays. If Christmas has always been a time for the convert and his or her siblings to congregate at their parents' home, that does not have to stop now that Christmas no longer belongs to one of them. Of course, different ground rules may apply, such as the convert no longer accompanying the rest of the family to midnight Mass. (That is not to say that a convert should never step into a church for weddings, funerals, or memorial services.) In most cases, the convert will want to discourage Christian family members from giving his or her children Christmas stockings or Easter baskets. Occasionally, some parents will continue the practice anyway, usually with no harm or spite intended. Depending on the circumstances, it may be best not to make a big issue out of such a gesture.

Balancing Cultural Differences

As much as religious differences between two families can cause problems, so, too, can cultural differences. Many married couples have stories of the difficulties in achieving harmony between both families, even when the couple comes from the same religious, cultural, and economic background! The situation becomes that much more complex when religious and cultural differences come into play.

The first potentially explosive encounter with such differences can surround the wedding. The experience of Joyce Brown, a Presbyterian from Mineola, New York, provides a case in point. Joyce had accepted her son's decision to convert and looked with great anticipation to his wedding. "Were we in for a shock!" she recalls. "The ceremony was lovely enough, but afterwards—we had never been to a more raucous event in all our lives! So much food! And the singing, dancing, and merriment were much too boisterous and, in our estimation, in very bad taste. The crowd got so carried away they even lifted the bride and groom off the floor in chairs. We had never been to a Jewish wedding and had no idea what to expect. Only later were we told that the dancing and the chair-raising were Jewish traditions."

To avoid misunderstandings or feelings of alienation similar to those of Joyce, particularly if one's parents have not had much contact with Jews and Jewish customs, the new Jew should explain in advance what they might expect. This principle should apply not only to the wedding but also to other Jewish events— a seder, a *brit milah*, a synagogue service—to which they might be invited.

Sometimes non-Jewish families worry unnecessarily about the impact of conversion on their child. This problem arises most frequently among Christians who have had little contact with Jews and harbor certain unflattering stereotypes. Such was the case with Hope Blackwell, an Episcopalian from a Chicago suburb. Her stereotypical image of Jewish women, few of whom she had ever actually met, was that they were loud, materialistic, and spoiled. She feared that her daughter, upon her conversion, would suddenly turn into that kind of woman. Ten years later, Hope feels ashamed for having worried that her daughter would change and now has met, through her daughter, many other Jewish women who do not conform to her earlier stereotypes.

So often our knowledge of another culture and religion is derived from popular media, through which stereotypes may be exaggerated rather than dispelled. It is into this backdrop of misinformation that conversionary couples may step as they seek to understand each other and each other's families, while trying hard to bring those families together.

Cultural differences need not present obstacles to a strong relationship between children and parents or parents and their in-laws. Misunderstandings are most often the result of ignorance or intolerance. Neither family is expected to alter its beliefs or convictions, but it is in the best interest of all parties involved to accommodate themselves to special situations, especially if they have been given the proper information and treated warmly and with respect.

The convert should be constantly aware of the need to inform the non-Jewish family about his or her new way of life, and non-Jewish parents should not hesitate to ask questions of the convert, in-laws, or a rabbi about any aspect of Judaism that the Christian family may not understand. The inquiry will almost always be interpreted as a sign of respect for the child's new religion. One call can often prevent embarrassment from saying or doing the wrong thing.

If achieving harmony and a lasting relationship become, as it will in more cases than not, prime objectives between converts and their families, then the means to achieving such harmony become easier. As one father who had a particularly difficult time adjusting to his daughter's conversion says, "It took me much too long, but I finally realized that our relationship did not have to change because she worships in a synagogue and I in a church."

In the same way that most parents do not wish to feel estranged from their child, they most certainly do not want to feel alienated from their grandchildren. If holidays exacerbate such feelings of separation, it may be a good idea for the convert to include his or her parents in other important events in the children's lives. Interestingly enough, the majority of Christian grandparents I have interviewed said they preferred that their grandchildren be raised as Jews rather than with no religion.

Some parents feel the same way about their children, glad that they have found some spiritual identification that may have been previously lacking. As one Methodist mother recounts, "I tried to impart our religious ideas to the children. But by the time they were teenagers, I knew they were just going through the motions. Our holiday celebrations were warm and fun but lacking in religious content. I worried they were growing up without a spiritual identity. When my daughter announced she was planning to convert to Judaism because Judaism meant so much to her, I was pleased. She was so enthusiastic, how could I be upset? After all, she now identifies with the granddaddy of three major religions!"

6

Raising children in a conversionary marriage

"How can I learn enough and feel comfortable enough with my own Judaism to raise Jewish children?" converts often wonder. One of the greatest fears they express is that they will not be effective in passing Judaism on to their children.

For sincere converts who become committed Jews, this concern usually proves unfounded. If both parents work to create a Jewish environment for their children, they will find little difference between their children and the children of two born Jews. Problems arise either if the born Jewish spouse is not supportive of his or her partner's efforts to incorporate Judaism into the family's life or, conversely, if the convert was pressured into becoming a Jew. In either situation the children will be confused by the mixed signals and the lack of conviction emanating from their parents. They may be labeled Jewish, but they will never truly feel Jewish.

The vast majority of children of conversionary marriages with whom I've had contact have grown up to become identifying and practicing Jews. However, there is no question that these families have had to work harder to achieve these goals. Converts have the added responsibility of continuing their own education as Jews while at the same time passing the tradition on to their children. Individuals from conversionary homes also face the challenge of instilling a Jewish identity while at the same time validating and welcoming into their lives the non-Jewish members of the family. Converts who have begun the process of developing their own Jewish identity and have established a positive relationship with their family based on that new identity will find it easier to transmit Jewish living to their children.

Connie Irwin shudders when she recalls how anxious she was that she would not be able to fulfill her son's spiritual needs. "Todd was already 2 years old when I converted, so I didn't get much of a head start before he began nursery school at our synagogue and started coming home with all kinds of questions. I pulled out my conversion class notes and headed straight for the library. I found that I sometimes learned more from the books targeted at Todd's age than I did from the adult books that presumed more knowledge than I had. Keeping ahead of Todd wasn't easy because he was so curious. The two of us learned together, baked our first challah together, lit Shabbat candles together, and burned our first Purim hamentaschen together. We were both proud of each other when we participated in his school's special Shabbat service!"

A conversionary home, like any Jewish home in modern-day America, must work to create a positive Jewish environment that inspires a strong Jewish identity for children.

The conversionary couple, again like other Jews in America, must strive to achieve a distinctive Jewish identity for the family while at the same time participating in the non-Jewish society in which they live. The task may be greater for converts, who, having grown up amid the dominant Christian culture, unaware of what it means to be part of a minority, find themselves unprepared to synthesize two potentially conflicting values—integration into American society and preservation of Jewish particularity. Jews by choice, then, face the special challenge of understanding that dichotomy both for themselves and for their children. Those who wrestle with these issues may find themselves better equipped to reply to an inquiring child who may someday come home and ask, "Why am I different from everyone around me?"

One of the ways to help children feel comfortable in both the Jewish and non-Jewish worlds is to expose them to both worlds, through family and community. A child who grows up in a completely non-Jewish environment may have difficulty assimilating his or her Jewishness. Such is the conclusion of 15-year-old Mike DeMateo, who grew up in an all-Italian neighborhood. "My father converted to Judaism before I was born," says Mike. "Our home was Jewish, but I always felt different wherever I went. On Ash Wednesday, I was the only kid on the block without an ash print on my forehead. And during Christmas, ours was the only house without Christmas lights or decorations. When I was 11, I was thrown out of the neighborhood street club because I was Jewish. After a few fistfights, they let me back in because I convinced them I was half Italian. Now that I'm older, I enjoy my dual heritage and feel equally at home with Italians and Jews. But it hasn't always been easy. I don't think I would have wanted to live only among Jews, but a mixed neighborhood might have been nice."

More than one preschool teacher has commented to me that children who come from conversionary homes tend to be more tolerant of differences among people and open to new ideas. Reba Dowlinsky, a teacher at an Ohio synagogue preschool program, makes these observations: "Children who come from conversionary households seem genuinely interested in learning about other people. Differences seem to fascinate rather than threaten them. From an early age, they learned that the whole world is not Jewish. They were forced to confront differences within their own family structures. This does not make them less Jewish, just more receptive to new and different foods, languages, and holiday celebrations."

INFORMING CHILDREN

Children of converts will probably spend the first few years of their lives unaware of any difference in background between mother and father. Parents themselves may be noticing different approaches to parenting based on their separate cultural back-grounds, but these distinctions, which have to be worked through, should have little impact on the extent to which a child is raised Jewishly.

In an active Jewish home, children will begin to associate specific rituals with certain times, such as candle lighting and challah with Shabbat, a menorah with Hanukkah, and matzah with Passover. They will have no idea that one of their parents did not grow up with the traditions associated with these customs.

At some point, probably when the child is around age 4, and particularly if the non-Jewish family is a central part of the child's life, the convert should explain the differences between the two sets of grandparents and extended family members—one Jewish and one non-Jewish. It is best to name that religion specifically—be it Lutheran, Catholic, Buddhist, or Muslim—so that the children will begin to identify it with their parent's family. Parents should emphasize to children that their religion and culture differ from those of other family members but that theirs are neither superior nor inferior. They are equally important.

Converts should always feel free to discuss their non-Jewish heritage with strangers as well as with their children. Converts should explain their background to the degree that their child is capable of understanding. They may even want to tell their children when and why they converted, as did Edwin and Claudia Boynton of Mellmor, Long Island. Claudia recalls:

"We borrowed the family albums from both of our parents and used them as catalysts from which to launch a discussion about my conversion and Ed's childhood. Our 5-year-old daughter was surprised to see childhood pictures of me standing by a Christmas tree or dressed up as an Easter bunny. I explained to her that I grew up as a Methodist but became interested in Judaism after I met her father. I was careful not to denigrate Christianity and tried to explain that her grandparents were still Methodist. I highlighted all the positive aspects of Judaism that she could relate to. I concluded by saying that I found more personal meaning in Judaism and that I wanted us as a family to share one religion."

Problems may arise if there is tension between the in-laws or if one side of the family is belittled or isolated. Such was the experience of Hank Ackerman, whose childhood memories of Judaism were not very positive, in large part because of the tensions between the two sides of his family.

"My mother converted soon after she married Dad, mostly because she wanted to be able to raise her children in one tradition. But my father's parents always considered her a *shiksa*. My brothers and I felt tremendous tension during the holidays. The two sides of our family never got together, even for our birthday celebrations.

"Dad didn't help matters because he tried to keep us away from Mom's family. He feared we would be influenced by their Christian ways. He made up all kinds of excuses why we couldn't visit them during Christmas. Once he even lied and said we were allergic to Christmas trees! As a result of all the tension that emerged around holiday time, we were never even able to enjoy the Jewish holidays. There was little joy or enthusiasm for the prayers and rituals. The result was that I lost a great deal of respect for my father. I never could understand why he didn't defend Mom against attacks by his family or why he tried to keep us away from her family. His actions served to drive me away from Judaism, exactly the opposite of what he had hoped for. Only now, at the age of 29, and after my father's death, am I beginning, with the help of my mother, to rethink my Jewish connection."

The lesson here is the importance of treating both families with equal time, love, and respect. These feelings must be transmitted from the parents.

Children's questions about religion should never be ignored. If they are receiving positive Jewish signals at home, in the synagogue, and through Jewish education, then curiosity about other religions, especially when they see them being practiced by family as well as friends, should not be viewed as threatening. Does it really matter if they see a Christmas tree in their grandparents' home in addition to the neighborhood bank and shopping mall?

In explaining to children that they can share the holidays with their non-Jewish relatives but cannot celebrate them, I often find the analogy of a birthday party to be helpful. Children can share in the fun and excitement of a friend's birthday, knowing full well that it is not their birthday being celebrated. They can have the pleasure of choosing and wrapping a present, playing games, and singing songs while knowing that the celebration belongs to someone else. The same can be said about visiting non-Jewish grandparents and family during Christmas, Easter, and other non-Jewish holidays.

My own children have helped to decorate Christmas trees at local hospitals, without feeling either uncomfortable or envious. They were able to separate the tree from their lives because of their positive Jewish upbringing, because their own holidays are more familiar and meaningful to them. The conversionary families who are most threatened by their children being exposed to non-Jewish family or activities tend to be those in which Jewish values, rituals, and customs are not reinforced at home.

Occasionally I receive a letter or report about Christian parents trying to influence their grandchildren by bringing them to church or exposing them to activities without the approval of the children's parents. As Bernie and Sandra Pollack gradually became more observant as a result of what they learned together during Sandra's conversion process, they encountered resistance from both sets of parents. Bernie says:

"When our children visited my wife's parents, they continued to give them nonkosher food after we had explicitly asked them not to. When we asked them to stop, they accused us of depriving our children of good old American staples like cheeseburgers and cheesesteaks. The hard part was explaining the situation to our children without making them feel they were being forced to choose between their parents and their grandparents. My wife was understandably disappointed with her folks. But imagine my predicament when my children informed me that they regularly ate cheeseburgers when they went out with my Jewish parents!"

In such cases it is the convert's (or in Bernie's case, the child's) role to confront his or her parents, emphasizing that the children are Jewish and are being raised accordingly. Calmly, but firmly, they should be asked to refrain from such activities. If the situation persists, it may be necessary to limit visits or else inform these grandparents that they will be able to see their grandchildren only under supervised conditions.

The relationship between grandparent and grandchild may be affected by the relationship between parent and child. If parents have come to accept their child's decision to convert, they most likely will accept their grandchildren as Jewish as well. Others, however, especially religious grandparents, may feel that because they have no control over their child's decision to convert, they will instead concentrate on "saving" their grandchildren.

Based on the history of Peggy Glazer's parents' response to her conversion, Peggy was not surprised when her daughter returned from visiting her folks with Christian coloring books and rosary beads around her neck. When confronted, Peggy's mother responded that her granddaughter, Jennifer, had selected the book herself—"probably because something was missing from her life"—and that the beads had been intended only as a pretend necklace. Peggy says, "I knew better, but I did not want to make a scene. I calmly but firmly told my mother that since Jennifer is Jewish, these items would have to be returned. I told my daughter that Grandmom had given these things to her only temporarily so that she could see what her cousins were learning about in school." Peggy correctly did not blame her child for accepting her grandmother's gifts; instead, she emphasized that they did not belong to her because she was Jewish.

Except in extreme situations in which the convert is unsuccessful in convincing the parents of the futility of their mission—in which case, extreme measures may be warranted—he or she should try to be patient and nurture the relationship. Grandparents have a special role in all families. In conversionary families, in particular, grandparents provide an important link with the converted parent's past. The heritage of a Jew by choice should be legitimized in the eyes of his or her children.

Jews by choice should demonstrate to their non-Jewish family members that they and their children are involved and happy with their Judaism. With patience, persistence, and a little luck, the non-Jewish family may come to feel like Clarinda O'Hara, a Protestant grandmother with two Jewish grandchildren, who says, "I don't think of my grandchildren as Jews, Catholics, or Protestants. I think of them as my special, wonderful, loving grandchildren!"

CONVERTING WITH OLDER CHILDREN

Although most people who decide to convert after marriage do so before they have children, it is not uncommon for a non-Jewish spouse to decide on conversion after the children are born. In such families, it is important not to introduce sudden, drastic changes into the lives of children. Even if most of the family's practice had focused on Judaism prior to conversion, it is important to involve the children in the process and not force them to make sudden changes in their lives without thorough explanations. The story of Sara Darron, who is now 18, is telling:

"I think that being the child of someone who converts is difficult. My mom decided to convert eight years after I was born. She told me and my sister Lou Ann, who was 10, that she thought it would be easier for everyone if the whole family shared one faith and that she had decided, after doing a lot of reading, that Judaism was going to be it. We hated the idea. Until then, we had been savvy enough to use the two faiths in our household as we pleased. We were Jewish when it was convenient and Protestant when we deemed that to be more acceptable.

"I remember that for months my mother would leave the house once a week to study with a rabbi. Unfortunately, however, she did not share her learning with us. She couldn't understand why we didn't share her enthusiasm. Not only did she not explain things to us, but she also made abrupt changes in the house and expected everyone to accept them. After having spent thousands of dollars on beautiful Christmas tree ornaments that she had always told us were to become family heirlooms, even

Dad winced when we watched them being carted away. At first my sister and I resisted Mom's efforts in our own ways. We refused to give up bacon and carried on very loudly at synagogue.

"Soon we realized that this was serious business. One thing Mom did that helped was to invite other Jewish families for Shabbat and accept invitations elsewhere, so we became familiar with the way other Jewish families lived. Mom told us that although she wanted us to be Jewish also, she did not want to force us into it. We could take as long as we needed, she said. My sister converted two years later. But even though I saw how happy everyone was about her decision—they even threw her a big party—I was determined not to become Jewish. Maybe it was my stubbornness, or my feeling that I should be loved whether I was Jewish or not, or maybe it was just plain adolescent rebellion. At one point I even announced to my family that I was going to become a nun!

"Finally, when I was 16, I read my sister's copy of Devorah Wigoder's autobiography, *Hope Is My House.* It tells the story of a Christian woman who defied her home and heritage to discover herself in Israel as a Jew. Perhaps I identified with the rebellious nature of this particular convert to Judaism. The next day, I started my preparations to become Jewish."

EDUCATING CHILDREN JEWISHLY

Telling a child "You are a Jew" does not go very far in instilling a sense of belonging or ensuring a strong Jewish identity. As Hayim Halevy Donin writes in his extremely helpful book, *To Raise a Jewish Child: A Guide for Parents:*

> The sense of belonging and of having a strong Jewish self-identity is not achieved by merely telling the child "you are Jewish" and then letting him wonder in what way he is different from people who are not Jewish.
> Being different without himself being able to notice the differ-

ence and to be proud and happy about it can be very disturbing to a child. How often have we heard the complaint, I know I'm Jewish because I've been told so or because all my friends are Jewish, but aside from that it doesn't mean very much to me.

An appreciation of differences is achieved by seeing and doing those things that are decidedly Jewish in character: observing Jewish holidays, learning Hebrew words of prayer, coming in contact with Jewish symbols and feeling at home in a synagogue. These Jewish associations must provide warm and happy memories, to which there must later be added feeling about worth and importance of Jewish life.

Jewish education can go a long way toward developing that sense of Jewish worth. Jewish education, both formal and informal, should begin as early as possible for children of conversionary parents. These children generally encounter religious differences early in life because of contact with non-Jewish family members. Although an understanding of religious differences can be healthy for children, it can also be confusing. A continual reinforcement of Jewish identity that begins early in life will help assuage that confusion.

Grace Brown, the 18-year-old child of a mother who converted, thinks that it was a combination of her strong Jewish upbringing and her close relationship with her non-Jewish family members that "satisfied my curiosity about other people." She thinks that this exposure in part explains why she, unlike most of her Jewish friends, has no desire to date non-Jewish men. "I have the jump on my friends," she says. "I wish they understood how different non-Jewish beliefs are. They may end up getting hurt in the end."

Children of conversionary couples also usually have fewer Jewish contacts, stimuli, and role models from whom to learn. Aside from friends and community, they have at most one set of Jewish grandparents and relatives with whom to learn and experience Jewish tradition and culture. Those grandparents themselves may not be knowledgeable or practicing Jews, thereby thrusting the entire responsibility back on the parents. If the parents begin too late, there is much to catch up on. The task becomes overwhelming to the parents and bewildering for the children.

Occasionally, children of converts encounter insensitive Jews who question their or their parent's legitimacy as Jews. One day, when my son was 7 years old, he came home from school, marched right up to me, and said, "I'm not really Jewish, am I?" I was completely thrown off guard until he explained that one of his classmates had been told by his Orthodox parents that one can only be born Jewish and therefore I was not really Jewish, nor was my son. I responded that his friend's parents were wrong, that there is more than one way to be Jewish, and that "you, my son, are as Jewish as your friend." That's all he really needed to hear.

Several years later, my son overheard a guest of ours, someone who didn't know I was a convert, say to another guest: "I would just die if my child brought home a non-Jew. Even if he converted, he would never really be Jewish." This time my son spoke up. "Why can't you be really Jewish if you convert?" he challenged her. In his younger years, he would have wondered if she were right. Now he just thinks, how ignorant can she be?

Sometimes the Jewish family itself makes life more difficult for the conversionary family, which was the experience of 13-year-old Melissa Marks: "Being the child of a convert can be tough at times. I think my parents are paranoid about what the rest of the family says about us. Why do we always have to do more to show how Jewish we are? When I grow up, I'm going to marry a born Jew so that my kids won't think they're different!"

Deciding how to educate children, through a Jewish day school or supplementary synagogue program, is a very personal matter that parents must determine according to their philosophy, commitment, location, and financial situation. In addition to providing a formal education, they can take advantage of activities offered by the Jewish community. If the relationship with members of the Jewish family is strong, they can be important sources of information and support.

TIPS FOR CREATING A JEWISH HOME

Whatever children learn at school or synagogue needs to be reinforced in the home. To create a Jewish home where children will develop a positive Jewish identity, here are a few suggestions that have worked for conversionary families in the past:

1. Begin a photograph album for each child, including photographs from the *brit milah* or baby naming ceremony, a Hanukkah party, each child's first Purim costume, marching in the Israel Independence Day parade, decorating the sukkah, and so on.

2. Assign each child a specific task for Shabbat such as picking flowers to put on the table, setting up the candles, or making the *motzi* over the challah. Make Friday evening a special time by having a nice Shabbat meal, reading a favorite story, or serving a special treat. Before Shabbat begins, you may want to contribute a little *tsedakah*, charity, to a special box so that your children will learn the importance of giving in Jewish tradition.

3. Visit places of Jewish interest. Buy postcards to keep in a personal scrapbook of Jewish places and things.

4. Supplement daily conversation with significant Hebrew or Yiddish phrases.

5. Display Judaica items throughout the home, including *mezuzzahs*, Sabbath candlesticks, menorahs, seder plates, and plenty of Jewish books.

6. Use tapes, records, and books to expose children to a variety of songs and activities.

7. Join a synagogue and investigate other Jewish communal centers. Participate with your children in activities as often as you can.

8. Encourage your children to share their holidays and activities with other children, including, when appropriate, their Christian neighbors.

9. Take a family trip to Israel. Expose your children to Israeli foods and culture to help create an identification with Jewish peoplehood.

In determining the children's education, both the born Jew

and the convert must ultimately come to terms with their own Jewishness. After all, who knows us better than our children? Children will quickly detect their parents' attitude toward learning, Torah, and Jewish communal responsibility. What do the children hear at home? What do they see? What is the conversation at the dinner table? What books does the family read together? The educational process begins at birth and continues throughout a child's lifetime. Parents should strive to instill—with creativity and enthusiasm—a love of Jewish tradition. Books can provide formal training, but it is parents who, by their own example, must also provide the environment in which the Jewish training becomes a cherished way of life.

7

Finding acceptance as a Jew

WHERE DO I FIT IN?

Finding a niche in the Jewish community is a process that begins prior to the actual conversion and continues for years afterward. The divisions among the different branches of Judaism often make integration more difficult as the convert attempts to sort out the different ideologies and patterns of Jewish practice. Sometimes converts find themselves torn between the teachings of a rabbi on one hand and the practices and levels of commitment on the part of their Jewish spouse and in-laws on the other. Great confusion can develop as they listen to one interpretation of Jewish law and then another. Most difficult of all is when a convert encounters different reactions from different Jews to the conversion itself.

Bertha Turner, for example, a 39-year-old Reform convert from Buffalo, describes her frustration at receiving mixed reviews of her conversion. In her own Reform synagogue, no one questions her Jewishness. Yet when she visits her sister-in-law's Conservative synagogue in Delaware, she encounters skepticism about the authenticity of her conversion because it did not require immersion in a *mikvah*. And in the Brooklyn Orthodox synagogue of her husband's grandparents, there is no doubt at all. "There I am not even considered a Jew," she laments.

It is natural for recent converts to be baffled by the abundance of Jewish views, especially over the question of "Who is a

Jew?" Some segments of the Jewish community, both here and in Israel, use their nonacceptance of certain conversion processes as a means to delegitimize other groups. Converts, though clearly not responsible for today's growing schisms among Judaism's different branches, are forced to accommodate themselves to this fact of modern Jewish life.

Many converts, once they become more aware of the many options available, may explore paths of Judaism different from the ones with which they were originally acquainted. Some even decide, as an outcome of this exploration, to undergo another conversion process within a different branch of the community. A majority, however, are usually content to remain with their original choice.

The important thing to remember is that each convert must seek his or her own Jewish identity through individual methods, not through the methods or opinions of others. Each individual's knowledge and experience will help determine how Jewish practice meshes with daily life.

The process of forming an identity and finding a comfortable community is a hurdle that each new Jew must confront in the quest for integration. A second hurdle—finding acceptance within that particular community as well as in the broader Jewish community—can often pose an even greater challenge.

A PAINFUL PROCESS

One of my most devastating experiences as a convert was my encounter with rejection at a Conservative synagogue near Rye, New York. Rejection, from all corners of Jewish society, is nothing new for a convert. This particular experience, coming four years after my conversion and two years after my very Jewish wedding, was particularly traumatic. It points to one of the most serious problems facing all converts: lack of acceptance by other Jews.

There I was trying to prove to everyone—and mostly myself—that I was an authentic Jew. I was one of those excessively enthusiastic converts who, having wholeheartedly accepted Judaism, was looking everywhere for affirmation of my Jewishness. Like many others, I became a fanatical joiner. I joined loads of organizations—the Zionist Organization of America, Hadassah, and more. I subscribed to scores of Jewish publications from *Commentary* and *Present Tense* to *Sh'ma.*

Despite my obvious commitment, the consensus in my family was that it would be better that my "past" not be made public knowledge. My husband would say things like, "Maybe it would be better if we didn't talk about your past." My mother-in-law would say, "Aunt Sadie doesn't know, so it's best that you don't say anything. You pass for Jewish anyway." I began to think I was walking around with some sort of disease.

With my past presumably tucked safely behind me, I plunged into active Jewish communal life. The synagogue, particularly the sisterhood, became my special domain. I did the baking, the flower arrangements, everything that needed to be done. For two years, members of the sisterhood called on me for anything and everything. They knew I would never say no. Then, in the third year, the other members decided it would be nice to elect someone like me—young and full of energy—as sisterhood president. Nice, that is, until my secret was revealed.

It happened rather innocently: a friend in whom I had confided and who didn't realize that my conversion wasn't public knowledge unwittingly passed the word on to others, including at least one member of the sisterhood who apparently did not approve. This woman, whose identity I did not discover until years later, made it her business to annul the election and unseat me as president. It was the synagogue's non-Jewish secretary who delivered the crushing news. "You are no longer sisterhood president because one of the members does not think that a convert is a real Jew," she told me quite matter-of-factly.

After three years of giving my all, I couldn't believe this treatment. I was so hurt and angry, I couldn't even tell my husband. I was afraid he was going to explode. He was already so tired of it all, tired of feeling that we were living a lie. So, since he hadn't even known I was elected in the first place, I just went on as if nothing had happened. I didn't write to the rabbi or to the rabbinical seminary. I often wondered, in retrospect, whether I should have done something—anything—to protest. But I didn't. Without a word, I buried my pain and, in fact, became even more active.

I didn't want revenge. I didn't—and still don't—wish harm to that woman or others who have continued to deny my Jewishness. I feel like the Italian poet who, after achieving fame and fortune, was asked by his servants how he wished to get back at his enemies who had tried to thwart his success. The poet replied that all he wanted was to take away their ill will.

That is all I want: to dissolve the ill will that many born Jews feel toward me and toward thousands of other Jewish converts.

As converts struggle with their search for identity and integration, they are often unprepared for the reactions of those who try to negate their Jewishness. For the skeptics, the bottom-line question nearly always comes down to this: Is this person really Jewish?

This familiar concern was expressed to me by a father whose youngest son was engaged to a non-Jewish woman. The woman was taking classes in Judaism with the intention of converting prior to the wedding. The man, an unreligious Jew who was pained when his elder son married a Christian who did not convert, wondered aloud: "How can she ever be a real Jew if she doesn't share our heritage? I just can't envision accepting her as one of us."

Similar feelings have been echoed by countless born Jews, many of whom find it difficult to rationalize their visceral reactions. "Jews are born, not made," declared Marty Ross, the father-in-law of a recent convert. "The Jewish people fought long and hard to survive the ravages of history. Why should an outsider, after a few months of study, be entitled to claim our inheritance?"

Four thousand years of Jewish history have cast a unique perspective of the world on many Jews—a perspective that above all emphasizes the uniqueness of a people who have triumphed over repeated periods of persecution, alienation, aloneness. For some, this sense of uniqueness is threatened by one who tries to "join the club." This belonging is seen as a birthright, not something that can be learned or transferred. As the protagonist in Mordecai Richler's *Joshua Then and Now* tells his WASP lover, who offers to convert for him: "You can learn to play tennis, but you can't learn to be a Jew."

Other Jews, particularly those for whom the Holocaust weighs heavily on their worldview, wonder whether converts are "fair-weather Jews" who would renounce their Judaism should another such trauma occur.

Some born Jews try to appear accepting but nonetheless feel uncomfortable around converts. Martha Firstein explains how her family reacts to her sister-in-law, Christine: "We all love her, but I'm not so sure we accept her as a Jew. Maybe there are too many reminders, including her name, of her non-Jewish, Irish-Scottish past. Her fair skin and dirty-blonde hair stand out like a 'notice me' sign among the curly- and black-haired relatives. Her painstaking efforts to belong are so obvious that it further sets her apart. When she opens her mouth and intersperses Yiddish phrases with her 'Golly!' and 'Heavens me!' I just shudder! Sometimes I ache for her because she is left out of so many inside jokes and experiences. Once a group of friends were all sitting around relating stories of our bar and bat mitzvah antics. Christine obviously could not participate. Usually at times such as those, I resolve to make her feel more welcome, but I'm ashamed to say I'm not always as patient and diligent as I should be."

Often acceptance may just require time, as Stanley Benjamin well recognizes when it comes to his brother-in-law, Steve. Stanley says: "I think people don't accept converts because they feel so uncomfortable around them. I have a hard time relaxing and being myself around Steve, even though we have a lot in common. I often find myself searching for the right words so that I don't insult him and embarrass my sister. I think in time that I'll feel as comfortable with him as he feels with me. Recently, he told me two jokes, one about a non-Jew, one about a priest. I never would have had the courage to tell them to him. Maybe it was his way of telling me he is one of us."

Some born Jews may think they are welcoming, but only if the convert conforms to their own notions of what it means to be Jewish. Maggie Austin, a medical student in Vermont, is facing such difficulties with her in-laws, who think she should define her Judaism in their terms. "One minute they label me fanatic because I keep a kosher home; the next day they say I'm not a 'full Jew' because I don't have a palate for gefilte fish and lox."

Boston orthopedist Edward Flynn is encountering similar experiences with his newly acquired family: "My New York Jewish family was elated when I agreed to convert, but I'm not sure they realized what would *not* happen: I did not lose my southern drawl; my eyes and hair are still light; I read Hebrew like an elementary school child; and just as I didn't care for Chinese food before I converted, I still don't care for Chinese food—kosher or not. My in-laws wanted me to become an instant Jew, molded into their idea of a social and religious success. How do I tell them it just doesn't happen that way?"

New Jews feel pain when they encounter the attitude that says "We don't accept you because you weren't born one of us." Sheila Galant, a Jew by choice who is studying to be a rabbi, is adamant about her feelings. "I don't think of myself as a convert. I'm a Jew. I'm not ashamed that I'm a convert, but I'm going to choose whom I tell that to. I wish that it didn't make any difference, but I know sometimes it does." Sheila has found a warm, loving *havurah* community where all that matters, she says, "is that I'm involved."

Sara Lithgow, a Classics professor at a small liberal arts college, quickly found her niche as part of a traditional equalitarian havurah that meets in a Conservative synagogue. Since her conversion three years ago, she has also continued to be involved in serious reading and discussion of Jewish texts. When asked to give a presentation for the group on the eve of Simhat Torah, Sara spoke movingly about what the Torah means to her as a Jew by choice and how it has enhanced her life as someone whose work is centrally concerned with literary interpretation.

"When I sat before the Beth Din as part of the conversion process, I wondered what the rabbis would ask me. The first question was this: You have the Classics; why do you need Judaism? It seems to me that the rabbis knew what they were asking, and I might now re-cast their question as follows: If what drew me to the Torah was in part its being an emblem, a sublime version of all literature and of all interpretation, then why, if I have secular literature, do I need the Torah?

"Perhaps, however, I have already answered this question by the words in which I have asked it. We need the Torah precisely because it is not secular but sacred; and if the Torah is a sublime version of all literature, then perhaps in some sense other books are cast in the Torah's image as we are in God's. I cannot fully explain either of these answers—but that simply means that they call me to further study of the Torah."

Here, then, is a convert who not only has attained a sophisticated appreciation of Torah but, like a born Jew, is already comfortable with the realization that Jewish study is an open-ended and unending process. To paraphrase the great sage, Rabbi Tarfon: We are not required to finish the work of Torah study, but we can never consider ourselves to be finished with the learning—each of us at our own level.

HOW BORN JEWS CAN HELP

Whether one actively embraces Jewish tradition and culture immediately, prefers to integrate slowly, or chooses to be a passive observer, all converts yearn for acceptance. But just as the convert requires time to become familiar with Jewish practice and actually feel Jewish, so too does he or she require assistance in pursuing the path toward acceptance. The people most able to help or hinder a convert's successful absorption into the Jewish community directly are the Jewish spouse, if there is one; the new Jewish family or Jewish friends; and the converting rabbi. We have already discussed how all these people in the life of a convert cannot only affect the initial decision to convert but also provide the necessary support and encouragement throughout the conversion process. When it comes to integration and absorption, these are the individuals who can help ease the convert's entry into Jewish life and serve as important role models.

The Spouse

As we discussed in Chapter Three, a Jewish spouse's attitude regarding his or her own Jewishness greatly influences the convert. A convert whose spouse is knowledgeable about and committed to Jewish life will often find the transition to Judaism much easier than one whose spouse is indifferent and removed from things Jewish. Compare the case of Eva Fleischer to that of Janet Braverman. Eva's husband knew very little about the history and culture of the Jewish people. "When I questioned him," she recalls, "he became defensive. He had wanted me to convert but resented that I showed real interest in Judaism. He hardly ever attended synagogue, so I didn't either. Later on, I forced myself to go without him so that our children could have the experience. It was a lonely time for me."

Janet, on the other hand, recalls her husband's support and encouragement throughout the conversion process and afterward. "He explained everything during my conversion class. He was deeply interested in my learning, and he even learned a thing or two himself. Together we explored the tradition. I could not have done it without him."

Family and Friends

In the same way that a spouse can provide an important avenue for integration, so, too, can the spouse's family. When a convert's Jewish family has a strong Jewish identity, the welcome is often warmer and the opportunities to learn about and share in Jewish tradition more abundant. Paul Raskis's second marriage was to a woman whose family considered religion a central component of their lives. Paul did not convert until three years after his marriage to Denise, because he wanted to know more about Judaism before he made his decision. In retrospect, Paul says that it was partially due to the influence of his in-laws, who included him in all holiday and family celebrations and helped him learn more about Judaism, that he finally decided to convert.

Sometimes if the family is not able or willing to provide the assistance necessary for integration, Jewish friends can step in. Ellen Berman is someone who depended on her friends more than family to introduce her to the Jewish community. She still feels resentment when she recalls that it was her nonobservant in-laws who insisted she convert before she married their son, Eric. Ellen recalls: "Before long, to my own surprise—and certainly to theirs—I became more and more interested in Judaism. They were not prepared when it became evident that I wanted to be a knowledgeable and practicing Jew. They tried to talk me out of becoming what they called a 'fanatic.' It was with the help of supportive Jewish friends that I was able to find my way in the Jewish community. Now my husband and I are both active in our synagogue and in Jewish organizations. My in-laws have remained on the sidelines of our Jewish existence. I know that while we are at Shabbat services on Saturday morning, they are out on the golf course."

The Rabbi

As we will explore in greater depth in Chapter Eight, the role of the rabbi prior to and during the conversion process is often critical to both a convert's outlook on Judaism and ultimate level of involvement in the community. A rabbi's continued interest in and communication with a convert, after the conversion itself, can often provide the impetus for active participation in Jewish life, especially in the cases of single converts or converts whose spouse, in-laws, and friends are unequipped or uninterested in providing the necessary support and know-how.

When Anita Keating, a single convert, enrolled in a conversion course, she felt very lonely. She remembers being the only convert not taking the course with a partner, the only one converting out of conviction rather than for the sake of marriage. Anita credits her rabbi for taking a personal interest in her, matching her with a host family from his synagogue, responding to her questions and her needs. After the conversion, Anita moved to a different city to finish her graduate work but corresponded with her rabbi regularly, always assured of a quick response to her letters. Two years later, Anita returned to Baltimore and joined her rabbi's synagogue because she knew she would be welcome there. Her host family went out of its way to include her in all the communal activities, and today Anita heads the adult education program for the congregation. "Converting on my own was a difficult challenge," Anita says. "I honestly don't know if I would have become so involved if not for my friend, my rabbi."

Gail Heller's experience was slightly different, but it illustrates how the influence of her converting rabbi facilitated not only her own integration but also that of her previously uninvolved Jewish husband.

"My husband is the first to admit that he is not religious. To this day, he is unable to explain why he felt so strongly about my converting before we were married. It was not through my husband but through my converting rabbi that I became so excited about Judaism. This rabbi is so enthusiastic and inspiring that it is almost contagious. His enthusiasm has affected not only me but my husband as well—the same husband who at one time was disdainful of organized religion and who now doesn't miss a Shabbat service. I also know that it is because of our rabbi's influence that my husband has agreed to send our children to Jewish day school. What is particularly special about this rabbi is that he is always telling his congregants that the convert, the *ger tzedek*, should be loved and welcomed. It is his attitude that I believe has helped both my husband's family and our congregation to fully accept me."

Others have not been so fortunate in their experience with their converting rabbis. Consequently, they have found it more difficult to find a place where they feel welcome and accepted beyond the family environment.

One convert remembers being so turned off by the rabbi who was teaching her conversion course that if she had not met other supportive rabbis along the way, she probably never would have joined a synagogue. In another case, a woman named Christine resented her rabbi for trying to persuade her to change her name to a more Jewish-sounding one. When she refused, he stopped speaking to her and ultimately made her feel so uncomfortable in his synagogue that she was forced to start all over with a new congregation.

A Word about Role Models

It is not surprising that the very people who contribute most to a convert's Jewish practice and integration into the community are also the same people to whom a new Jew looks for information and guidance. To the convert, every Jew is a potential role model. The best role model—whether spouse, in-law, friend, or rabbi—is one who provides support, information, and opportunities for learning in a personal, nonthreatening, joyous environment. A positive role model in this context communicates Jewish values and practices by words and deeds, by including the convert in celebrations and involving him or her in Jewish experiences that are meaningful, interesting, and fun.

Not every Jew, however, is comfortable being thrust into the position of role model. I often hear families express discomfort, worrying that their degree of commitment to Judaism is being scrutinized and questioned by the new Jew in the family. One Jewish mother—who, though unobservant, strongly identifies as a Jew—wrote: "I was eager for my daughter-in-law to learn as much as possible about Judaism. But when she bombarded me with questions, I became defensive and nervous. Should I immediately transform my home into a religious place? I don't want to be viewed as a hypocrite."

My experience has shown that if Judaism is presented with warmth and sophistication, radical changes on the part of the role model—in this case, the in-laws—are not warranted. Alterations in life-style that are made solely to impress the convert rarely work to the benefit of either the convert or the family. The only time when change is positive and worthwhile is when Jewish parents, spouses, or any other role models initiate reform based on their own personal introspection and reassessment of their Jewish life-style.

In addition, Jewish in-laws and other potential role models are often not equipped with the explanations and answers that are sought by a convert who is thirsty for knowledge. One Jewish mother expressed the concerns of a hundred when she said: "I was able to show my daughter-in-law how to light the Shabbat candles and the Hanukkah candles, but I was embarrassed when I could not answer her questions on why we do these things." My advice is to be honest. No one should pretend to be something he or she isn't. If one knows the answers, they should be shared in a simple, straightforward manner. If one does not, then it is often meaningful for the convert and the role model to seek the answers together.

There *are* answers to the questions that converts ask. It is merely a matter of finding the resource—a rabbi, a book, a knowledgeable friend—to provide those answers. Helping the convert seek those answers is the responsibility of every potential role model.

The fact is that a knowledgeable Jew does not automatically make a good role model. One such example is provided by Henry Thornton, a convert whose wife is a Hebrew school teacher. The knowledge was there, Henry says, but "when my wife came home at night she was too burned-out to continue playing teacher to me. I felt cheated, like she was hoarding all the Jewishness, keeping it all to herself. Eventually, I found other role models and teachers, and at my initiative, we have brought more Judaism into our home."

Unlike a born Jew who grows up with many role models, a convert must find and adopt them. Sometimes, as in the case of 56-year-old Janis Krupnick, any number of role models can influence and help shape a convert's Jewish existence. "The Jew I am today," Janis says, "is the result of my many role models. From my mother-in-law, I learned the basics of Jewish cooking; from my husband's grandfather, my love of Torah; from my rabbi, the power and beauty of prayer; and from my husband, I learned to be an ardent Zionist. And from my brother-in-law, I learned what kind of Jew I didn't want to be!"

THE SYNAGOGUE AS PORT OF ENTRY

A synagogue, as a central address for Jewish activity, can in its own special way often provide the best environment for a convert to integrate and begin to feel a true part of the Jewish community. The first steps toward synagogue affiliation can often be truly intimidating for the convert, who is generally still unfamiliar with the ritual, the liturgy, and the customs that surround Jewish worship and other synagogue activities. I remember feeling absolutely petrified the first day I entered my rabbi's Orthodox shul. I was all alone and felt that the building might swallow me up. As soon as I saw my rabbi's welcoming face, I felt much better. Everyone wished me "good Shabbes" and treated me with warmth and respect. A few of the women seated near me were kind but not patronizing when they leaned over to make sure I was on the right page of the prayerbook.

Though it is a challenging task, I believe that conquering the fear and unfamiliarity of the synagogue by becoming involved can be an important step toward creating a meaningful Jewish life. Born Jewish couples who may not feel the need to affiliate with a synagogue can still get a certain degree of positive Jewish reinforcement from familial and cultural connections, but converts don't have that foundation from which to build Jewish lives. The synagogue, and the community it provides, can offer affirmation of a convert's Judaism as well as opportunities for increased Jewish involvement. Some converts prefer the more intimate setting of a small synagogue or a *havurah*, finding it more comfortable than a large synagogue. A *havurah*, which usually functions without a rabbi and with a small group of people either independently or as part of a large synagogue, offers a more participatory and personal Jewish environment. It is important to explore all the options in one's community.

Synagogues, for their part, must work to eliminate the ambivalent attitudes toward converts and conversion. The ambivalence that prevails at many synagogues stems from the dual concern of not wanting to appear too encouraging of intermarriage while at the same time not wanting to single out the convert, who should, according to Jewish tradition, be considered a full Jew. The delicate balance of meeting the needs of converts while not setting them apart is an issue that synagogues must address. In today's Jewish America, most synagogues count among their members at least one convert or conversionary couple.

Synagogue attendance often goes hand in hand with the conversion process, since most conversion programs require the convert or conversionary couple to attend Shabbat services regularly. Some programs even recommend that the convert attend services at synagogues affiliated with movements other than the one sponsoring the conversion. It is an excellent idea for all converts to do this, even if it is not suggested or required, in order to obtain a greater understanding of the differences in content and style among the branches in Judaism.

Once the conversion process is over, however, the conversionary couple's interest in the synagogue often wears off. This is particularly true if, as is often the case, the convert is involved with a Jew who was not previously affiliated with a synagogue. Often, the Jewish partner's last real involvement was with bar or bat mitzvah preparations or with a youth group. The Jewish partner, who has not maintained or seriously reevaluated his or her own attitudes toward the Jewish community, often influences the convert not to continue his or her involvement. Some converts are content with this attitude. Others, however, having gone through the conversion process with only a taste of what Judaism is all about, are eager to persevere and acquire greater understanding of what it means to be Jewish. In some cases an influential rabbi or role model has inspired continued synagogue involvement. Sometimes these determined converts begin to develop their own Jewish lives, apart from a spouse, attending services alone and participating in various aspects of synagogue life. Although these converts usually express the desire for their spouses to participate with equal fervor, they continue alone, hoping that their enthusiasm might eventually prove contagious.

I know personally of many cases in which converts have influenced their spouses to become active in synagogue life after many years of absence and apathy. Converts with ambivalent spouses should try to gently coax them back. A simple "I would love for you to accompany me to services" would naturally be received more favorably than "What kind of Jew are you?"

The fact that a majority of conversionary couples end their affiliation once the conversion is over is not surprising, given that most endogamous Jewish couples in America also do not affiliate with a synagogue. The percentage is relatively low, according to most Jewish population studies. Many of the convert's stated reasons for not affiliating with a synagogue are similar to those of born Jews: It is too expensive; we don't have time; we find services boring and meaningless; we will join when we have children; I don't feel welcome as a convert; and the synagogue does not meet my needs.

Better Now Than Later

Since synagogue or *havurah* affiliation has the potential to provide positive reinforcement for the convert as well as a burst of energy and commitment for the community, both the convert and the congregation should be seeking ways to encourage involvement among new Jews. I would suggest dealing with some of the reasons for resistance in the following ways:

"It is too expensive." All converts should be given a one- or two-year free membership in a synagogue of their choice as a way to encourage attendance. Membership cards or invitations might be given out at conversion classes along with a list of area synagogues and their locations. After two years, if the cost of affiliation is still a problem, a sliding scale system, already employed

by many synagogues, could be applied to the individual or couple.

"*The service is not meaningful to me.*" Many converts, for whom the synagogue experience is new and exciting, tend to be more tolerant and patient with regard to services and sermons than their spouses. But if the sermon is not meaningful, it is possible to tactfully and politely tell the rabbi so. Rabbis are human beings. They do not read minds, and they need to be inspired and challenged by interested and concerned congregants. Many rabbis would welcome suggestions and comments rather than the routine, "I really enjoyed your sermon." It is important to keep in mind, however, that rabbis address a diverse group of people and cannot possibly meet the needs of everyone all the time. It is also important to remember that Jews in large metropolitan communities have a choice of synagogues with which to affiliate. There are many kinds of synagogues—some large, some small, some more personal than others, some with *havurot*, and some with more participatory religious services and activities. If the services, the rabbi, or the congregational activities are not meaningful, then keep searching; explore all the options until the right one is found.

"*We don't have children.*" Many Jews between the ages of 20 and 40 wait until they have children to affiliate with a synagogue. They view the synagogue primarily as a vehicle for providing their children with a Jewish education. Converts, who encounter many sources of stress surrounding the birth and raising of children that born Jews do not have to deal with, will have a much easier time of it if they have already established themselves in a Jewish community. Friends from a synagogue or *havurah* can provide wonderful support in times of celebration, such as the birth of a child, or in times of need, such as the death of a loved one. It is preferable to try to establish a Jewish network prior to those times when a community support system becomes invaluable.

Despite the trend toward developing programs geared for

singles and young couples without children, most synagogues still cater to the family structure. More need to engage in active outreach toward adults without children, born Jews as well as converts, so that these valuable individuals will not feel estranged from the synagogue.

"My needs are not being met." People often shy away from a synagogue that does not seem to meet their needs without realizing that if they came forward and articulated their needs and desires the synagogue might be very responsive. For example, a group of recent converts and their spouses in Philadelphia gathered to discuss their feelings of awkwardness during Shabbat services. They all agreed that although they wanted to participate fully, their conversion courses had not adequately prepared them to follow the Hebrew prayers. Instead of confronting the possible embarrassment of not being able to participate or recite the blessing over the Torah if asked, these people often felt more comfortable just staying at home. They needed some experience with the service in a nonthreatening atmosphere. They approached their rabbi, who responded enthusiastically by helping them to form a learners' service. There, with the guidance of some experienced teachers, these converts became confident enough to integrate gradually into the main sanctuary. The rabbi made sure they were called up to the Torah for *aliyot* when *they* were ready.

In another congregation, conversionary couples formed a support group for their parents, with the encouragement of the rabbi. The program was so successful that it attracted parents of conversionary couples from other synagogues in the area as well, thereby meeting the needs of a large group of people.

"I don't feel welcome." A recent convert, often still insecure about Judaism, feels out of place at synagogue if no one makes a special effort to be welcoming. Sometimes a simple "Shabbat Shalom" can do wonders to make a newcomer feel accepted. The rabbi is responsible for setting the tone by welcoming newcomers and encouraging others to do so as well. Rabbis should openly address the issues of intermarriage and conversion. Congregants

will be better able to grapple with their own feelings toward converts if they are provided with honest information and encouraged to be sensitive. As Sheila Galant observes, "Changing the attitude of born Jews is a long process, but it has to start from the top down. Rabbis themselves have to decide that converts are real Jews."

Whether a synagogue should have special programs for converts depends on the individual congregation. Some converts welcome such programs. Others prefer to blend in rather than emphasize their conversionary status. Converts consider themselves Jews and want others to think of them that way too. On the other hand, some programs, such as learners' services, can benefit less knowledgeable born Jews as well. Each congregation could take an informal and anonymous survey to determine what programs, if any, are desired.

One of the most successful ways I have seen to help smooth the absorption process for the convert is to assign host families. Host families can provide all kinds of simple services with a personal touch. The host family can introduce the converts to other synagogue members, invite them to activities, and guide them through the prayer service until they feel comfortable. The hosts can answer questions about the synagogue and the community in a way that makes the converts feel welcome. Experienced conversionary couples often make good host families, but anyone can serve this important function.

ACCEPTANCE OUTSIDE THE SYNAGOGUE

I have emphasized the importance of synagogue affiliation because I believe that synagogues and *havurot*—with their religious and communal activities—can provide the best port of entry into the Jewish world. But for some converts the synagogue may not be the only connection, or the right one at all. Some find more fulfillment in Jewish organizations dedicated to social action, political activity, or Jewish culture. One young woman, a dancer, found her niche at weekly Israeli dancing sessions held at the local Jewish community center. From there, she became interested in the Hebrew music that accompanied the dances and decided to study the Hebrew language. Her active connection to the Jewish people began with dance but soon expanded to encompass a wide range of elements.

As we discussed early in the book, a conversion certificate may make one officially Jewish, but that is not enough. Only by actively participating in the Jewish community in one way or another can a convert really come to feel Jewish. Converts who convert into nothingness will flounder for much longer than those who actively pursue a Jewish identity. It is normal for new Jews to lack tremendous confidence about their Jewishness; this insecurity can be overcome only through active participation and practice.

Active converts usually find greater acceptance than passive ones. There is a double standard when it comes to converts. Those who convert do so presumably because they have found something meaningful in Judaism as a way of life—even if the initial decision was precipitated for the sake of marrying a Jew. Therefore, converts are expected to demonstrate that commitment in ways that are not expected of born Jews. This may seem unfair, but I myself have often wondered about the wisdom of converting people to Judaism who are going to end up like the majority of born Jews in this country—assimilated, uninvolved, and doing little to strengthen Jewish life and to ensure a Jewish future.

Converts should also be aware that they will generally be better accepted by born Jews who strongly identify with the Jewish tradition than by those who are more secular or unaffiliated. This phenomenon, confirmed by many converts, seems to occur for two reasons.

First, Jews who do not identify with Judaism have a hard time understanding why a non-Jew would want to join up. "I've spent my whole life trying not to act and look Jewish," Penny Zahavi says. "That's why I nearly died when my roommate at college, Patricia Margaret McGowan, showed up at school with all kinds of Jewish books! She told me she was studying to become Jewish because her fiancé was Jewish. She must be really dumb."

One convert says she encountered a Jewish man who was so puzzled by her conversion that he just didn't know how to deal with her. "He just couldn't imagine that if he ever had the option, that would be a choice he would make."

A second explanation for the lack of acceptance among unaffiliated Jews is their unawareness of the Jewish tenet that converts should be welcomed into the community and their non-Jewish past should never be referred to unless the convert initiates the discussion.

TIME TO REEVALUATE ATTITUDES

Integration into the Jewish community really is a two-way street. Although the motivation needs to come from the individual convert, signals of encouragement and acceptance must emanate from the community. As illustrated here, it is time to reevaluate the Jewish communal attitude toward converts. Converts, often at least as committed, as informed, and as involved in Jewish life as born Jews—and frequently more so—should be seen as positive influences and vital sources of strength and commitment for the community at large. At a time when more and more American Jews are assimilating and drifting farther away from their Jewish identity, people who have chosen Judaism as their way of life should be welcomed with open arms.

8

The challenge to rabbis

Whereas a born Jew may not need a rabbi in order to *feel* Jewish, a convert needs at least one rabbi in order to *become* Jewish. Since conversion is such an intimate and highly emotional experience, it is little wonder that the rabbis who encounter prospective converts at such a critical juncture in their lives can significantly influence their entire view of Judaism.

For this reason, the spirit in which conversion is provided is sometimes even more important than the content of a conversion course itself. From an initial call of inquiry made to the rabbi's office to the last day of formal study and beyond, the rabbis encountered by the prospective convert set the tone for that individual's entry into Jewish life. It is an awesome responsibility.

The influence that a rabbi may have on a prospective convert can, of course, be either positive or negative, and sometimes a little of both. First impressions count. When Jane Bodall decided to convert to Judaism, she called five Conservative synagogues and was rebuffed by each one, either by the rabbi himself or by a secretary who replied that this rabbi doesn't do conversions. "At the very least, I expected the courtesy of an appointment so that we could talk," Jane says. Being rather naive at that point, I assumed that all Conservative rabbis were uncaring, so I decided I did not want a Conservative conversion. A year passed before I mustered enough courage to start again, this time with Reform rabbis. My first call produced a human being on the other side who was warm and gentle and expressed interest in me. We made an appointment, and a year later I converted. My attitude about rabbis, even Conservative rabbis, certainly has changed."

Few rabbis fully comprehend the dynamics of conversion, including the conflicts it often generates within families, within the convert, and between the spouses experiencing the conversion process. Rabbis also don't always understand that prospective converts walking into their offices today tend to be older and more mature than their counterparts of even a decade ago.

From the increasing number of calls and letters I receive from rabbis all over the country, seeking advice or wanting to exchange ideas, I do sense a growing sensitivity to the issue of conversion. As the number of converts increases annually, rabbis—more than a few of whom have converts in their own families as well as in their congregations—are being forced to reevaluate their attitudes toward conversion, converts, and their impact on the future of the Jewish community.

Obviously, not all prospective converts experience the initial hurt and rejection that Jane encountered. But most converts agree that even those rabbis with sensitive souls have a great deal to learn about the complexities surrounding conversion. From their initial encounter in a rabbi's office—where prospective converts feel more comfortable when the rabbi makes the simple gesture of emerging from behind a desk to establish personal rapport—to the content of the conversion course itself, to the attitudes that succeed it, converts have a lot of good advice to give. *All* rabbis, not just those currently involved with conversion courses, would be well-advised to listen to what they are saying.

FIRST ENCOUNTERS

Couples in which one of the partners is considering conversion are often very apprehensive about their first encounter with a rabbi. The Jewish partner may be harboring feelings of guilt for being entangled in an interfaith relationship. The non-Jew may be feeling inadequate and nervous. Often, it may be his or her first contact with a rabbi. Couples generally have two fears going into this meeting: that they will be scolded or chastised for their involvement with each other and that the rabbi will reject their request for conversion. These fears are sometimes realized.

Carla Westover had already resolved to convert to Judaism when she and her fiancé, Michael Abrams, first entered the rabbi's study. The rabbi had known Michael since his bar mitzvah. He had already spoken to Michael's parents, who were anxious about the situation and were hostile toward Carla. Carla recalls that the rabbi had barely greeted them, practically ignoring her altogether, when "he launched into a tirade about the perils of intermarriage. He told us we were selfish and immature. He cast doubt on our love and reminded Michael of the pain he was causing his parents with his decision to marry me. Finally, he turned to me and told me that since my background was so different, I would never fit in or be happy with Jews. We did not interrupt the rabbi. But when it was clear he had exhausted his repertoire of intermarriage advice, we told him I was planning to convert. The rabbi stood from behind his great desk and said to me, 'You are a nice girl, but you have no business being Jewish.' He then turned to Michael and said, 'I promised your parents that I would talk to you. I have done my job. The rest is up to you.' "

This rabbi, clearly uncomfortable—as many rabbis are— with the idea of conversion, used his time to talk *at*, not *with*, the couple. He may have felt an obligation to Michael's parents, but he failed to recognize that he also had an obligation to the couple. Because of his obvious discomfort with the subject, he should have referred Carla and Michael to another rabbi or a Jewish counseling program where they could obtain further information and direction. Discouraged but undaunted in their determination, the couple finally located a Hillel rabbi who listened with compassion to what they had to say and referred them to a conversion program in their area.

Margie Opal's first encounters with rabbis were also disillusioning. A medical student involved with a fellow medical student, Margie had had little time to consider conversion seriously. Like many couples, she and her mate, Brett Klingsman, knew their religious differences were an issue but delayed discussing them. Then Brett's grandfather suffered a fatal heart attack, and Brett's world came crashing in on him. "I was extremely close to my grandfather," he says. "I was severely traumatized by his death. He was a Holocaust survivor, and in spite of the horrors he had witnessed, he still had tremendous faith in God and in Judaism. During the days when we sat *shiva*, I experienced a resurgence of Jewish feelings that had been buried under my medical texts. Margie was there for me. I looked around the room and everyone was Jewish except her. When *shiva* was over, I asked Margie to seriously consider conversion."

Margie remembers the moment well. "At first I thought he was talking through his grief, but then I realized how serious he was. I remembered seeing him saying *Kaddish*. Although I had known Brett for five years, I don't think I really knew him until I saw him put on his tallit and pray with such fervor.

"I didn't know what to say when he brought up conversion. I was caught off guard. Things were happening too quickly. I loved Brett, but I was unsure about conversion. I desperately wanted to talk to a rabbi. I located one in the phone book. He told me he was too busy to see me. I'd have to make an appointment in six weeks, but I needed to see him *now*. My pain was great, and I couldn't wait that long to talk through my feelings. I called another rabbi. He said he didn't do conversions and suggested I call a Jewish counseling agency. I repeated that I did not even know if I wanted to convert; I just wanted to talk. He finally agreed to see me the next day, but an emergency arose that I didn't find out about until after I had already canceled my clinic patients and driven forty-five minutes to his office.

"Finally Brett intervened and suggested I speak with his parents' rabbi. They were not thrilled about our relationship, and they somehow convinced the rabbi to let them come to our meeting. Early in the discussion, Brett's father asked the rabbi what he would do if his own son brought home a non-Jew. The rabbi replied, 'I think I'd kill him.' Just like that. The rabbi went on to say he didn't believe in 'willy-nilly' conversions, but if he had to, he would provide me with one. There was little direct conversation between me and the rabbi. He was cold and negative toward Brett and me and sympathetic toward Brett's parents. I was hopelessly torn between my love for Brett, the memory of his grandfather, and being true to myself. I was so confused. Inside I was screaming, 'Somebody, please tell me what to do.' "

Brett and Margie didn't say much on the way home from that first encounter. Margie had needed someone with whom to discuss her feelings about her relationship with Brett and what Judaism was all about before she could even consider conversion. But the rabbi, instead of meeting with her alone to focus on her feelings, had chosen instead to echo the outrage of Brett's parents. Neither Brett nor Margie raised the subject again for over a year.

One day, one of Margie's patients spoke of her plans to convert to Judaism. She raved about her rabbi. He sounded very different from the way Margie had assumed all rabbis must be. A few weeks later, Margie contacted him. They met privately three times and later with Brett. She told him of her feelings about her former faith, her personal ambitions, and her love for Brett. It was not long before she considered this rabbi a friend. A bond had been established. He gave Margie several books to read, the names of two converts with whom he had worked, as well as of a conversionary couple. After months of exploration, Margie was convinced she wanted to convert. After her conversion and marriage, Margie reflects, "I could have been Jewish much sooner if we had found the right rabbi. I was almost ready to give up. I'm glad I didn't."

Single converts, too, are often wary of their first meeting with a rabbi. Though, as a whole, single converts—more than those with a Jewish partner—have become more familiar with Judaism prior to their decision to convert, they too fear rejection from the rabbi or suspicion of their genuine desire to join the Jewish people.

A rabbi who is contacted by prospective converts or their partners should make every effort possible to arrange a meeting—whether or not he or she is directly involved with providing individual or group conversion courses. A referral alone can be done over the phone, but the course of study is only part of the process involved and, optimally, it should begin only after the prospective convert has had some prior contact with Jewish activities. Whether or not the rabbi will be providing the actual conversion, a first meeting should be an opportunity to establish a rapport with the prospective convert, to help explore his or her feelings, and only then to discuss details about conversion. During the first session, it is a good idea for the rabbi to encourage the non-Jew to talk about himself or herself. Posing general, open-ended questions such as "Tell me about your childhood" or "What are your plans for the future?" is a good way to get the conversation rolling.

Jewish partners often tend to be very protective of their mates, unconsciously monopolizing the discussion. If this happens, the rabbi should try to refocus the discussion on the non-Jew. Later, the same questions can be asked of the Jewish partner. Close attention should be paid to what the couple chooses to talk about as well as not to talk about. For instance, is the subject of family reactions omitted from the discussion? What about feelings toward the non-Jew's current religion? The rabbi should be an active listener and interrupt only to ask a question or seek a clarification. Converts most admire those rabbis who listen rather than judge.

Rabbis should be especially alert to situations in which the Jewish partner may not be very knowledgeable about or comfortable with his or her Judaism. The Jew may be a medical doctor working on a doctorate in physics, but when it comes to Judaism, his education and affiliation may have been tossed away along with the wrappings from his bar mitzvah presents. There may be past resentment and unresolved conflicts, such as those felt by one Jewish partner who still resented his parents for making his bar mitzvah "according to the halakhah of the local catering association." These feelings most likely have been transmitted to the non-Jewish partner, who is receiving mixed messages—encouragement to convert, on the one hand, and a dismal picture of what Judaism is all about, on the other. The convert may be approaching the whole matter with great confusion.

By the end of the first meeting, the rabbi should know why the non-Jew wishes to convert and, if there is a Jewish partner, how both individuals feel about it. The non-Jew should also have addressed his or her parents' attitude toward Jews and indicated what their attitude toward the conversion may be. At this point the rabbi and couple should determine whether there is enough uncertainty or hesitation to warrant further discussions. If both sides agree, steps toward conversion can begin. If this rabbi will not be the converting rabbi, because of either discomfort or lack of time, the individual or couple should be referred to a rabbi in the area who can provide preparation for conversion on an individual or a group basis.

Sadly, I have received more than a few reports of rabbis who are unwilling to recommend a colleague because of personal differences or territorial disputes. There are even situations in which rabbis who would like to perform conversions are discouraged from doing so because someone else has the area monopoly on conversions. This may be acceptable if the rabbi is a good teacher and the program is accessible. Occasionally, however, a well-established program has not been reevaluated, the rabbi's enthusiasm has waned because he or she has been teaching too long without revising the curriculum, or the location is inconvenient for the prospective convert. Some rabbis have confided to me that even with the knowledge of such factors, rabbinic politics still dictated their decisions to recommend the usual person. One rabbi said, "I know Rabbi X runs a mediocre program, but I do not have the time to do conversions. His is the only game in town."

In any case, those rabbis who will be guiding the conversion should tell prospective converts exactly what conversion will entail—costs, length of course, requirements (*mikvah, beth din, hatafat dam brit* or circumcision), and whether the convert's Jewish partner may be required to attend the course (something I strongly urge). The rabbi can also provide an outline or syllabus of the course for the prospective convert to peruse at home under less pressure.

Rabbis can also put the prospective convert in contact with other converts. Fellow converts can be a tremendous source of support and information. In addition, some synagogues have established host or hospitality groups to help prospective converts as they begin their formal entry into Jewish life. The host family can provide support as well as a bridge to others in the synagogue and community. Other converts or a conversionary couple with a similar background can serve as ideal hosts, since they can directly relate to the anxieties, conflicts, and joys that a prospective Jew experiences in the process of withdrawing from a past and forging a new future. A host who is also a convert can provide emotional support and suggestions, particularly on relating to one's non-Jewish family. Rabbis should carefully consider the qualifications and backgrounds of host families. I know of a few unfortunate situations in which the Jewish hosts vented their own frustrations on the convert and did little to provide the support needed. Although conversionary couples are ideal, any sensitive and knowledgeable person or family can act as a good supportive role model during the conversion process.

If, after the initial consultation, the rabbi refers the non-Jew to another rabbi or program for conversion, it is still a good idea to stay in touch with the convert throughout the course and even after official conversion. One prospective convert was grateful that he had his referring rabbi to turn to when the converting rabbi was not fulfilling his duties. He often came an hour late to class, did not follow the syllabus, and had canceled half of the first six lessons. The prospective convert was very concerned and decided to speak to his referring rabbi. The rabbi learned that several complaints had been made about this individual. Ultimately, the course was restructured and another rabbi assigned to teach it.

Others turn to their referring rabbi as a secondary source of information as well as for friendship and emotional support. Audrey Kimball was one such person who had established a special bond with her referring rabbi. "I felt very alone in my conversion class. Most everyone had spouses or fiancés with them. My fiancé was six hundred miles away. His parents didn't even know I was converting. Both my parents were dead. It was so important for me to have this wonderful rabbi take a personal interest in my progress, my thoughts and feelings. He was more than a friend. To this day he is my confidant."

PRIOR TO THE COURSE OF STUDY

Whether the conversion program is being conducted on an individual or a group basis, the rabbi involved should take the time to meet with each student to determine his or her level of knowledge and particular needs. Clearly, it is easier to adopt an individualized course of study in private sessions. In larger courses, rabbis often encounter very diverse groups of prospective converts—some young, some old, some converting out of conviction, others for marriage, some with a great deal of Jewish knowledge and experience, others with very little prior contact with Jews or Judaism. For some prospective converts, the first Jew they ever meet is the one they plan to marry. It can be difficult to assess and then balance the various needs of such a diverse class, but rabbis should make every effort possible to provide individualized time and attention. The daughter of a minister who seeks conversion out of conviction will have very different needs from those of a young man converting for the sake of marriage to a secular Jew or from a fianceé of a Jewish rabbinical student. Each convert should be seen as a unique individual with a distinct past, present, and future. The converts who find their course of instruction the most meaningful are those who receive a message from the rabbi that says, "I care about you. I want you to be a functioning Jew."

Rochelle Rebman received a very different message from her converting rabbi. A 42-year-old mother of five from Deerfield, Illinois, Rochelle says the rabbi met with her for less than ten minutes when she first sought him out for conversion. She found herself in a class with six other students, all in their mid-twenties, all converting for marriage. Rochelle had little in common with her classmates, and she found the instruction boring and elementary. The rabbi had not taken the time to learn that Rochelle had lived in Israel for ten years and was currently working as a Hebrew teacher. Her knowledge and practice of Judaism was quite extensive. After four lessons, she approached the rabbi with her concerns. He offered little sympathy and told her she would have to "suffer through it for conversion." Angry and disappointed, Rochelle stopped attending the classes. Thinking that no alternative course of action existed for her, she put conversion on hold for four years. At that time, she met by chance a rabbi who, when he heard her story, immediately offered to study with her. After twelve weeks of private instruction, Rochelle felt ready to convert. By then, conversion was simply a formality. "I had been Jewish at heart for a long time. The *mikvah* and *beth din* provided the last steps in making me a complete Jew."

Recognition is another issue that must be addressed prior to or at the very first session of each course of instruction. Every convert has the right to know whether the conversion will be viewed as valid and authentic in the eyes of all Jews. Rabbis sometimes neglect to discuss the different requirements among the various branches of Judaism, leaving the convert unaware of the discrepancies among the branches and the ramifications of such discrepancies, particularly as they relate to marriage and children. Several recent converts who have come to the Jewish Converts Network have expressed total shock when they learned that some Jews do not recognize their conversions because they were done under Reform, Reconstructionist, or Conservative auspices. More than one bride-to-be who converted under a Reform rabbi has been devastated when her fiancé's Conservative rabbi told her he did not accept her conversion and therefore could not marry them. Often, these rabbis consent to carry out the necessary rituals and study they feel was missing from the first conversion. Nonetheless, it is unfair for a convert to discover that he or she is not considered Jewish by other standards only when he or she is preparing to get married or perhaps to make *aliyah* to Israel.

To minimize feelings of rejection, alienation, and confusion that accompany such discoveries, all rabbis must present a clear and honest picture of the current thinking surrounding conversion both in the United States and in Israel. The fact is that even when provided with this information, converts for the most part will not get up and leave the class or change their course of action, preferring instead to deal with the consequences should they arise. But that doesn't make their right to know and understand the differences in opinion over "Who is a Jew?" any less legitimate.

Converts who are asked what they see as the best possible solution to the "Who is a Jew?" issue are nearly unanimous in citing the need for the development of a standardized communal conversion course that would be recognized by all branches of Judaism. In these days of internal strife, the prospects of such a program being widely implemented or succeeding seem a long way off. Still, the development of such a program on a local or national level would be one of the most important contributions rabbis could make not only to converts themselves but also to the Jewish community as a whole.

EVALUATING CONVERSION PROGRAMS

I once met a rabbi who told me he had been working with converts for fifteen years. His experience seemed impressive, given that there are no real experts in the field. But when I began meeting some of the converts whom he had taught, I discovered that for fifteen years he had not altered or reevaluated his teaching methods or his course content. For fifteen years he repeated the same mistakes over and over again. He had rarely taken the time to address individual questions, he had steadfastly refused to speak to the converts' families, and his recommended reading list dated back to the 1960s. This rabbi's greatest error, in my opinion, was to insist that converts not visit their families during Christmas for fear that such visits would stir up Christian religious ties.

In my travels, many rabbis who work regularly with converts have indicated the desire to have a network of their own. Many are interested in exploring new programming and exchanging ideas with their colleagues. Some have even suggested the creation of a manual or guidebook with suggestions for lesson plans and experiential workshops.

Published materials already in existence tell us what the conversion programs strive to teach. However, there is sometimes a huge gap between what the rabbis try to impart to their converts and what the converts actually learn. A convert does not become a Jew by the single act of enrolling in a conversion program. This person must be helped to think, feel, and create Jewishly. The prospective convert must be taught that Judaism is much more than a system of beliefs that can be learned from books. For some potential converts, this becomes the most difficult notion to absorb, especially if they are coming into the process without much prior Jewish knowledge and experience. Converts who are leaving a Christian faith often find it difficult to comprehend that they are adopting more than a religion when they decide to make Judaism their own.

The conversion course provides the ideal opportunity to begin the process of creating committed Jews who are as concerned about the Jewish past and the Jewish future as they are about learning how to light the candles on Shabbat. The concepts of Jewish peoplehood, of *tsedakah*, of justice and compassion must be stressed along with spirituality and prayer.

During the conversion program, the prospective convert should be exposed to two areas of learning, cognitive and affective. There should be a healthy balance between the cognitive—acquisition of information relating to prayer, holidays, and history—and the affective—the emotional absorption of the Jewish value and behavior system. The inclusion of both aspects of learning goes a long way toward solving many of the postconversionary problems that converts experience.

Those involved in working with converts must excite and enthuse the convert (and often the partner) to appreciate and enjoy Jewish living and learning. The rabbi can do this only by going beyond the academic aspects of Judaism and showing interest in the converts' emotional states—their feelings, values, and character. When converts express the need for further discussion on the Holocaust or how to relate to their non-Jewish families, rabbis cannot ignore these issues simply because the syllabus doesn't allow for it.

The time constraints surrounding conversion courses as they are currently constructed, particularly the group programs, severely limit the ability to include as full a curriculum as desired. But the length of the program is often less important than the content and the way the information is presented. No matter what its length, a conversion program can only provide the foundation for what ideally will turn into a lifetime of Jewish learning and living. The most important thing the rabbi can pass on to the convert is not the meaning of words in a book, but a love of Judaism and a thirst for a Jewish way of life so that the process of absorption will continue. As Benjamin Nathan Cordozo once said, "There is education in books but education in life also; education in solitude, but education also in the crowd; education in study, but education even greater in the contagion of example."

RECOMMENDATIONS FROM CONVERTS

More than five hundred converts from all over the United States and Canada responded to a questionnaire I developed, asking them to evaluate their conversions and to reflect on some of the areas in which they felt, based on their own experiences, that changes and improvements would have made their transition to Judaism easier and/or more meaningful. The results reflect the experiences of those who at one time or another have come into contact with the Jewish Converts Network and were motivated enough to respond voluntarily. Although the findings in no way represent a statistically comprehensive or sociologically sound analysis, they provide suggestions that rabbis who work with converts might take into consideration.

As a whole, those surveyed reported that their conversion courses were too academic and impersonal and lacked the essential experiential component of how to "do Jewish." Some of the suggestions to remedy the deficiencies included the following:

1. Incorporate hands-on workshops as an integral part of the conversion program. Many converts expressed frustration that when all was said and done, they were unequipped with synagogue skills and unable to light Shabbat or Hanukkah candles, dress the Torah, put on tefillin, build a sukkah, make a seder, or prepare for the holidays.

2. Implement a "buddy system" for converts to attend synagogue services in pairs or small groups. Going to a synagogue alone can be a frightening and lonely experience. Also include in the discussion about synagogues the roles of the rabbi, cantor, and ritual director and how they function in each branch of Judaism as well as how their roles differ from those of priests and ministers.

3. Provide a list of recommended books for converts to buy as well as a Jewish calendar and a list of Jewish places of interest in the community. Converts like to have these for future reference.

4. Match prospective converts with other new Jews or born Jews in the community who are willing to act as hosts. This is especially important for converts who do not have Jewish in-laws or friends who can serve as role models.

5. Arrange visits to Jewish museums, kosher meat markets or bakeries, a *mikvah* (before the actual conversion), a Jewish funeral home, and other places of Jewish interest. If such field trips cannot be arranged with the whole class, host families can help the convert locate these places and provide companionship and explanations during visits.

6. Provide access to qualified professionals and resource people in the Jewish community who can discuss issues of concern

such as personal and familial conflicts, divorce, and child rearing. Rabbis should also tell their students when they are available for consultation outside the class setting. Rabbis sometimes assume that students know they are available, but the fact is that many converts say they are reluctant "to bother the busy rabbi."

7. Provide opportunity for discussion of issues relating to families, both Christian and Jewish. In addition, many rabbis avail themselves to both families throughout the conversion process. Those who provide a special session for parents to interact with each other as well as with the rabbi receive special kudos from their converts. Other rabbis, who believe that it is either not appropriate or not their responsibility to get involved with families, leave some converts feeling very frustrated and ill equipped to approach their families on issues of Jewish theology and ritual.

8. Add to the course curriculum (if they are not already included) such topics as the history of conversion and intermarriage, the branches of Judaism, patrilineal and matrilineal descent, and anti-Semitism. Many converts also expressed the desire for some introduction to Jewish culture, including Jewish art, music, dance, and Yiddish. Although the converts understood that time restrictions do not allow for full exploration of these topics, they suggested that reading and resource lists could provide for further study after an initial exposure. Several converts suggested that students be given the opportunity to research and report to the others on subjects not generally discussed in class. Topics beyond those already mentioned could include Soviet Jewry, Jews of other lands, modern Israel, righteous gentiles, as well as Jewish views on homosexuality, AIDS, surrogate motherhood, organ transplants, infertility, and death.

9. Pay special attention to Jewish partners. In general, converts would like to see attendance of their Jewish partners in the conversion class made mandatory. If sickness, distance, or work precludes partner participation, there should be a requirement to meet with the converting rabbi or another rabbi at least three times prior to the conclusion of the program.

10. Invite converts who have become involved in the community to address the class, providing insight into their own con-

version experiences and answering questions that other converts may be best equipped to handle.

11. Keep abreast of recent literature and programming on conversion and intermarriage. Refer prospective converts and their families to existing support groups, or, if they don't already exist in a particular area, establish new ones. Three-quarters of the respondents either had access to a support group or expressed the desire to join one. Others who felt they didn't need support groups said they would like to see one available for parents, both Jewish and non-Jewish.

12. Provide a list of synagogues in the area, with a brief description of each. A bit more controversial was the repeated suggestion that converts be provided with free one- or two-year memberships in local synagogues and community centers. Many converts also expressed interest in learning about *havurot* as an alternative to membership in larger, more established synagogues.

Most of the converts agreed that the ideal length of a conversion course should be a year so that the convert can experience an entire Jewish calendar of events. Many, however, added that they did not have the time or willingness to commit themselves to a year-long conversion. An excellent suggestion was that the program be divided into two six-month periods—the first being mandatory, the second voluntary.

A general rating of the courses by the five hundred converts surveyed was satisfactory but far from outstanding, except in the evaluation of about seventy-five people. Most agreed that rabbis could use more guidelines as well as financial and emotional support for the crucial role they are playing in ushering non-Jews into the Jewish world they have chosen.

Because of the widespread discontent I detect among converts, I will add my own suggestion here. At least in the larger Jewish communities, a few nonpulpit rabbis should be designated to take responsibility for all matters relating to conversion, including counseling, courses for children, organizing support groups, and serving as a resource coordinator for converts who are continually seeking Jewish-related literature. Such a system would eliminate the burden felt by some rabbis, particularly those who are uncomfortable with conversion or extremely busy. It would allow those rabbis who are truly interested to focus their energies on this growing segment of the Jewish population.

CONVERSION CEREMONIES

Converts should be given the option of whether or not to be involved in public conversion ceremonies. Whereas some find the idea of publicly affirming their new Jewish identity both moving and meaningful, others resent being part of what some have called "a public spectacle" or a form of entertainment. Many would prefer a more personal conversion ceremony. In discussing this with rabbis, I always recall the story of twin brothers, Tim and Tom Richards, who enrolled in the same conversion course but had very different ideas about how they wanted to culminate the process. Tim, who wanted to shout and let everyone know about it, welcomed the opportunity to share his happiness at a public ceremony in front of two hundred congregants. Tom, the more reserved of the two, regarded his conversion as a deeply personal and private affair. He was content to sit with the rest of the congregation while his brother and the others publicly proclaimed their Jewishness.

POSTCONVERSION FOLLOW-UP

Postconversion follow-up was suggested by over half the respondents to my survey. Such follow-up could include personal contact from the rabbi or host families as well as invitations to seminars and retreats.

Keeping in touch means a great deal to converts. When I

reflect on my own postconversion years, I see how invaluable my relationship with the rabbi who converted me has been. A special bond was formed the day we met—even after he rebuked me for showing up at his Orthodox shul with a scarlet red sleeveless dress! The ties were strengthened as my studies continued. The day I converted in his presence, that bond became permanent. Since then he has always been a tremendous source of support, wisdom, and encouragement. He has earned my love, respect, and admiration for many reasons, but mostly because he has always demonstrated an interest in me as a person.

Clearly, not all rabbis will form special relationships with all of their converts. At the very least, however, they should maintain some contact. It is a good idea to maintain a personal file on each convert. The file should be updated at least once a year with a simple letter or phone call. Later, if the convert should come back to discuss issues such as marriage, children, or death, the rabbi will have immediate access to information on the individual. One rabbi has developed a form letter that asks questions requiring simple answers in spaces provided. This rabbi then replies to those he detects may need a personal letter or phone call. He also sends holiday cards and cards of congratulations at appropriate times. It is not surprising that 80 percent of the converts from his classes become members of his congregation—active and enthusiastic members at that!

Sometimes, after a few years, if it appears that the convert has adapted well to his or her new Jewish life and has found a network of support from family and friends, a community, and perhaps another rabbi, the converting rabbi may find it appropriate to decrease correspondence gradually, feeling confident that the convert has found a niche in Jewish life. The rabbi should make it clear, however, that he or she will always be available if necessary. The rabbi should also be sure to send a change of address after a move or retirement. Many converts have told me that when they went looking for their converting rabbis years later—often to share good news such as the birth of a child or their own adult bar or bat mitzvah—they had a hard time tracking them down.

LEADING THE WAY
TOWARD ACCEPTANCE

Nearly all rabbis in America today, from every branch of Judaism, will encounter converts either in their congregations or in their congregants'—and often their own—families. There is no escaping this reality. How rabbis and the rest of the Jewish community react to converts will significantly influence their long-term involvement and contribution to Jewish life. Rabbis who take the lead in demonstrating warmth and acceptance toward converts can be important role models for their community. This does not mean singling out converts and their families. They will feel comfortable only if they are treated like other Jews. Rabbis should teach about every Jew's obligation to love and welcome the convert. They should condemn those who reject converts. Rejection and lack of respect, however, will not dissipate until the rabbi has helped to replace suspicion with education and mere tolerance with genuine acceptance. One rabbi recently told me that his congregation's president scolded him for spending too much time with converts. The president's primary concern was whether these converts were going to become members of the synagogue; if not, he said that the rabbi shouldn't be wasting his time on them. This is precisely the attitude that rabbis, with the support of other Jewish leaders, need to counter.

Rabbis must emphasize that their concerns about intermarriage are separate from the issue of conversion. Conversionary couples are not interfaith couples, and they resent being lumped together. The problems they and their families face differ greatly from those of interfaith couples. Unlike interfaith couples, converts yearn for acceptance and participation in the Jewish world around them. Whether they realize those dreams will depend in large part on whether they are given the chance.

9

Israel: adopting a country

Rabbi Abraham Isaac Kook, an important Zionist thinker
and first Ashkenazic chief rabbi of modern Israel, once said that
"deep in the heart of every Jew . . . there blazes the fire of Israel."
For the new Jew, that fire may take time to kindle. As converts
discover very early in their journey, choosing to become Jewish
means much more than accepting a system of religious beliefs.
Being Jewish is a way of life. Intrinsic to that way of life is identification with the Jewish people as a nation that transcends geo-
graphical borders. This sense of peoplehood explains why Jews
in America demonstrate on behalf of their brothers and sisters in
the Soviet Union or contribute money to aid small Jewish communities in India, Uruguay, and China. The notion of peoplehood is best embodied in the talmudic principle: "All Jews are
responsible for one another."

As difficult as it may be to assimilate Jewish rituals and customs, it is even harder to adopt the intangibles that bond Jewish
people together wherever they may be. One of those intangibles
is love for the State of Israel.

JEWS AND ISRAEL:
AN ETERNAL RELATIONSHIP

Throughout the millennia, since the destruction of the first Temple in Jerusalem in 586 B.C.E. when the Jews were exiled and dispersed, the Jewish people have yearned for the return to the land of their Biblical ancestors. The Jewish people's steadfast refusal to relinquish the concept of one nation rooted to a specific land has mystified historians for centuries. This connection to the land and the love of Zion is repeated throughout Jewish prayers. Every Passover seder ends with the words "Next year in Jerusalem!"

Thus the return of the Jewish people to the land of Israel with the establishment of an independent state in 1948 was a historic triumph culminating centuries of Jewish longing. Though Jewish immigration to what was then called Palestine had begun decades earlier with Zionist pioneers, primarily from Eastern Europe, it was no coincidence that the state became fact as the world woke up to the atrocities of the Holocaust and the annihilation of six million Jews. Jewish perseverance, despite the destruction of one-third of world Jewry during World War II, converged with world sympathy and guilt to allow for the creation of a state where the Jewish people could begin the process of rebirth.

The security that the establishment of the Jewish state provided and the assurance that no future Adolf Hitler could attempt another extermination of the Jewish people as long as the Jews had their own sovereign state further explain the universal Jewish attachment to Israel. If Israel had existed prior to World War II, the Jews would have had a place to seek refuge. There they would not have been turned away as they were by so many countries of the world, including the United States. Likewise, if Jews should ever again need such a haven, Israel will be there to provide it. Thus Jews all over the world, most of whom would never consider living in Israel and have not even visited there, derive comfort knowing that a Jewish state now exists.

The return of the Jews to Israel is a chapter in Jewish history that continues to unfold before us. The building of the state, the draining of the swamps, the development of sophisticated technology and agriculture, and the absorption of Jewish immigrants from over a hundred countries into a vibrant democracy have been part of a miraculous process in which Jews everywhere take pride.

Along with the miracle of building has been the pain of war as Israel has had to cope with a sea of hostile Arab neighbors who resented the return of Jewish sovereignty to the Holy Land. As a result, Israel, in its short history, has been engaged in five wars, beginning with the War of Independence, which its surrounding Arab neighbors waged almost simultaneously with the declaration of Israeli statehood. The history of the Arab-Israeli conflict is complex, and it continues to this day, with the focus of the conflict having shifted to the Palestinians in the West Bank and Gaza Strip. These territories, outside the boundaries of the state that was created in 1948, have been administered by the Israelis since the Six-Day War in 1967, when Israel defeated its Arab neighbors in their further attempt to destroy the Jewish state.

Because of their deep-seated attachment to the State of Israel, American Jews react to the political and military events that shape Israel with more than passing interest. Though an estimated 85 to 90 percent of American Jews have never once visited the state, fund-raising for Israel is such an extensive part of American Jewish life that it links diverse groups of American Jews. American Jews do more than give money, however. They register pride in massive Israeli Independence Day parades throughout the country; they grieve at the loss of Israeli life; and when Israel's interests are threatened, they unite behind Israel by lobbying in Washington, writing letters to the editor, and staging pro-Israel rallies. Also out of love and concern for the Jewish state, American Jews sometimes pass judgment on its policies, criticize its actions, and express disagreement directly to its political leaders. In short, Jews view Israel not only as a state but also as a center of Jewish life in which all Jews share a vested interest.

Although most converts may be superficially familiar with

the country of Israel, through history lessons and news reports of the current political events of the Middle East, few have had reason to consider Israel on a personal level. Or if a convert has thought of Israel beyond the headlines, it may have been in the context of the Holy Land where Jesus lived and preached.

One man, David Allen, in describing his visits to Israel to his non-Jewish girlfriend, Chris, discovered that she had traveled on a Christian pilgrimage to the "Holy Land." They compared notes and discovered that both had been in the same places but were looking for different things. When he said, "Your Holy Land and my Israel are the same place," she was surprised. He had been familiar with non-Jews referring to Israel as the Holy Land, but she had never thought of the Holy Land as Jewish.

INTERNALIZING THE CONNECTION

For Chris, like most converts, Jewish attachment to the State of Israel is a foreign concept and a seemingly unattainable feeling. Whether in the course of discussion with Jewish friends and family or during the conversion course, the realization that there is this country one is expected to adopt as one's own can be a startling discovery for the convert. As Karen Canuzzi recalls: "It wasn't until the rabbi brought in a guest speaker to talk about Israel that it dawned on me that I would now inherit a new set of roots. Since I had already claimed roots to Italy, I wasn't sure how to think about Israel or what it would eventually mean to me."

Like Karen, many converts at first find it awkward to integrate Israel into their new lives as Jews. A lot of the awkwardness stems from lack of knowledge. The conversion course, owing to time constraints, provides only limited discussion about Israel. Thus it is up to converts to read what they can about the history and culture of the Jewish state. The convert's Jewish family and friends can help by providing opportunities to learn more. Synagogues, Jewish organizations, and community centers offer a wide variety of programs, courses, and speakers related to the myriad facets of Israeli history, culture, politics, and international relations. Participating in Israeli Independence Day celebrations can inspire stronger ties not only to Israel but also to the local Jewish community.

I also recommend that converts take a beginner's course in Hebrew, the ancient biblical language resurrected and adopted as the official language of modern Israel. Hebrew is the language of the Jews. Learning it not only facilitates the study of Jewish prayer and Torah, but also helps create a bond with Jews in Israel and throughout the world. It is a tremendous feeling to walk into a synagogue in Buenos Aires, Rome, Istanbul, and, of course, Jerusalem and realize that the same prayers are being said in the same language by Jews everywhere. That is what Jewish peoplehood is all about. Courses are offered through synagogues, through local Jewish educational institutions, or even through instructional tapes and books.

The process of adopting Israel, like the process of adopting Jewish ritual and custom, takes time. Dorothy Collins, a stewardess from Grand Rapids, Michigan, compares her gradual affinity for Israel to a stray dog that stuck around so long that it succeeded in worming its way into her home and heart. Dorothy says, "I cannot say that I embraced Israel as soon as I became a Jew. But as I became more Jewishly involved both at home and in my community, the survival of Israel was a constant topic of discussion. I couldn't deny it or escape it; it permeated my life. My children brought home papers with stickers of Israeli flags; they were assigned all kinds of projects that focused on Israel. Together we listened to the news reports about Israel. We talked about what we heard and saw. We marched in the Israeli Independence Day parade as a family. We bought Israel bonds and enjoyed photos from our friends' trips to Israel. Just as that puppy wormed itself into our home and hearts, Israel has wormed its way into my life. I could never turn my back on Israel. In fact, I can't imagine what it would be like being Jewish without Israel."

PLANNING A VISIT

Above all, the best way to discover what Israel is all about is to visit. A hundred books and dozens of lectures cannot provide a glimpse into Israeli society the way a visit can. Only by being there can a Jew bask in the glory of the miracle that is modern Israel, the Israel that intertwines the old and the new so that each step is a new discovery, a journey into the Jewish past and future. This marvelous experience is one that no Jew should miss—especially not the convert.

Nancy Conley, a 32-year-old advertising account executive from Saratoga Springs, New York, describes how her first visit to Israel helped establish the connection she had been seeking: "After conversion, Israel was suddenly thrust on me by my husband and his family, all ardent Zionists. I read the papers and was familiar with the perpetual Middle East crisis, but it all seemed so remote. I tried to talk myself into looking upon Israel as 'my' country, but deep down I was really neutral about it. I just couldn't understand the role of Israel and its connection to the Jewish people. I began to feel guilty because my feelings were not deep and genuine. I couldn't tell my husband because I was afraid he would think I was not a good Jew. One day in the midst of a heated family discussion about the current political situation in Israel, I couldn't hold back my frustration any longer. 'I don't understand what's going on!' I cried. Everyone tried to explain at once, until my father-in-law said, 'Hold everything! For your first anniversary, I'm sending you to Israel.' We were thrilled. I learned so much on that trip, most of all that there is much more to Israel than politics and war. I truly feel a personal connection to the Jewish state now. I recommend a trip to every new Jew!"

Mark Calabrese, a 36-year-old language professor from Ohio, was surprised by the intensity of his feelings during his first visit to Jerusalem and one of Judaism's holiest sites: "I felt an intense emotion praying at the Western Wall for the first time. I discovered a whole new world and felt a oneness with the Jewish people. I became a Zionist. I may never choose to live in Israel, but I finally understand its centrality to the Jewish people. I now understand that the Jewish past is inexorably linked to the Jewish present and the Jewish future. All of this is part of the inheritance I have chosen."

When planning a trip to Israel, do some background reading and research. Consult with friends and family who have been there for suggestions on what to see and do and where to stay and shop. Taking an organized tour is a good idea for any first-time visitor because there is so much to experience. Many Jewish organizations and travel agencies sponsor package tours. While there, do not hesitate to call the friends and relatives whose names and numbers you most likely will have been given. Most Jews know someone in Israel. Israelis are known for their warm hospitality, and such contacts provide an excellent opportunity to get to know some of them.

Proficiency in Hebrew should not be a prime concern. Although a visit to Israel provides a good opportunity to use what one has already learned and to improve on that elementary knowledge, the fact is that most Israelis know at least some English, and many speak it fluently. One conversionary couple was anxious to use what little Hebrew they knew but felt disappointed when everyone spoke English to them. "Finally," they recall, "we made a pact with our tour guide, a student who was eager to learn more English. He would speak only Hebrew to us, and we would speak English to him!"

Spouses who have been to Israel may find themselves surprised by the depth of their own feelings when returning to Israel and seeing it through the eyes of a new Jew. Such was the experience of Robert Gross, a 28-year-old nuclear physicist: "I was not too anxious to return to Israel with my wife, Jane. As a rabbi's son, I had had ample exposure to Israel—at least ten trips. But after Jane converted, she insisted that we go. My stories were not enough for her. She wanted to see it on her own. Five years after we were married, we finally made it there together, and I was shocked at my own feelings. I began to see Israel from a different perspective, through Jane's eyes, and it seemed more vibrant, more exciting than I remembered. It was as if I, too, were experiencing Israel for the first time!"

IS THE CONVERT A JEW IN THE EYES OF ISRAEL?

Let's be up-front about this thorny issue, which has made more than its share of headlines in recent years under the title "Who is a Jew?" A non-Orthodox convert is not recognized as authentic according to Israeli law, under which the Orthodox rabbinate has jurisdiction over matters of personal status, marriage, and divorce. Until recently, the practical consequences for converts and their children were limited to not being able to marry inside Israel. In recent years, this question has exploded into the public arena as extremist Orthodox groups have sought to extend this nonrecognition to any immigrant who was converted under non-Orthodox auspices. These groups are trying to amend the Israeli Law of Return—which grants automatic citizenship to any Jew born to a Jewish mother or converted—to include the words "according to halakhah" (Jewish law), in effect excluding non-Orthodox converts from this automatic right to Israeli citizenship.

The issue has precipitated tremendous debate, particularly among American Jews, the majority of whom resent the allegation that non-Orthodox converts—and, by implication, their rabbis—are not legitimate Jews in the eyes of Israel. Many American Jews, the majority of whom identify with non-Orthodox Judaism, also resent the issue being thrashed out in Israel's political, rather than religious, arena. Thus far unsuccessful in its attempt to formally change the law, the religious sector has used its growing political power to exclude non-Orthodox converts in other ways, such as refusing to register them as Jews on their identity cards or even refusing to issue them Israeli identity cards at all. These tactics are being vigilantly monitored and challenged in the courts by the non-Orthodox movements, which have increased their visibility in Israel in recent years.

The fact is that very few converts immigrate to Israel, so the practical impact of such changes is minimal. But for the American Jewish community as a whole, this fact does little to quell the outrage over what it sees as an affront to so many American Jews.

For those converts who do consider making *aliyah*, the issue is a painful one. Sheila Galant says: "I had a valid Jewish conversion even if it wasn't Orthodox. Making *aliyah* is a real possibility for me, so I thought long and hard about having an Orthodox conversion as well. But I really feel that if I did that, I would be invalidating my rabbi and my community, which I know to be authentic. I honestly don't know what I'm going to do when the time comes."

Other converts, however, seem less incensed—and more confused—by the whole issue. For them, it is no greater a concern than the related "Who is a Jew?" issues that hit closer to home, that is, nonrecognition by Conservatives of Reform conversions or by the Orthodox of Conservative conversions. Many say they will worry about the Israel question if and when they decide to live in Israel. Georgia Ferry takes such an approach, thinking "maybe I would get an Orthodox conversion if I ever decided to immigrate to Israel." Still, like Sheila, it bothers her that she would not be recognized as Jewish and that she would be forced to act against her convictions. "It's such an emotional blow when someone says you're not Jewish in my eyes. There are very good reasons I did not go for an Orthodox conversion in the first place. I am very committed to liberal Judaism, and I felt it would be hypocritical to pretend to be something I'm not."

The whole issue reconfirms the belief among many converts that there should be a standardized conversion process acceptable to all branches of Judaism and to Israel.

Despite the potential alienation from Israel over this issue, most converts do not feel that it has inhibited the development of a positive relationship to the Jewish state. With one couple, in fact, it was the born Jew who was so upset by the thought that his wife, a Conservative convert, would not be accepted in Israel that he did not want to visit there again, despite the strong attachment he had always felt for the Jewish state. "If they amend the law, it would be hard for us to visit Israel, just out of principle," Paul Weiss says. To which his wife, Marilyn, responds, "It would be really hurtful because it would mean they were questioning my Judaism and my Jewish commitment. But I don't know if we shouldn't go because of it. I've never been, and I really do want to see what it is all about."

THE RIGHT TO CRITICIZE?

The debate over whether Jews who live outside Israel have a right to criticize some of its policies has been exacerbated over the past decade as an outgrowth of both internal divisions in Israel and a new willingness among growing numbers of Jews in the Diaspora to express discomfort with some of the political and military policies being pursued. The question of Jewish dissent over Israel's policies has a special twist when it applies to converts, who may fear they might not be considered "good Jews" if they openly criticize Israel. Gerald Tyler puts it this way: "Before I converted, I felt comfortable entering into lively debates about Israel. Now my wife becomes annoyed when I become critical of Israel. She would rather that I display unquestioning support and actively defend all of its policies. But I feel that as a Jew, I have developed a closer bond with Israel, and because of that bond I can and should be critical when necessary. I, too, feel threatened when Israel's enemies want to deny its legitimacy and annul its existence. I think Ruth is afraid that some Jews may be suspicious of a convert who criticizes Israel."

Whether critical or defensive of a particular Israeli policy, the point of departure that most American Jews share is their inherent love for the state and concern for its physical safety and moral well-being. For born Jews, this concern is often instinctive, even if not always articulated or acted upon. The new Jew, on the other hand, must take steps to ensure that an understanding about Israel develops. In time, the learned response of caring will eventually give way to a more instinctive approach. As Mary Berman puts it, "When I first converted, my approach to Israel was purely academic. It seemed like an interesting but complex place. After several years of learning and two visits, I can now honestly say I feel a deep sense of identification with Israel. Now I can talk about the Jewish state as mine."

10

The Holocaust: inheriting an awesome legacy

Auschwitz, Treblinka, Babi Yar. The memory of the Holocaust tugs at the heart of each and every Jew. It is the greatest tragedy that has befallen the Jewish people. The atrocities perpetrated by Adolf Hitler and his Nazi regime led to the systematic extermination of six million Jewish men, women, and children during World War II. The German Reich murdered others besides Jews, but it was the Jewish people as a whole who were targeted for annihilation under Hitler's "Final Solution." In concentration camps throughout Europe, Jews were murdered in gas ovens designed by sophisticated German scientists. The Holocaust remains embedded in the Jewish psyche, irrespective of one's level of commitment or affiliation. It is a chapter of Jewish history that no philosopher or theologian can explain—and that no Jew can forget.

This is the awesome legacy a new Jew must struggle to come to terms with. In ways similar to support for the State of Israel, the history of the Holocaust creates a strong bond among Jews everywhere. Like Israel, as well as other emotive rather than cognitive elements of Jewish identity, the Holocaust is not easily assimilated or understood by new Jews. Having been spared the tragedy of murdered relatives, shattered families, and the collective grief of Jews of all generations—whether or not they were personally touched by the horrific genocide—converts inherit this legacy with a unique perspective. They denounce, as do many non-Jews, the crimes against humanity and wonder at the human capacity for destruction and complacency. They view with horror the films and the television documentaries filled with piled corpses, mounds of hair, extracted gold fillings. But the convert's view is the view of an outsider, shielded by an accident of birth that both protected and excluded, leaving the convert yearning to identify and to empathize with this Jewish tragedy, but wondering whether he or she has the right.

AM I WORTHY?

"Am I worthy of this legacy?" is a question often posed by converts. They know their pain may never equal that of their fellow Jews, so many of whom personally lost grandparents, aunts, siblings, friends. Still, with the convert's desire to stand up and be counted as a Jew comes the realization of what that identification means: the burden of the past and a responsibility for the future.

As converts acquire deeper knowledge about the Holocaust, they often respond on several levels. First comes an overwhelming horror and disbelief as the jumbled facts and sketchy details they may have once learned come into focus with vivid descriptions and survivors' testimonies. Jill Lebowitz came away stunned from a visit to a Jewish nursing home where she met several Holocaust survivors. "The Holocaust was a senseless, illogical event," she says. "Adequate explanations can never be found."

Converts express deep curiosity about questions of Christian responsibility as they discover the complacency and complicity of large numbers of Christians during the Holocaust. At the same time, converts seek to reevaluate Christian attitudes toward Jews and Judaism, focusing on traditional and revised Christian doc-

179

The

Holocaust:

inheriting an

awesome

legacy

trines toward Jews, modern Christian attitudes toward the Holocaust, and an exploration of the root causes of anti-Semitism and aggression.

Converts often experience sensations of revulsion and shame, because of their identification with the oppressor and feelings of guilt. They wonder if they would have had the courage and strength to react like the "righteous gentiles" who risked their own lives to save Jews. Some converts say these feelings intensify their desire to convert. They view conversion as a means of atonement or, in some cases, as a symbolic act of replacing one Jew who perished in the Holocaust.

Martin Paulson says it wasn't until he began reading about Jewish history that he considered converting, although his girlfriend had insisted she could not marry him unless he did. "I could not justify converting for the sake of faith alone, but the idea that I could act as a replacement for a Jew who had lost his life really appealed to me."

Maria Giovanini's path to Judaism began when her high school class was assigned to read several books about Nazi Germany and the Holocaust. "The books really affected me. I felt embarrassed and guilty because there were Germans in my family. I feared my classmates would find out and hate me. I went out of my way to be extra solicitous toward my Jewish classmates. I wanted to make amends, but I didn't know how. I stopped celebrating Protestant Christian holidays, which upset my parents, but they dismissed it as 'teen-age' rebellion. When I was 18, I approached a local rabbi about converting because I really felt that I wanted to replace the soul of a Jew killed in the Holocaust. His reaction was to tell me that I had overreacted to the books I was reading. 'Guilt is not a valid reason for converting,' he told me, adding that if I still felt the same way in three years, I should come back. I cried but did not forget my fellow Jews.

"When I was 21, I returned to the same synagogue only to discover the rabbi had retired. The new rabbi listened to my story and seemed very understanding. Still, he said that while my intentions were noble, they were not enough. Emotion alone would not sustain my Judaism. I had to show him that I was truly committed to Judaism. After studying with him for a year, I can honestly say that my decision to convert was based on study, practice, and feeling. If I am responsible for starting a new generation of Jews, I will feel a certain measure of satisfaction."

LIVING AS A GERMAN CONVERT

There is another type of convert who may not choose Judaism out of a sense of guilt, but whose family background hangs like a cloud over the decision. I have worked with a handful of German Christians, some of whom fear that they may always carry the burden of their past with them. The greatest nightmare that one such woman harbors is that when her parents die, she will not get to their house in Germany before her husband does so that she can throw away the Nazi memorabilia that she knows still adorn their living room. She has never revealed to her husband what she knows of her family's past.

Another German woman, Sandra Bond, was very nervous before she met her husband's family, half of whom fled Nazi Germany in 1939. She had met her husband while he was a student in Germany. "A week after my arrival here and six months before our wedding, I met Mark's family at a big Hanukkah party. I was immediately inundated with all their stories from Germany, the hard times they had, and how they managed to escape just in time. I was sitting there just thinking, 'It's not my fault. I can't help it. Please don't tell me all this. I *know* all this.' "

In retrospect, Sandra feels that Mark's family wasn't trying to put her on the spot. "They all just wanted to get rid of their stories one more time. Now it's not an issue at all. But those first few meetings were very difficult. I was so conscious of their history—and mine."

Sandra's mother, who still lives in Germany, says she had no problems with her daughter's conversion, since she wasn't religious herself. But her biggest concern was how Mark's family would react to the fact that Sandra was from Germany.

Four years after her conversion, Sandra gets along fine with her husband's family, but she still feels uncomfortable when the subject of the Holocaust comes up with them or anyone else. "I even feel uncomfortable telling people I'm from Germany. Here everybody knows it. But we're moving from Pittsburgh to Baltimore soon, and when people ask me where I'm from, I really don't know what I'll say—Germany or Pittsburgh. I think I may just leave Germany out of it."

QUESTIONS OF LOYALTY

New Jews also worry about the possibility of another Holocaust. If it did occur, would they continue to identify with the Jewish people enough to die with them? The question is usually posed by converts to themselves or by each other. But occasionally they are asked by a rabbi, a spouse, or a parent what they would do if they found themselves in such an imponderable situation. It is a question that causes considerable anguish. It is a hypothetical scenario for which very few of us, born Jew and convert alike, could predict our actions. Indeed, the history of the Holocaust contains many accounts of Jews who renounced their Judaism or even contributed to the death of other Jews in order to save their own lives. Doreen Johnson, a 25-year-old convert and mother of twin boys, says, "I would have no trouble admitting my Jewishness and dying for my people, but I think I would do everything in my power to protect my children even if it meant denying their Jewishness."

For other converts, the hypothetical is particularly troubling because it calls into question their commitment to the Jewish people. It is especially painful when the question lurks below the surface of one's relationship with a partner's Jewish family. Cathy Greenfield says, "From day one, I sensed that my husband's family did not trust me. At first I thought it was the religious differences, but it clearly went deeper than that. Scott tried to explain to me that his parents were Holocaust survivors and that they had never recovered from the fact that the non-Jewish world had allowed such an abomination to take place. I knew they did not hate me personally, but I was seen as a representative of the oppressor. They wondered if another Holocaust occurred, whose side would I be on? I had this sinking feeling that no matter what I said or did, they would always be wary of me. It's been several years now and my relationship with Scott's family is strong, but no matter how good a Jew I have become, I still wonder if they really think of me as one of them."

Above all, thinking and learning about the Holocaust serve to remind converts that they have chosen to identify with a tiny minority that has, throughout history, been the target of irrational hatred and persecution.

THE NECESSITY FOR DISCUSSION

Before converts can begin to come to terms with the Holocaust they need to confront it on both an intellectual and an emotional level. Many non-Jews, especially those born after World War II, have pathetically little knowledge about the Jewish experience during the war owing to the dearth of Holocaust education in both public and private schools. For some converts, their first real encounter with the subject comes only during the conversion course. Though an essential element of the course, it is generally given only cursory exploration because of time constraints. If rabbis who teach conversionary courses do not have enough time to delve into the issues, they should provide a bibliography of Holocaust literature. Scores of first-rate books and films depict the historical events leading up to Hitler's ascension to power in Germany, his plans for purging the world of the Jewish "race," and his devices for their systematic extermination. Per-

183

The
Holocaust:
inheriting an
awesome
legacy

sonal accounts of survivors of the concentration camps, both written and oral, provide powerful descriptions of the forced labor, the conditions under which they lived, and the mad methods of murder by which so many died. A trip to a Holocaust museum, if one is nearby, can serve as a catalyst for discussion.

Still, the intellectual part of confronting the Holocaust is easier than the emotional. Wrestling with the Holocaust on an emotional level can come only after plenty of discussion with friends, family, or rabbis. Some conversionary couples, particularly in which the born Jew's family was not directly affected by the atrocities, may spend several years together before the subject ever arises. Then a problem may ensue, as it did in the case of Mary Ellen and Jeffrey Shrager, when the new Jew displays a lack of knowledge about that painful period of Jewish history. Two years after Mary Ellen's conversion, the Shragers were visiting Jeffrey's extended family for dinner. When a discussion about the Holocaust arose, Mary Ellen began asking all sorts of questions because she had never learned about the Holocaust. Instead of encouraging her interest, Jeffrey was embarrassed by her lack of knowledge and called his wife a "stupid shiksa." She felt angry and rejected. He felt confused. Mary Ellen had learned so much about Judaism—he assumed she knew everything. Deep down, he also resented the reminders that his wife had not always been Jewish. Some unresolved guilt about not marrying a born Jew still lingered within him. This episode brought it to the surface. The Shragers clearly had several issues to resolve, which they sought to do through counseling. On the Holocaust issue, Jeffrey felt that the whole episode could have been avoided had he been more open to discussing the Holocaust with Mary Ellen to begin with.

Some Jewish partners express reservations about raising the Holocaust, uncertain of what kind of reaction to expect. Jewish partners must understand that the convert must be educated in all aspects of Judaism, even the painful ones. Attending a movie or a lecture on the Holocaust can serve as a springboard for discussion. Joel Canon, of Nebraska, wanted his fianceé, Paula, to understand why his grandparents were so upset about their upcoming marriage even though Paula had converted. He did not share his grandparents' mistrust of all non-Jews, but he wanted her to try to understand where those feelings came from. So he bought a few books by Elie Wiesel and other survivors and together they read them, discussing their reactions and emotions. "We forced ourselves to read them," Joel says. "It was a very painful experience, but we made ourselves continue. There were long silences and tear stains on the pages. Later, I told my grandmother what we had done. She was surprised and didn't quite know how to respond. We hugged and felt like we understood each other a bit more. I won't say that Paula was welcomed immediately, but I could discern a change in my grandparents' attitude toward her. They were at least willing to give her a chance."

ATTITUDES OF BORN JEWS

In addition to dealing with their own feelings about the Holocaust, converts must learn to deal with the thoughts and feelings of born Jews both toward the Holocaust itself and toward converts who seek to inherit this chapter of history that remains uniquely Jewish. The legacy of the Holocaust has shaped the consciousness of Jews in very different ways. There are Jews who live in perpetual fear of another Holocaust even in America, where, despite sporadic incidents of anti-Semitism, it is not widespread and unlikely to threaten Jewish survival. For these Jews who have never really recovered from the devastation wrought by the Holocaust, their Jewish commitment remains fierce. However, two very different manifestations of commitment can be discerned among this group of Jews. On the one hand are those who publicly demonstrate their Jewishness, never hesitate to speak up for Jews in trouble, and cast unquestioning support behind the State of Israel. On the other hand are those who, also permanently

185

The

Holocaust:

inheriting an

awesome

legacy

shaken by the Holocaust, have withdrawn from Jewish life, are reluctant to openly identify as Jews, and fear that public Jewish activism will spark new waves of anti-Semitism.

Sara Gant, a 39-year-old convert from Chicago, tells of her experience with a Holocaust survivor whom she had met at the laundromat on several occasions. Sara told her new friend she was in the process of becoming a Jew. "He tried to convince me not to do it," Sara recalls. "He kept telling me I was safe and that if I became a Jew, I would no longer be safe. No matter what I said to try to convince him that Judaism had added a tremendously positive dimension to my life, he wouldn't listen. He would just shake his head and mourn for my safety. He was trying to protect me."

Some Jews, having sought but not found answers to explain how the Holocaust could have happened, have retreated from Jewish life altogether and have become alienated or even self-hating Jews.

The impact of the Holocaust on the Jewish psyche is often hard for converts to understand. Some converts without much knowledge of the Holocaust's history say they think Jews are overly obsessed with the Holocaust and fears of persecution. Others don't understand the reluctance on the part of many who lived through the trauma to talk about their experiences. Only after serious grappling with the issues can the seeds of understanding begin to grow.

In one unusual case, Paul Kael, a convert from Delaware, could appreciate the horrors of the war in ways that many born Jews could not. Paul's father, the son of a Dutch diplomat, spent five years in a Japanese concentration camp in Indonesia when his family was caught behind enemy lines as the war broke out. Paul's elderly grandmother still carries her passport with her, a lasting remnant of the sense of insecurity seared into her consciousness during her years in the prison camp. "Because of my family's experiences, they knew that the position of the Jews can be a precarious one and couldn't understand why I would, as they put it, want to put myself in such potential danger," Paul says. Because of that slice of his family's history, Paul feels deep identification with the Jewish experience of the war.

QUESTIONS WITH NO ANSWERS

The fact is that the Holocaust raises unanswered and unanswerable questions for both converts and born Jews. The concerns that arise among converts are similar to those posed by younger generations of born Jews for whom the personal links grow fainter as time goes on. I hear statements such as: "It is so hard to imagine how such a thing could have happened. Why were the Jews so passive; what kind of resistance was there? Why did the world stand by? Where was God? How did the Jews find the courage to pick up the pieces and go on? If it happened once, couldn't it happen again? We must keep the memory of the Holocaust alive so that it will never happen again."

More than one convert has expressed confusion and dismay over a comment made by Jewish in-laws or grandparents who say that the high rate of intermarriage will give Hitler a posthumous victory. What Hitler didn't accomplish through his death camps, goes the argument, Jews will achieve by themselves: the gradual elimination of the Jewish people. The argument is often employed as a means of dissuading the Jewish partner from marrying a non-Jew. The fact that a conversion is taking place holds little weight among Jews with such attitudes. One grandfather asked his grandson, in the presence of his fianceé, "How could you marry into a faith that was responsible for our destruction?" In another instance, a Jewish father reminded his daughter that the Pope had done very little to help Jews during the Holocaust. She was marrying a man whose sister was a nun and whose brother had just entered the Catholic seminary. In both cases, the Jewish partners responded by impressing upon their respective families that they saw their fiancés as individuals who should not be held responsible for the actions of their former co-religionists.

CONVEYING THE LEGACY TO CHILDREN

Many converts who have not studied the Holocaust are caught off guard when their children raise questions about it. Such was the case with Vivian Freeman, a 26-year-old convert whose 5-year-old son, Jacob, came home from school one day with all sorts of questions. "Why did they hate us? Why did it happen?" he wanted to know. "Like most young people, I had read the *Diary of Anne Frank* and had studied some European history," she recalls. "But that was about the extent of my knowledge. Even though my husband's parents are survivors, they rarely discussed their experiences, and when they did, I couldn't bear to listen. When Jacob came home with questions, I was caught unprepared. Part of me thought it was too morbid a subject to dwell on, but the rest of me knew better. 'Coward,' I said to myself. 'You don't deserve to be a Jew.' I called my son's teacher and asked for some books to read. She was glad to help me. We don't dwell on the subject, but our discussions are well thought out. I always follow any Holocaust story with a story of Jewish triumph."

Another young mother, a German Protestant by birth, was also unprepared when her daughter, Susan, came home from Hebrew school one day and asked her why her mother's people had killed the Jews. After a moment's shock, Lindsey Hertok recalls "mumbling something about the fact that my own relatives were not directly responsible but that they should have tried to stop the situation. I told Susan that what had happened was horrible but that there were some good Christians who tried to help the Jews. My answer satisfied her for a while, but I knew I needed to do a lot of thinking about how to discuss the subject with Susan as she grew older. I also knew it wouldn't be long before she noticed the numbers etched in her grandfather's arm."

In time the convert's outrage and deep emotions relating to the Holocaust become real. My own transformation became apparent when I found that I could no longer bear to read any

Holocaust literature or watch a Holocaust-related movie. Whereas I used to feel deep anger, such experiences were now emotionally ravaging.

There should never be a question of whose pain goes deeper—that of the convert or the born Jew. There exists no Richter scale with which to measure the claims of empathy by the convert. What matters is the converts' desire to identify with the minority people they have chosen as their own, their constant vigilance against anti-Semitism, and their contribution to preserving the memory of the Holocaust. As Jill Lebowitz says, "There may be certain depths of understanding and emotion that converts and Jews of later generations may never be able to reach. However, all converts and all born Jews can make it their responsibility to keep the memory of the Holocaust alive—not only among Jews but among all people."

11

Homosexual converts: double hurdles

When Edwin Mayer called to inquire about conversion, he sounded similar to the hundreds of prospective converts who contact me each year. He voiced the typical concerns, and I asked the usual introductory questions: "Are you converting out of conviction, or is there a Jewish partner in your life? Are you getting married?"

"My partner is Jewish," Edwin replied.

"Would the two of you like to make an appointment to see me?"

"No," he said rather emphatically. "My partner has erratic hours."

I gently persisted but sensed some hesitation on his part. I suggested that he call again after reading the literature I would send him. I didn't think much of Edwin's hedging. Many prospective converts are nervous about embarking on the process; others find little support from their partners and are therefore reluctant to include them in the initial process. I didn't think much of it, that is, until I received another call a few weeks later. This one was from Michael Stern, who called to investigate conversion for his partner. This, too, was not unusual. Often, the

Jewish partner makes the initial connection with me. After a lengthy discussion during which Michael asked unusually poignant questions about conversion and its implications, I invited him to make an appointment with his partner. His answer was direct: "My partner is Edwin Mayer. You spoke with him a few weeks ago. Do you still want to meet with us?"

Trying to conceal my shock, I hastily responded, "Why, yes, of course." We agreed on a date and time, and as I hung up the phone, I said to myself, "This surely is a first for the Jewish Converts Network."

Until Edwin and Michael contacted me, it had never occurred to me that people involved in gay or lesbian relationships would actually consider conversion for the sake of the partnership. I also was aware of the traditional Jewish view of homosexuality, with the Torah condemning it as an "abomination." I felt a certain ambivalence about encouraging conversion for those who would be likely to experience rejection on two fronts—as converts and as homosexuals. I was aware that several gay synagogues had formed in cities throughout the country. I was also glad to see that as the AIDS crisis proliferated, some rabbis and Jewish communal leaders had taken steps to reach out to Jews affected by AIDS and to denounce the myth that AIDS is God's punishment for homosexuality, particularly in light of the fact that gays are by no means the only people to contract the deadly disease.

Still, I had my own personal prejudices to confront. I also felt myself facing a potential quandary: Would it be my responsibility to inform a rabbi that a person I was referring for conversion was gay or lesbian? Didn't I have a greater obligation not to betray a personal confidence? The answers, I soon came to believe, were no to the first question, yes to the second. Still, I was very confused and decided to broach the subject at the next meeting of the Jewish Converts Network. I wanted to ensure that if Edwin and Michael decided to join us, they would feel comfortable. They were coming to talk about conversion, not gay issues, and I wanted the group's support in making them feel welcome. We had an open, honest discussion during which I found my own barriers of discomfort breaking down as the reality emerged: gays and lesbians could be as Jewishly committed as anyone else. After the meeting, Rita Fountain, a JCN member for over three years, approached me. "What you said tonight was very important and long overdue. As a lesbian, I thank you."

CONVERSION FOR ALL THE SAME REASONS

Among homosexual converts, the reasons for converting cover the same spectrum as for all converts. Many of those interviewed converted out of an honest expression of love for their partners. For others, like Rita, it was a matter of personal conviction. Her lesbianism had nothing to do with her reasons for becoming Jewish. Rita, in fact, had converted after reading some Holocaust literature and feeling ashamed of her mother's German heritage. "I felt I was born with tainted blood," she told me the first time we met. "I wanted to erase half of my ancestry but I couldn't, so instead I chose to make my personal amends by converting." Interestingly, Rita's mother, at age 59, converted for the same reasons.

Another lesbian, Carmen Mills, also converted out of conviction. The 64-year-old grandmother from New York had been married and had raised three children before she discovered her lesbianism. Her sexual coming out coincided with her quest for Judaism. She had been raised as a Catholic, but her father was Jewish. She always felt closer to her father and his Judaism but had never been permitted to express it. She married a Jewish man who knew little about Judaism. Carmen says: "I should have converted sooner, but it wasn't until I came out about my lesbianism that I felt I could totally affirm who I am and what I believe. It has finally all come together for me."

Others are committed to a Jewish partner and want to share Judaism as an extension of love or an affirmation of a deep commitment. Gay converts usually decide to convert after several years with a partner and are often, therefore, more familiar and comfortable with the Jewish partner's holidays and rituals than a heterosexual converting for the sake of marriage may be. Gay converts do not have in-laws to please or a wedding date to honor. Without these additional pressures that other converts might experience, gays generally have more time to explore Judaism fully and feel wholly comfortable with their decision.

Ronald Jenson's path to Judaism evolved out of his commitment to his partner, Steve Jacobsen. Ronald had moved to Boston from Des Moines, Iowa, where he had experienced a difficult childhood knowing he was somehow different. "I didn't even have a name for my feelings or a vocabulary to explain them," he says. "I knew I wasn't like the others. I dated girls but my first attraction was to my gym teacher. In my early twenties, I read a psychology book about gays and was convinced I was abnormal. I thought it best to move to a bigger city far away where I could seek some help. Steve was the psychiatrist a friend had recommended. He was kind and patient and told me there was nothing he or I could do to change my homosexuality. I should accept my fate, he told me, and he would help me improve my self-esteem.

"Two years later, I met Steve at a gay party. I finally understood his patience, kindness, and compassion toward me. Twenty years separated us, but in less than six months we were living together as lovers. Steve was the first Jew I had ever really known. He was a deeply religious man, but it troubled him that traditional Judaism did not accept homosexuals. His father wiped Steve out of his life by saying kaddish, the prayer for the dead, when he discovered his son's sexual preference. But Steve had found his own Jewish community of both gays and straights. They warmly welcomed me, and we celebrated all the Jewish holidays together. It became increasingly clear to me that I had already adopted a new religion—I was a lapsed Methodist—although I hadn't yet seriously considered a formal conversion.

"Several years later, when Steve suffered a sudden heart attack, I panicked, because I was not only afraid to lose him but also worried who would say kaddish for him. On the way to the hospital, I decided it was time for me to undergo formal conversion. He survived that first heart attack, and I went ahead with my conversion anyway. We spent seven more wonderful years together as Jewish partners. When he died following a second heart attack, my pain was unbearable. Being able to say kaddish in Hebrew for him felt extremely important to me."

Other homosexual couples, like their heterosexual counterparts, decide on a conversion simultaneous with their decision to become parents. Peggy Gorf and Michelle Swan had been together for over seven years when they decided to adopt a baby from Columbia. "Our concerns were just like any other parents," Peggy recalls. "Both of us were religious in our own ways—I was raised a Quaker, Michelle was Jewish—but we didn't want to confuse our child with two religions. Michelle was basically a nonconformist Jew, but after the baby arrived, her inner feelings about Judaism surfaced along with her maternal instincts. She recalled the holidays she had celebrated in her youth and wanted us to share them as a family. I decided to convert to please Michelle."

TO TELL OR NOT TO TELL

The conversion process can be more complicated for gays and lesbians than for other prospective converts, especially as they wrestle with the decision of whether to confide in their converting rabbis about their sexual preferences. Many, like Ronald and Peggy, never reveal their life-style, preferring not to risk rejection. Ronald says, "I had a hard time finding a rabbi I liked with whom I could study. When I did, I was afraid to find out his attitude toward gays. Maybe he would have accepted me as his student anyway, but I never did tell him I was a homosexual or that my initial motivation for converting had been for my friend, Steve."

Peggy also chose to conceal her life-style from her rabbi. "When I enrolled in a conversion course, I told the rabbi that my fiancé lived in another state, so he was unable to attend with me. In class, I made up stories about our disagreements with family so that I would blend in with the others. When I was pressed to show everyone a picture of my fiancé, I pulled out a photo of my brother. As luck would have it, my apartment was the closest to the synagogue, and I couldn't refuse when the rabbi suggested we have a Shabbat dinner for the class at my place. The next morning, I went to Sears and bought a cot just in case someone decided to snoop around. I told everyone Michelle was my cousin visiting from Denver. We were both walking on eggshells until the last person walked out the door. We fell on the floor roaring with laughter, though what we really wanted to do was cry.

"The most painful part was being alone when the conversion ceremony finally arrived. I so wanted Michelle to be there, and she too wanted to share the special moment with me. But she couldn't leave the baby, and we were afraid of too many personal questions and puzzled stares. So I was alone.

"To make matters worse, the rabbi was beginning to get very friendly. He urged me to attend services regularly. He kept offering to officiate at my "upcoming marriage." Finally we couldn't stand the pressure anymore, and we moved to the next town without telling anyone. I still can't forgive myself for running out on the rabbi. He was really a nice guy, except for the joke he made one day in class about gays and AIDS. I laughed along with everyone else, though deep down I felt a knife in my heart."

In contrast to Ronald and Peggy, Martha Allison's circuitous route to Judaism almost ended at the entrance to the *mikvah* because, she says, "I let down my guard in a moment of friendship." A 58-year-old divorced grandmother and journalist, Martha had only recently begun to explore her lesbian identity when she was assigned to cover a gay rights demonstration for her newspaper. "I was horrified at the sentiments of fear expressed by so many homosexuals," she recalls. "I decided I needed to be myself, to come out of the closet, to love and live openly. The honesty cost me my job, but I did submit a great story!

"While searching for another job, I found a part-time secretarial position at a nearby synagogue. I was a great typist, but I knew absolutely nothing about Judaism. I was raised as a Baptist but had never considered it my personal faith. The rabbi and the director of the synagogue were very patient with me. I became fascinated by the Jewish world swirling around me. I read and studied as much as I could. My initial motivation was to enhance my knowledge in order to be more effective on the job. Later I realized I had found a religion that made sense to me. I decided I wanted to become Jewish. I had no idea I would not be accepted because I was a lesbian.

"The rabbi and I had become good friends. When I told him I was considering conversion, he was very encouraging. The class lasted about twenty weeks, and I loved every minute of it. I was one week away from the scheduled *mikvah* and *beth din*. In my great joy, I lowered my guard and revealed to my rabbi that I was a lesbian. I was looking for advice about how to resolve religious differences with my Catholic lover. Instead I received a cold, hard look of utter contempt. The rabbi told me I had deceived him, and there was no way he would consent to convert me now. I was fired from my job the next day. I was devastated. I could not reason with or talk to him. He refused to listen and just kept quoting passages from the Torah.

"I was so depressed that I drove away my lover and sought refuge, for the first time ever, in a lesbian bar. I found a friend who later took me to New York to attend my first Jewish service in a gay synagogue. There I found security and support, love and acceptance. I also met a Reform rabbi, another lesbian, who sympathized with my situation. She helped me to find a Conservative rabbi who would complete the conversion process I had begun. This time I did not let on that I was a lesbian. I love Judaism and never again want to be branded as my first rabbi had branded me—'a sinner who must be condemned.'"

In more than one instance, I have tried to intervene on behalf of gays or lesbians who revealed to their rabbis their sexual orientation and were turned away as a result. The comments I have heard are shocking. In one such instance, as soon as I mentioned the convert in question, the rabbi leaned over and said to me, "Homosexuals just mean trouble. They are sick in body, mind, and spirit. We have to be more discriminating. We are supposed to take in converts who will be assets to the Jewish people. We don't need detractors."

Other rabbis have said things like, "If we encourage homosexuals to convert, Jews and Christians will think we are condoning their behavior. Jews have enough problems"; "I can more readily accept a Jew who is gay than a gay reject from Christianity"; and "How do they expect to be Jewish openly if they can't even come out of their own closets?"

There are, of course, other rabbis who are more accepting, with views similar to the one who said, "A sincere convert can be a Jew. Sexual orientation is secondary." More than one rabbi, by the way, has suggested that it is unwise for me to permit gays and lesbians into JCN. Whenever that happens, I thank him for his advice and walk out the door.

FINDING A NICHE

If finding a receptive Jewish community is difficult for converts in general, it can be doubly difficult for gay and lesbian converts. Homosexual converts are made to feel like outcasts from two societies—the straight one and the Jewish one. They stand accused of violating society's norms as well as Jewish law because of the way they express their love and sexuality. Whereas becoming Jewish entails a clear choice, being homosexual, according to most gays, does not stem from the same selective decision-making process, yet the repercussions of being the "other" are felt in both worlds.

Being gay adds one more skeleton to the convert's closet that one must continually opt to reveal or to conceal. The difference is that for the heterosexual convert who becomes increasingly involved in Jewish life, his or her non-Jewish background gradually becomes irrelevant in the eyes of other Jews. Being gay, however, continues to shape one's current identity and therefore cannot be relegated to the past. Thus, choosing whether or not to reveal one's otherness—both as a convert or as a gay—adds to the complexity.

Many gay converts say they tend to find acculturation to Judaism easier in a primarily gay Jewish community. As Ronald Jenson put it, "Only with my gay Jewish friends am I accepted both as a gay and as a convert. Elsewhere, I find myself hiding either the fact that I am gay or the fact that I am a convert. Sometimes both central elements of my being just get swept under the rug."

Audrey Gilman agrees. "My gay and lesbian synagogue is one of the few places where I can truly express myself and explore my total reality," she says. "Nothing has offered me anything so intensely life-enhancing as Judaism." Audrey converted at the age of 22, prior to marriage, in order to please her fiancé's family. Despite her husband's indifference toward Judaism, Audrey became increasingly involved in Jewish activities. After ten years of marriage and the birth of a son, she discovered her affectional preference and filed for divorce. Wishing to raise her son in a Jewish environment while also wanting to meet other Jewish lesbians, she joined her gay and lesbian synagogue.

Only a limited number of gay congregations exist throughout this country, primarily in large metropolitan centers. Thus such an option is available to a limited number of people. Even among those gays who have a homosexual congregation accessible, some express ambivalence about limiting their Jewish experiences to a gay and lesbian community. Although they may find greater outright acceptance at a gay synagogue, many yearn for a larger, more diverse community where they can be surrounded by children and adults of all ages and outlooks.

Gay converts, to a certain extent like gay Jews in general, must choose between coming out of the closet and joining the more secure environment of a homosexual community and joining a heterosexual community where both their homosexuality and, to some degree, their non-Jewish background may need to be suppressed. Many of the gay converts I interviewed, again like gays in general, developed elaborate halfway measures: hiding their secrets from most of society and confiding in only a few trusted friends. Those who choose to become part of a heterosexual community, either a *havurah* or a synagogue, often must engage in a delicate balancing act. The difference for converts is that they are faced with the added burden of adjusting to a new tradition and culture while at the same time worrying about concealing their homosexuality.

Anton Peus converted to Judaism at the age of 19, with the rabbi who served as his army chaplain. "The Vietnam War was doing horrible things to my head and my heart," he says. "I needed religion to get me through, and Judaism made the most sense to me." Anton went through tough times following the war. He was deserted by a lover and struggled to find work. During his most difficult times, he found comfort in Judaism. He floated to various Jewish communities, both gay and straight, but ultimately found his deepest spiritual fulfillment at a straight synagogue. After a few years, says Anton, "I told my rabbi I am gay. He looked surprised but didn't respond harshly. He did say that he thought it would probably be best if I didn't broadcast my gayness to anyone else. So I put up with the elderly ladies trying to arrange dates for me. I feel I can permit my sexual preference to be submerged but not my love of Judaism."

Brian Green, a 36-year-old convert, has had a difficult time adapting to public Jewish life, despite the constant support he gets from his partner, Lonnie, and even Lonnie's family. "Things are so different when we're with Lonnie's family. I know they would prefer it if I were a nice Jewish girl instead of Lonnie's male lover. But still they have come to accept us, and they treat me like a son. When we're together for Jewish holidays, the rituals and celebrations are very meaningful. But we are both committed to making Judaism part of our daily lives. Belonging to a straight synagogue has been somewhat of a strain. My fear of being discovered intrudes on my ability to achieve maximum spiritual fulfillment. Each Shabbat morning, Lonnie and I leave our home together, get into our separate cars, and arrive at synagogue ten minutes apart. In the synagogue, we greet each other with a handshake and a hearty 'Shabbat shalom.' This charade has been going on for nearly ten years."

Like Brian, 62-year-old convert Martha Raker has made the conscious decision to conceal her true self in her Jewish community. Knowledgeable, observant, and highly committed, Martha has contributed much time, money, and energy to supporting her synagogue's activities as well as those of the greater Jewish community. No one who works with her at fund-raising events for Israel or rallies for Soviet Jewry knows she is a lesbian. Her lover masquerades as her sister. Martha feels neither bitter nor alienated from Judaism. But she is saddened by her circumstances. "I have to live a lie," she says. "My Jewish life means so much to me I cannot risk losing it by revealing who I really am. Instead, I live in two separate worlds."

Some younger converts take advantage of the activities for singles that are increasingly being offered at community centers and synagogues. "While some of my straight friends attend singles services with the hope of finding a date, I go along because it's the only time I can really enjoy the services, without feeling like an outcast," says one lesbian convert.

COPING WITH FAMILY RESPONSES

Some of the family issues faced by homosexual converts are similar to those faced by converts in general. Others are very different. For parents of gay converts, the news that their child is converting may be seen as a second blow of rejection, the first having been the discovery that their child is homosexual. Parents who may still be having difficulty accepting their child's sexual preference may react to news of conversion with deeper resentment. Others may be more understanding having already been forced to accept that their child's path has deviated from that of their expectations.

One Catholic mother was still reeling from the news that her daughter was a lesbian, wondering "How could I have given birth to such an anomaly?" when she later learned, as she puts it, that her daughter had "forsaken Jesus and converted to be a Christ-killer." According to her daughter, "My mother was ready to disown me when she found out I was a lesbian. My conversion provided the final impetus to sever all ties."

Sometimes gay and lesbian converts have never even told their parents of their homosexuality, and it is not until they are converting that the truth comes out. Such was the case with Vicki Lewis, whose story is told by her lover, Olga Thomas. "Vicki and I knew we were lesbians as early as high school, but no one suspected it. Everyone just thought of us as best friends. We did the usual best-friend things—spent the night at each other's houses, exchanged clothes, participated in the same activities. After college, we shared an apartment.

"The only difference between us was religion. I'm Jewish, and Vicki is Presbyterian. But it never much mattered. I spent Christmas at her house; she joined my family for all the Jewish holidays. When we hit our mid-thirties, our parents began to nudge us about getting married. They were itching for grandchildren. They continually tried to arrange dates for us. We were torn. We both loved our families and were extremely close to them, but we were afraid to tell them about us.

"At about the same time, Vicki began seriously considering converting to Judaism. She really fell in love with Jewish ritual and tradition, especially the ones centered around the home. She loved to say that being Presbyterian was like cream of wheat compared to rugelach! One day, while her parents were visiting, they spied the Jewish books she was reading. We were forced to give them some explanation. One thing led to another, and we wound up telling them about our true relationship. Her family was shocked, but much more accepting than mine. My family reacted with hysterics and chest-beating for several weeks. Later they acquiesced. I think they loved us too much and really had no choice but to accept us if they didn't want to lose us. A short time later, we invited both sets of parents to Vicki's conversion ceremony. Later, they stood underneath the *chuppah* with us at our commitment ceremony, held under a beautiful pink magnolia tree. The ceremony was performed by a Reconstructionist rabbi who was sympathetic to our needs. I think our parents understood that we were establishing a holy union. It was our way of saying we were married to each other."

The reaction of Olga's parents to their daughter's sexual partner is reminiscent of the reaction of many Jewish parents to the news that their child is involved with a non-Jew: shock gives way to anger, denial, and guilt, followed by a period of personal introspection. As with many Jewish parents of an interfaith couple, Olga's parents' initial lack of acceptance and attempt to discourage the relationship ultimately gave way to acceptance, albeit without approval. Likewise, Vicki's parents, like many Christian parents, were resentful that their daughter was converting to Judaism. But they had the double burden of having, at the same time, to face the reality that she was a lesbian. Both sets of parents, meanwhile, secretly blamed the other for having the daughter who initiated what they regarded as illicit sexual behavior.

Now that they are open about their relationship, Vicki and Olga experience some of the same strains of other conversionary couples, including the need to balance holiday celebrations. "After some difficulty navigating the family dynamics, we now just take turns to try to please both families during the holidays and at the same time maintain our Jewish identity," Olga says. "We spend Thanksgiving, Christmas, and Easter with Vicki's folks and all the Jewish holidays with mine. Sometimes, both families come to us for a holiday. This means tremendous work for us, but it also provides a meaningful symbol that we are recognized as a couple."

Rebecca Hart also made the difficult decision to confide in her Orthodox Jewish family about her Swedish female lover, and she is glad she did. Rebecca, a professor of Jewish studies, took a sabbatical in Israel the year after her father died. There, on a nonreligious kibbutz, she met Sven Johannson, a non-Jewish volunteer. Rebecca says: "We were opposites in every way. I am dark, short, and stocky; she is blonde, tall, and willowy. I could fill volumes with my Jewish knowledge; she knew absolutely nothing about Judaism but identified strongly with Zionism. I admired her dedication and unselfishness, her warm and gentle ways. She helped me through my worst depression. By the end of the year, I realized that I loved her and could not leave her behind. I was ecstatic that she felt the same, and she even agreed to convert. We flew back to the United States, where I arranged for a discreet Orthodox conversion. We also sent for her 6-year-old son, who was living with her mother in Sweden, and arranged for his conversion as well. The rabbi was told only that Sven had been studying with me.

"I felt that I couldn't hide all this from my mother. At first she was shocked and blamed herself for not pushing me toward marriage. But after the emotional trauma subsided, she began to adjust to the reality of my sexual orientation. She loves me without fully accepting my life-style. My decision to share my life with my family has resulted in a much stronger relationship. I've adopted my partner's child, and my mother loves him like she would any grandchild."

Other Orthodox families have a much harder time coping, as was the case with Reuven and Sarah Kaplan. The Kaplans, residents of Boro Park, New York, could not understand why their son, Shmuel, had not taken an interest in any women since his divorce three years ago. They were saddened that his marriage to Chana, which had been arranged for him, did not work out. They knew he had never really loved her, but they had hoped he would learn to. They were worried about their son. He seemed so preoccupied and was spending inordinate amounts of time studying Torah with his friend Jack. Jack, now known as Jacob since his conversion, was considered a righteous man in their Orthodox community. He had approached the rabbi several years ago about converting. His only motivation was his deep love for Judaism. He was respected, accepted, and popular with the older men, who could always count on him to show up for afternoon and evening prayers.

One day, Shmuel's parents said to him, "Learning is good, but you're spending too much time with Jacob. You can't marry Jacob. Let us at least introduce you to some nice girls."

Shmuel could hold back no longer. "It is too bad that I can't marry Jacob because I truly love him," he confessed. "I could never love a woman the way I love him." Sarah and Reuven were shocked and outraged. "You are sick," they told Shmuel. "We'll find you a doctor to straighten your head out. The divorce must have been more devastating than we thought." Shmuel tried to explain to them that he had told his wife about his feelings, she was grateful for the truth, and the marriage had ended amicably. But they refused to listen. Eventually the anger led to complete rejection. His parents disowned him. All emotional and financial ties were severed. Shmuel was forced to move to another city with Jacob.

Today Jacob and Shmuel own a religious bookstore. They pass themselves off as brothers. Shmuel believes that his parents' Orthodox religious beliefs will always serve as a barrier to any future reconciliation. Jacob, feeling a certain sense of guilt for the family breakdown, has unsuccessfully tried to reach out to Shmuel's parents. His letters have been returned unopened. They have no family to turn to, but both Shmuel and Jacob say they are happy that they can be together. They continue to study Torah and Talmud and live observant Jewish lives. When I asked them to comment on the traditional Jewish attitude toward homosexuality, they both declined.

Despite the pain that open confrontation can bring, conversionary gay couples who don't confide in their families about either their homosexuality or their religious orientation may be setting themselves up for a devastating fall, especially if illness or another crisis arises and the family is unaware of their child's hidden life. Mary Ann Worth experienced just such pain when her lover, Ellen, was in a car accident. "She was in the intensive care unit for several weeks. Her family thought I was just the roommate, so after I notified them they totally ignored me. They called in a priest. They had no idea we had converted together several years earlier. I was not even allowed in to visit Ellen. I wanted to shout to them, 'I am family. I love her. You don't even know her.' But I kept silent, tears burning me inside. I had promised Ellen I would never reveal her Jewish, lesbian truth.

"Her death was even more devastating. We had been to-gether for fifteen years and had lived a full Jewish life. I couldn't bear to go to the Christian funeral her parents arranged. I prayed for help and wrestled over whether to reveal Ellen's true identity. I consulted a rabbi, who advised me to leave well enough alone. There was already enough pain, he said. My unsolicited revela-tions would only cause more. There was no one I could turn to for comfort. No one asked if I needed help. How could they have known?"

After Ellen's death, Mary Ann moved from Houston to San Francisco, where she became involved in a gay synagogue. "I needed my Judaism very much. In synagogue, I felt closer to El-len. I received tremendous support from the members there. They were like family to me. The rabbi in my community teaches that we should not be regarded as violators of Jewish law but, rather, that we should be seen as victims of circumstances be-yond our control!"

JEWISH ATTITUDES TOWARD HOMOSEXUALITY AND AIDS

Many gay converts express deep dismay over the Jewish view of homosexuality as a sin. The book of Leviticus (18:22) is ex-plicit on the subject: "Thou shall not lie with a male as one lies with a woman; it is an abomination." There are several references to the consequences of homosexuality in the Bible. It is interest-ing to note that the Bible does not mention female homosexual-ity, from which one may infer that either lesbianism was not widely practiced or perhaps that it was not considered such a gross transgression because it does not involve the same "wasted" spilling of seed that applies to men. Still, Jewish law prohibits lesbianism, though it does not apply the same penalty of death as it does to male homosexuality. The argument offered by some modern Jews in defense of homosexuality is that although pro-creation is an important purpose of Jewish marriage, it is not the sole purpose. Homosexuals are made in God's image as much as every other human being, and so they should not be denied the right to a full life.

Many homosexuals mistakenly assume that synagogues would be the first among Jewish institutions to encourage love of all Jews. One lesbian convert, Judy Stone, laments: "For years I asked myself, why am I gay? Why did God give me these feelings? I don't want to be different, but I recognize that I am. God can't hate me. He made me this way."

Distress over the Jewish view of homosexuality is exacerbated when it is translated into Jewish attitudes toward AIDS. When Francis Farber, a 36-year-old gay convert from Lancaster, Pennsylvania, learned that his lover, Mark Newman, was dying of AIDS, his pain intensified as he saw the isolation his friend was experiencing while his family and other Jews backed away from him. Francis says: "My lover was a very committed Jew. He wanted to return to die near his family in Pittsburgh, but they would not hear of it. His parents had finally accepted his homosexuality because he was far enough away to conceal it from their family and friends. But they were bitter and angry that he had contracted AIDS. They told him that Judaism could not recognize him and that his sin was unforgivable.

"I was a new Jew at the time and was just beginning to appreciate Judaism, but I was appalled at the ostracism that Mark experienced. In his desperate attempt to find a sensitive rabbi, Mark contacted someone in Pittsburgh who agreed to talk to him but at the last moment canceled the appointment. After calling several other rabbis, he finally found one who agreed to come to the hospital to see him. When this rabbi arrived, he requested a mask, gloves, and a gown and would come no closer than five feet from the bed. It was hardly the comfort Mark was seeking.

"My friend died peacefully in his sleep after a torturous three-year battle with the disease. I convinced the doctor to write 'pneumonia' as the cause of death because I feared that Mark would be denied a Jewish burial. He died a broken man, rejected by the family that he loved and the tradition that he cherished. I continue to practice Judaism, but I'm closeted and will remain that way because people are not ready to face the reality of my true existence."

FROM HOMOSEXUALITY TO CELIBACY

More than one gay or lesbian convert I met had felt unable to reconcile Judaism with homosexuality and, as a result, had come to lead a celibate life. Melanie Thompson, a 33-year-old sales representative, tells her unusual story this way: "Mine is a sordid past. For several years, I worked as a model and a prostitute. I was in three pornographic films and posed naked for *Playboy* magazine. My horrible experiences as a prostitute led me to discover that I was actually a lesbian. I spent several driftless years courting lovers in Europe. After I returned home, I met a friend who invited me to a Passover seder. I knew virtually nothing about Passover or Judaism or about any real religion. As a child, I moved at least fourteen times with my family. Wherever we landed, my parents had to 'have religion,' so they joined whatever church was convenient—Lutheran, Baptist, Catholic, Quaker. Since it made little difference to my parents which church they prayed in, I certainly never felt connected.

"That seder was a turning point in my life. I decided right then that I wanted to find out more about Judaism. I wanted to experience the warmth and love and sense of history over and over again. My friend's uncle helped me find a job, and I devoted all my spare time to learning about Judaism. A year later, I began studying with a wonderful Orthodox rabbi. He charged me nothing. When I told him about my past, he just nodded his head. 'Your past is behind you,' he told me. 'Now you are a new person.' I promised him I would never have another lesbian relationship. My conversion took place eighteen months later.

"Today I am happy as a Jew. My sexuality is repressed. I have no lovers. I have no desire to marry. Judaism has extracted a high toll from me, but it is my choice. I am happy in other ways. My family and friends support my decision. For the sake of Judaism, I will remain celibate."

Reginald Fineman, 29, came to Judaism and celibacy via a different route. The only child of missionary parents, Reginald spent most of his early years in various parts of Africa, India, and Southeast Asia, where his parents tried to spread the word of Jesus to the native inhabitants. Religious indoctrination and strict moral codes were imposed on him for as long as he could remember. At age 15, he contracted malaria and was sent to the United States for treatment. Angry at his parents for not visiting him once during his illness, Reginald resolved not to return to Africa. "I enrolled in college and pursued my interest in linguistics and theology," he says. "It was there that I had my first homosexual experience—with a young man who was planning to become a Catholic priest. I never knew I was gay before, although I did have strong feelings for men and none for women. It just happened, and I let it happen because it seemed so natural.

"I entered the seminary with my friend but found it too stifling. I had discovered a new world during college, and the seminary reminded me too much of my previous missionary experience. I left before the year was finished. I resumed my religious studies and decided to explore Judaism, a religion my parents denigrated. The more I read, the more Jesus receded into the background and Moses stepped forward. Before long, I decided I wanted to become Jewish. I had great difficulty finding a rabbi to study with. One rabbi refused because he thought I was motivated by revenge against my parents. I'd made the mistake of telling him too much. Another rabbi suspected that I still worked for a missionary group. Others said they didn't have the time. One day I was sharing my troubles with a group of guys at a gay bar. A balding man in his fifties handed me his card as he walked out the door. The card indicated that he was a rabbi. I called him the next day, and he helped me contact another rabbi who would do my conversion. That first rabbi made it clear that his payment would be in the form of sexual favors. After my conversion, the relationship ended, but I was left feeling embittered. I felt like an overgrown boy in a man's body. I resolved not to become like that rabbi. Instead, I devoted my energies to being a good Jew. The more I learned, the stronger I felt that I could no longer pursue homosexual relationships. It's not that I'm no longer attracted to men; it's just that I have chosen to be true to my Judaism first."

Both Melanie and Reginald say they no longer consider themselves homosexual. Their primary relationships have been forged with Judaism rather than with a partner, but they seem content to have thrown themselves wholly into their Jewish communities and synagogues. The sad part is that although Judaism may chastise homosexuals, it certainly does not condone celibacy. These two have been forced to choose what they see as the lesser of two evils.

A PERSONAL NOTE

After interviewing over a dozen homosexual converts for this book, I have come to realize that some of the same prejudices and ignorance that preclude understanding and acceptance of sincere converts by the mainstream Jewish community also work to exclude gays and lesbians from society in general and Jewish society in particular. I still feel uncomfortable with the idea of two men or two women making love. But whatever my own personal prejudices may be, my heart says that all gay converts should be welcomed into the Jewish community to be given the opportunity to express their commitment as Jews. Some of those who shared their stories with me are wonderful people who demonstrated tremendous strength of character as they overcame one obstacle after another in their search for recognition as legitimate Jews. The Jewish community can only benefit from such strength and commitment. Time and knowledge are forcing me to reevaluate my own thinking about homosexuality and Judaism. I hope others will begin to reevaluate their own attitudes as well. Outreach has already begun in certain parts of the Jewish community, especially in response to the AIDS crisis. Let us hope that the crisis will spark further outreach not only to homosexual Jews who are dying, but also to those who are living, so that we may help them lead full Jewish lives without denying who they are.

12

Black converts:
double jeopardy

"I sat in synagogue on this first day of Rosh Hashannah and knew myself once again to be an outsider. . . . If people didn't know anyone else was there, they knew I was there, with my black self. How can I become a part of the Jewish people when I don't look like other Jews?"

The question, posed so poignantly by Julius Lester in his book, *Lovesong: Becoming a Jew*, is one voiced by nearly every black convert with whom I have spoken. Their stories demonstrate the tremendous courage and conviction necessary for a black person to become Jewish. Well aware that their darker skin will always prevent them from easily blending into a Jewish crowd, blacks enter the covenant of the Jewish people with their eyes wide open. They know, after all, that the eyes staring back will also be wide—wide with amazement. Unlike their white counterparts, who may or may not choose to publicize their non-Jewish past, black converts do not have that choice. Some of the issues black converts will face are similar to those encountered by all converts, especially those converting primarily for the sake of marriage. Yet the black convert must contend with additional pressures in a society that continues to scorn interracial unions. The black convert, then, faces the dual challenge of transcending racial as well as religious barriers.

CONVERSION FOR ALL
THE SAME REASONS

Black converts become Jewish for the same variety of reasons that most converts choose Judaism. They may have fallen in love with the tradition, found identification with the Jewish people, or chosen to share a common religion with a Jewish partner. Brenda Holland, a 29-year-old dance instructor, converted four years ago, following a spiritual journey that began at a kosher catering hall and ended with the celebration of her own conversion. "At the age of 18, I went to work for a Jewish catering firm," Brenda explains. "My first exposure to Jews came through working at their weddings, anniversaries, and bar mitzvahs. At college most of my friends were Jewish. One of them invited me home one year for Passover. I was really scared. I had been around white folks but never in their homes as a guest. My friend's parents were waiting at the station, and they hugged both of us so hard I thought my ribs would crack! I had never felt such warmth growing up in my grandmother's house. At the seder I felt really comfortable. I even knew some of the Hebrew prayers I had heard so often at my catering job. My friend's family was really impressed, and they kept joking that they were going to make me into a kosher Jew. They were clearly just kidding, but the idea suddenly hit me that maybe I could become Jewish and share this tradition that I inexplicably had come to love.

"When I first approached a rabbi about the idea of converting, he tried to discourage me because he assumed I had a Jewish boyfriend. When I finally convinced him that I was doing this for me and me alone, he consented to study with me. Three months later, I was ready for *mikvah* and a *beth din*. When I returned to my college dorm, my whole floor had planned a party for me.

There were blue and white streamers, and they all chipped in to buy me a gold necklace with a Star of David on it. It was the happiest day of my life."

Priscilla Woods, a 42-year-old cancer researcher at a prestigious New York hospital, lived with her fiancé, Philip Rosenberg, for six years before they married because they both feared the familial and societal repercussions of their union. Priscilla wrestled long and hard with the idea of converting because she knew it would deeply hurt her parents. Her father was the minister and her mother was the choir director at a Baptist parish in Georgia. Priscilla also knew that a conversion would not make her problems go away. She and Philip would share a religion that they would be able to pass on to their children, but they would still be an interracial couple, an identity they felt would almost guarantee constant hostility, rejection, and, at the very least, puzzled stares from strangers.

"As much as I loved Philip, I wasn't always certain that I was ready to carry the burden of society's prejudices around on my shoulders throughout my life," Priscilla recalls of her early thinking on the subject. "I knew that I would encounter prejudices from my own black people and from white people. I wanted to be true to my African ancestry and still inherit the Jewish tradition. It was a tremendous task and I gave it a great deal of thought.

"Today, five years after my conversion and marriage, I have no regrets. It is difficult, I'll admit, balancing my Jewish and my black worlds. But we are passing on to our children with love and pride the two worlds that have for us become one. When my 3-year-old daughter asks me who she is, I give her a great big hug and say, 'You are a black Jew.' "

With nearly all the interracial couples I interviewed, I was extremely impressed by the tremendous thought and effort that had preceded any final decisions on conversion and marriage. Of the thirty-two couples I interviewed, only three said they had had no idea what they were getting themselves into. One of these individuals, Daniella Evans, says, "We were so blinded by love that we never really stopped to think what the consequences of our unusual marriage would be." Daniella and her husband Benjamin, who converted prior to their wedding, were divorced three years later. Both of them told me their divorce stemmed from differences in "values and priorities" rather than differences in cultural and religious backgrounds.

ENCOUNTERING RESISTANCE

Even when much thought has gone into the matter, the problems are no less real. For one thing, the fact of conversion does little to allay the fears of Jewish in-laws as a conversion might in noninterracial conversionary marriages. Race and culture become the defining characteristics, with religious identity being relegated to a matter of much less import.

Though such resistance generally does not come as any great shock to Jewish children, in some cases it does. Nina Skopnic was genuinely surprised at her parents' reaction to her boyfriend, Jim. "My parents have always been active in liberal causes, particularly in cultivating black–Jewish relations in my hometown. I really had no idea they were so bigoted. When I brought Jim home for dinner, they found him bright, witty, and charming—that is, until I announced that we were living together. They were appalled. They stopped paying my college tuition and wouldn't return my phone calls. Even later, when Jim decided to convert, they wanted nothing to do with us. It was very painful. I not only lost my parents, but I lost total faith in everything they had taught me to believe."

Nina's parents see it very differently. Carol Skopnic was in deep pain because she had been unable to accept her daughter's black husband. "I'm tired of fighting, but it hurts so badly," she told a support group of parents of interfaith couples. "I'm not prejudiced. I have black friends. But as hard as I try, I just cannot accept a black son-in-law. He is willing to convert, but the issue is not religion—it's race."

While the Skopnics' opposition to Nina's marriage is a typical reaction—although perhaps more extreme in that the familial ties were severed altogether—not all families react so forcefully. Emily Laserwitz's parents were thrilled when she told them she was bringing someone very special home to meet them. As a 42-year-old pediatrician, Emily had postponed marriage, and her parents had all but given up hope they would ever see their daughter marry or have children. Emily had raved about her fiancé, Arthur Brooks, for six months, even telling them that he was in the process of converting. The one thing she hadn't told her parents was that he was black. Emily describes their reaction when they finally walked in the door of her parents' home:

"My parents did a double take. But even though they were shocked, they never lost their composure. I was really proud of them. I suspect that my parents, both well-traveled academicians, would not have been so favorably disposed had I brought home an uneducated, coarse bookie even if he were white! Arthur is articulate, witty, charming, and gorgeous. My parents, as well as his mom, who is a widow, have been loving and supportive. They are concerned about the difficulties our children may face, and so are we. But at least as far as our families are concerned, we have penetrated the skin color barrier."

Despite Arthur's positive experiences, the fact is that most black converts will encounter resistance and sometimes downright hostility from other Jews. Most Jews will look twice if they walk into a synagogue and find a black person there davening. The first time John Grethen entered a synagogue, he had barely advanced a few steps before he was handed a coat and hat by an older woman, who sweetly asked him to "take care of it" for her. It was hardly the welcome he was hoping for. On subsequent occasions, he says, "I was mistaken for a driver and the caterer. But what I know best—how to read from the Torah—no one seemed to ask of me."

Black converts, whether converting for marriage or out of conviction, not only will encounter nonacceptance from white Jews but also must deal with the attitudes of family and friends, many of whom interpret conversion as an outright rejection of their black roots. Brenda Holland, who had converted out of conviction, was afraid to tell her primary guardian, her grandmother, of her action.

"I knew she would interpret my conversion as a rejection of all the black pride she had tried to instill in me," says Brenda. "Sure enough, when I wrote her a letter telling her of my decision, she appeared at my dorm a week later. She accused me of turning my back on my black heritage and my true kin. I tried to explain that although I was now Jewish, I would always be proud of my black heritage. It's been a difficult process, but she is gradually coming around to accept me as I am."

The volatile state of race relations in this country in general, and black–Jewish relations in particular, also contributes to the hostility that black converts may encounter when trying to explain their decision to other blacks. The black community may see them as traitors, as selling out to be on the "comfortable side."

"I know I'm just as black as they are—that I'm Jewish *and* black—but when I tell that to my family and friends, they just don't understand," laments one black convert, echoing the pain of many others. "When they tell me I can't be both, it hurts so much. They are denying me who I am."

Although the politics of race may remain with these converts forever, some see the positive side of being able to play the role of mediators between the black and Jewish communities, whose organizations continue to try to promote good relations. Black converts, who straddle the fence between the two peoples and identify with both, may in some instances serve as effective spokespersons and bridges.

BLACK SINGLES

For single black converts, finding a partner or even a date can prove to be one of the most difficult consequences of their decision to straddle two worlds. Julia Cohen, herself the daughter of an interracial couple, converted at age 22, not long after she discovered that her father was Jewish by birth and had all but rejected his Jewish past. His rejection of Judaism inspired her determination to explore it. The more she learned, the more she desired to reclaim the Jewish tradition as her own.

Now, Julia's biggest concern is "Who exactly should I date? Whites don't know I'm Jewish, and black guys are uncomfortable with it. My black dates usually never call back once they discover I'm Jewish. They, like my mom, resent me for what they see as a denial of my black heritage. Besides, if I ever did fall for a black guy, I would want him to convert and he would probably be reluctant to do so. I don't kid myself about white Jewish guys either. I know that most wouldn't date me even if they knew I was Jewish. They would only see me as black. I have this fantasy that some day I'll be swept off my feet by a Jewish guy who loves me as I am. For now, I try not to think about finding a lover because it seems useless. I have my work, my family, my friends, and most of all, I have my Judaism."

Winifred Davis had to bounce back from a series of painful encounters before she found a man she could love. The first incident occurred at synagogue, at the Oneg Shabbat following her first public reading of the Torah. "I had studied for months, and I knew I had done quite well. My rabbi was so proud," she recalls. "Suddenly, I overheard a lady from the congregation say: 'We shouldn't be very nice to her because she'll then tell her friends and soon they'll all want to convert. We can't have our children marrying blacks.' I'll never forget those words—they stung me like a bee.

"I'd never thought about who I would date before. I had just concentrated on becoming Jewish, something I'd always wanted ever since my childhood when we lived across the street from a synagogue. Somehow I knew then I wanted to be a part of what was going on there.

"After this incident, I called my rabbi, who didn't know what to say to me. At last he suggested that maybe my best bet was to find a black male who would be willing to convert. That wasn't much help. Soon after that, I attended a singles service at a nearby synagogue. I was the only black person there. Only one man approached me, and the only thing he had to offer me was directions because he thought I had wandered into the wrong building! He seemed totally oblivious to the fact that I was wearing a very large Star of David around my neck!

"I began to feel very lonely and sorry for myself. I had no regrets about becoming Jewish, but I also knew that I very much wanted to get married. Months later, I impulsively put an ad in the personals column of a local Jewish paper. I received six responses, including two from black men. One of them was just wonderful. Bruce, also a convert, and I were going through the same things. Two years later, we were married. We live a traditional Jewish life and have found a small community that accepts us. We have decided, however, not to have children."

BLACK-JEWISH CHILDREN

Nearly every black convert interviewed said that one major concern revolved around children. Some, like Winifred and Bruce, decide from the outset that they will not have children for fear of subjecting them to the hardships of living in two different worlds. Winifred believes that although it will be painful not to have children, it will be even more painful to have them. "I'm afraid that I won't get the support necessary, that my children might hate me for making their lives so difficult, that they might even end up rejecting the Judaism I have come to cherish. That would probably upset me more than anything."

Other black converts and interracial couples also indicated that even if they, as adults, can handle the prejudice and the stares they frequently encounter, they are afraid to bring children into such uncomfortable circumstances. Winifred herself acknowledges feeling helpless and inadequate when unkind comments are tossed her way. "How could I possibly be helpful to my child? It would be a double burden to bear," she said.

Another recent convert spoke for many when she said, "Neither society, black nor Jewish, is ready for my children."

One interracial couple said they had adopted two interracial babies because they knew those children would have trouble finding homes.

Hope and Morris Mandelbaum had long discussions about how they would raise their children. But even with all the planning, Morris says, "I still feel occasional twinges of doubt, wondering whether we did the right thing subjecting children to hostile looks and words." Morris and Hope, who converted right before she gave birth to their first son, feel they need to protect their two children not only from a disapproving world but also from their own families, who have been less than supportive. "Since our marriage, my parents don't want to know about my existence," Morris says. "We have tried everything to bring about a reconciliation, but nothing has worked. I have to lie to my children and tell them that their Jewish grandparents are in a nursing home and can't be visited. Eventually I will tell them the truth, but while they are still so young, I don't want to inflict unnecessary pain on them by telling them my family has rejected them because they are half black."

Another convert, Sam Woods, relayed how unhappy his daughter, Beth, was in a racially mixed public school. "Beth considers herself mostly white, because she identifies as a Jew and most of the white children in her school are Jewish. But the white kids, except for a few, see her as black while the black kids see her as white."

Ephraim Goldblatt, the 8-year-old son of an interracial couple, has a different problem: identifying with his black heritage. "I'm the only black kid in my school, so I can't be hanging around other blacks. There are no blacks; even the janitor is white. My mom tries to teach me about my black roots, but I live in a white world. Half the kids in my class are Jewish and the other half are Christian. We don't talk much about religion, but everyone knows I'm Jewish."

Rebecca Lynne's experiences as the daughter of an interracial Jewish couple confirm the worst fears that many couples express for their children. But her story also attests to the strength of conviction, for after a long quest for an identity she could call her own, Rebecca came to affirm her Jewishness. Rebecca, now 28, tells her poignant story:

"I'm black, but I look white. Because of my heritage—my father was Russian, my mother part Indian, part black—I experienced a very difficult childhood. We lived in a white neighborhood and I was passed off as white, even though I thought of myself as black. Most of my schoolmates thought I was white. When they saw my mother, they mistook her for a nanny, since many of the kids had black nannies. As I grew older, I tried to tell everyone I was black, but no one would listen. It hurt because the message I was getting was that it was better to be white. It was a message that confused me, since my mother, whom I loved very much, was black. I felt both anger and shame.

"My mom converted to Judaism for my father's sake. They raised me Jewish, but my mom seldom accompanied us to public Jewish observances or to synagogue. I used to think she didn't come because she did not want to embarrass us. I knew nothing of black culture and began to explore on my own. I tried to find books that would help me integrate my Jewish self with my black self, but no such writings existed. I felt like the missing piece of a puzzle, and I didn't know where I fit in.

"My dad died when I was 14. People in our community were nice to us, but my mother felt uncomfortable staying there, so we moved to a black neighborhood. My direct association with blacks helped me establish a sense of roots. I began to overcome some of the internal conflicts that had plagued me, but school was still difficult. My new school was mostly black, which excited me at first, but my fair skin set me apart from the others. I tried to gain acceptance by making fun of the white kids. This helped for a while, but still my Jewishness created a barrier. Some kids taunted me by calling me 'richy' because they thought I identified with rich Jewish children. My mom and I continued to practice Judaism at home, although occasionally I would accompany my few friends to the Baptist church. Mom didn't approve of this, but she understood that I was trying to be like other blacks.

"It has taken me many years, but today I proudly identify as

a black Jew. I realized that my father's Jewishness had a profound
impact on me, although it took me many years to uncover it.
Unfortunately, my father was unable to help me forge a personal
identity that incorporated both my Jewishness and my blackness.
I have finally found that the Jewish people did not choose me,
but I have chosen them. The destiny of the Jewish people is my
destiny. I now know this is where I belong."

Children of wealthier families sometimes seem to be protected by their affluence and their parents' status in the community. Malcolm and Melinda Johnson, black converts who met in
conversion class, live in a fashionable suburb of Los Angeles.
They say that neither they nor their children encounter prejudice
on account of their blackness or their Jewishness.

Malcolm's and Melinda's reasons for converting were very
different. Melinda had pursued conversion after being influenced
by the writings of Dennis Praeger, a contemporary Jewish writer
whose work she had discovered while working toward her Ph.D.
in philosophy. The more she read, the more she wanted to know
about Judaism and Jews. "I was raised in a Catholic home but
had always felt wishy-washy about Catholicism. I must have encountered Judaism at a time in my life when my mind and heart
were open to it. Judaism really made sense to me."

Malcolm, a 45-year-old physician, quips that his reasons for
converting were "less admirable" than his wife's. "It's really very
simple," he says. "I have always felt very comfortable around Jewish people. I always felt a certain connectedness, even a kind of
brotherhood with them. It's hard to explain. Maybe it's that both
blacks and Jews bear the mark of pain. Slavery was the black
people's Holocaust. Hell, for as long as I can remember, most of
my friends and colleagues were Jewish. It just made good sense
to join my friends."

Most of the Johnsons' friends are white and Jewish. They
describe themselves as cultural Jews who occasionally attend synagogue and are generous supporters of Jewish causes. Their two
children, ages 6 and 10, attend a private school where the majority of the students come from Jewish homes. When asked their
thoughts about interdating, Melinda responds: "Sometimes we

joke about that. God knows who they'll bring home. We will encourage our children to date Jews, but given the choices we made in our life, we would never think to forbid other partners. The fact is, they think of themselves as blacks first, then Jews. If I have to be honest, they will probably marry blacks, and there will be very few black Jews available. Maybe we could encourage them to convert! When we converted, we hoped that we would be the first Jews in a long tradition of Jews in our family. But I guess reality dictates that we'll just have to wait and see."

BLACK OR WHITE NEIGHBORHOOD?

Deciding where to live is difficult for any couple. It can be more complicated for conversionary couples, and doubly so for black conversionary couples. With few successfully integrated neighborhoods in this country, interracial families are often forced to choose between their mixed identities when choosing where to set up a home. Many fears often arise: Will the white wife be accepted by the black community? Will the black husband be accepted by the white community? How about the children? Identifying as Jews exacerbates the tensions of an already complex situation.

Of those I interviewed, the middle-class families living in racially mixed neighborhoods and large university towns seemed to encounter less prejudice than those living in all black or all white neighborhoods. Joseph Reed, a retired English professor, converted after thirty-five years of sharing a Jewish life with his wife because "only then was conversion being talked about in the open, as an acceptable option." He and his wife raised three children near a New York university town, and he attributes his children's well-adjusted natures to the more tolerant university environment.

"My children knew no barriers of race," he says. "They consider themselves black Jews. They don't pretend to be white, which I think is healthy. Problems result when an interracial child wants to be considered all white. We and our children both have friends of all races. Most of our white friends are Jewish. Although initially they were curious about our religious identification, they accept us as we are."

The majority of the professional, more affluent couples interviewed tended to settle in areas that were predominantly white. Some reported encountering overt discrimination, whereas others felt it on a more subtle level. Ethel Feinstock, a black convert in Minneapolis, recalls the shocked look on the face of her real estate agent when she told her she had just joined her synagogue.

In another instance, Adra Moore was confronted by reality two days after moving into her new Boston home. A white neighbor, carrying a plate of cookies, knocked on her door and asked to speak to "the lady of the house, Mrs. Finkelstein." Adra smiled and said, "Mr. Finkelstein is my husband. I'm Adra Moore. Won't you come in?" The woman turned bright red, stammered out a welcome and ran down the steps. "She even forgot to leave me the cookies!" Adra recalls.

Other more affluent families, like the Johnsons, say they encounter little prejudice in their neighborhood. The greatest difficulties were described by those who had settled in working-class neighborhoods. Two couples, one in Philadelphia and one in Detroit, gave practically identical accounts of the verbal and physical abuse both they and their children had suffered. In both instances, the families had moved to poorer white neighborhoods, where just a few elderly Jews remained in an area that had once boasted a large Jewish community. The neighbors complained about the "intrusion" into their neighborhood, broke windows, and sent threatening letters. Their children were harassed on their way to school. When word got around that they were Jewish, the situation only deteriorated. Both families then moved to mostly black neighborhoods, where they encountered virtually the same hostility. As a last resort, each of these families settled in a racially integrated neighborhood, with mixed results.

One family, the Kleins, found a measure of acceptance in their Detroit locale, especially at the neighborhood synagogue, whose membership had dwindled significantly because many

Jews were moving out of the area. Dora Klein, speaking with hard-earned relief, says, "Our son's bar mitzvah was the first bar mitzvah the synagogue had witnessed in a decade. They were so glad to have us, no one seemed to care that I am black and his dad is white. We're Jewish and that's all that mattered."

The Philadelphia family wasn't quite so lucky. The Georges found initial acceptance in their middle-class housing development—that is, until the neighbors learned they were Jewish and would not be joining the local Baptist church. "From then on," says Sue George, "the greetings on the street were a bit icier."

EXTENDING A WELCOMING HAND

Despite the potential problems that black converts face, their numbers seem to be increasing each year. Although it's easy to spot them once they emerge into the Jewish community, it's not always easy to find them before they do. Many, fearing ostracism and isolation, express reluctance to become publicly involved in Jewish communal activities. As Julius Lester said during his pre-conversion days when he wrestled with whether he as a black could become a Jew: "My blackness burns my skin when I think of walking into a synagogue where I don't know anyone."

Thus the initial responsibility of welcoming black converts will fall on individual Jews who encounter them through friends or work rather than in the organized Jewish community. When a born Jew does see a black person at a synagogue or public event, he or she should extend a welcoming hand, a "Shabbat shalom," an invitation to lunch.

Black Jews often express strong religious convictions following their conversions. Therefore, it is not Judaism as much as Jewish peoplehood that they have the most difficulty embracing. The challenge to feel a part of the Jewish people—a challenge facing all converts—is especially formidable for blacks.

With most converts, I believe that the process of identifying with the Jewish people is a two-way street. It requires as much determination and initiative on the part of the convert as it requires an openness on the part of the Jewish community. Although black converts, too, must demonstrate Jewish commitment, the responsibility for encouraging acceptance falls largely in the hands of the Jewish community. Optimally, the Jewish community should devise programs in which black Jews can explore these issues among themselves and with other Jews. In addition, rabbis and other communal leaders must lead the way by emphasizing the importance of welcoming all Jews into the fold.

Black Jews are not a new phenomenon. The discovery of the black Jews of Ethiopia, who for centuries had practiced Judaism unaware of a wider Jewish world that was oblivious to their existence, brought wonder and joy to the hearts of many. The rescue efforts that brought thousands of these Jews to Israel in the early 1980s sent a ripple of excitement throughout the Jewish world. It reaffirmed the oneness of the Jewish people. Although we in America tend to think of all Jews as coming from Eastern and Central European descent, the fact is that Jewish communities exist all over the world, where shades of skin color may vary. We never question their Jewishness.

Blacks who today choose, in the face of so much adversity, to cast their lot with the Jewish people, should be admired for their courage and embraced wholeheartedly.

13

Special for singles

When I fell in love with Judaism twenty years ago, people considered me a rather odd phenomenon. "Why would you want to become a Jew?" was a question I encountered almost daily from Jews and non-Jews alike. A common, though mistaken, assumption was that I had a Jewish man hidden away somewhere. Surely my conversion wasn't something I was doing strictly on my own! Today the notion—and the number—of conversions is more widely recognized, though still not always accepted.

But single converts still may find themselves in a paradoxical position. One who converts for the sake of marriage, though ultimately a personal decision, nonetheless had the idea implanted by a Jewish partner or family member. Often the conversion process coincides with wedding plans, so the idea of becoming Jewish is just one more item on the list of things to do before the big event. Only when the wedding is history can such a convert begin to assimilate into practice what was learned and observed during those hectic prewedding months. To help guide that process, there will, it is hoped, be a new Jewish family, ready and waiting to serve as conduits to Jewish life. At the very least, the convert generally has an automatic invitation to a Jewish home for the holidays.

In contrast, the single Jew by choice has no time pressures dictating the conversion process. There is time to explore, to question, to absorb. Thus by the time a single Jew converts, he or she is fully certain in mind and heart that being Jewish is the desired goal. Conversion may be the culmination of years of Jewish discovery so that, when it happens, this convert is often ready to plunge into Jewish life with the intensity of an infant just learning to crawl. New avenues never before accessible, new opportunities never before known lie waiting to be explored. The problem is that, unlike infants, whose parents will be there to rejoice at each new discovery, single converts may not find anyone or any place waiting to nurture the enthusiasm.

The category of single convert can encompass many situations beyond never-before-married singles who convert out of conviction. Under the same rubric, but with some differing needs and complicating factors, are widowed and divorced converts, single parents, and singles with no desire to mate and marry, including homosexuals. I will address the special needs of these groups later in the chapter.

FINDING A COMMUNITY

Judaism is deeply rooted in the family, the home, and the community. For any Jew, it is hard to be Jewish alone. For the new Jew who is alone, it is not only hard to *be* Jewish, it is even harder to *feel* Jewish.

"I feel like I've been left dripping at the *mikvah*," says Marla Owens, echoing the frustration felt by many new single converts. "It reminds me of being 16 years old and looking for a job. No one would hire me because I didn't have experience. But I couldn't get experience until someone hired me. I don't have a Jewish family to go home to for the holidays and have yet to make Jewish friends to invite me to Jewish celebrations and functions. My Jewishness so far is limited to vicarious living through books and movies. I keep wondering when I will get a role in the plot."

As a recent convert, Marla is an intellectual Jew. She can tell you more than most born Jews about Jewish history and Jewish law, but the experience of "doing" Jewish still eludes her, especially since she has no friends or family to guide and support her.

Celebrating Jewish holidays ranks right up there with finding a Jewish partner as the greatest difficulties of being a single convert. Viola Hamden recalls her first Yom Kippur as a Jew. "I really felt connected sitting through the services, but afterwards everyone quickly greeted each other and rushed right out of the synagogue. They were all going home to break the fast with their loved ones. I went home alone and shared my food with Jake, my cat."

Geoffrey Gordon panicked as Passover approached and he had yet to meet one fellow Jew in the Nebraska town where he had been transferred soon after his conversion. "The thought of sitting home alone during the first seder made me cry," he recalls.

Without a family with whom to share Jewish ritual and tradition, the single convert must first and foremost seek a community where he or she feels comfortable—whether a synagogue, a *havurah*, a Federation singles group, or a university Hillel. In Philadelphia, for instance, some single converts have found the most warmth and welcome at one of the several *chavurot* that exist. One convert considers herself very lucky to have found a "loving and protective" *havurah* that has helped boost her confidence as a Jew. "Now my problems as a single convert are the same as those of any single Jew, no more and no less," she says.

PROGRAMS NEEDED FOR SINGLES

Other single converts may prefer the atmosphere of a larger, more diversified synagogue. But as one recent convert suggests, with a mixture of innocence and wisdom, synagogues without singles programs are missing the boat. "They think we need them, but in reality they need us!" says 28-year-old Stephanie Mulligan. "Aren't we going to be the next leaders of the Jewish people? If we do not feel comfortable joining a synagogue now, why would we join a synagogue in later years? If we don't establish a certain level of comfort now, they shouldn't assume we're going to join later, when we are married and have children. Besides, not all of us will choose to get married and have children. We can still be important, contributing members of the community.

"As a convert, I look to synagogues to fill both my spiritual and social needs. I have an awful time finding Jewish guys. With red hair, green eyes, and tons of freckles, I don't look Jewish and my name doesn't sound Jewish. I often wear my Star of David necklace so that Jewish guys will know I'm kosher. I worked hard to become Jewish. I certainly don't want to negate it all by marrying a goy."

Most single converts with whom I speak agree that any city with a significant number of Jewish singles should establish singles programs through either synagogues, community centers, or other organizations. Many communities already run successful programs. They should be consulted by other places that wish to start such programs.

Across the country, those rabbis whose synagogues provide singles programs all agree on the importance of these efforts. They agree that such programs succeed once the proper leaders are found. They view such services as one way to help stem the rising tide of intermarriage in their communities. Many reported the special joy they experience when officiating at marriages of couples who have met through the singles services.

Several rabbis alluded to the initial concerns of the synagogue's lay leadership that the programs would be too costly to the synagogue. Much to everyone's pleasant surprise, most of the synagogues were able to recoup the expenditures and, in some cases, even add extra revenues.

Most synagogue-based singles programs are started in large synagogues because they have ample facilities. But smaller synagogues also could consider offering some activities. Brunches, study sessions, and Shabbat dinners are among the popular programs. Northern New Jersey and other areas have established a successful model of rotating Friday evening services especially for singles. The system gives each synagogue only an occasional responsibility and allows singles to enjoy a certain variety, but on a regular basis.

Those synagogues that cannot provide special programming might consider offering reduced rates for singles, even beyond the one- or two-year free membership that may have been given to converts. The special rates should be openly advertised, since many singles, especially single converts, are reluctant to ask for them. Many singles do not even consider joining a synagogue because they assume the rates are prohibitive. Synagogues could advertise in local general and Jewish newspapers, at local college campuses, and in libraries and health clubs.

Needless to say, the personalities of the rabbis and cantors, as well as the formats used, will help determine the success of these programs. Traditional services may not succeed with young singles; many say they prefer more participation and discussion. But the success of these programs should not be measured only in terms of the number of marriages that result. They can also go a long way in strengthening the bond between singles and Judaism. Single converts, especially, want desperately to feel at home in the synagogue as they engage in Jewish prayer.

Some single converts may feel the need to relocate in order to strengthen their new Jewish identity. Ramona Sands moved from South Carolina to New York for just that reason. "There weren't too many Jews in my hometown in South Carolina, so I didn't expect special programming. Intermarriage was a big problem and a major concern to the small Jewish community, but they all just fretted and wrung their hands. Even my born Jewish friends had trouble meeting Jews there. As a recent convert, I needed to find a stronger Jewish community, so I moved to New York. It's wonderful to be Jewish in New York. On Friday nights there are many singles services to choose from. Since I don't have a Jewish family, these programs are my only vehicle for practicing Judaism and feeling that I really belong somewhere. Right now I don't have the funds to join a regular synagogue, and I also don't feel quite ready. I still feel strange and anonymous in a regular service. Singles services have become an integral part of my life."

Armando Virgilio also found his port of entry to Judaism through singles programs in New York. Several years ago, Armando had converted to please a Jewish girlfriend whom he thought he would marry. When the relationship ended, he found himself with a broken heart and a piece of paper declaring that he was a Conservative Jew. He didn't think much about it until one day a friend encouraged him to come along to a singles service. "I took my certificate of conversion with me in case somebody asked to see it for entrance purposes," he recalls. "What did I know? Before I knew it I was making friends and dating. I even became somewhat of a celeb once people heard I had converted. Soon it became apparent to me that my four-week conversion had not taught me much. I was embarrassed and ashamed for knowing so little. I resolved to learn more and joined a Torah study group for singles. As a community project, we made a seder for twenty senior citizens. It was my first seder. I don't know who enjoyed it more—the older folks or me. It was wonderful. The singles group helped me to become Jewish for real, beyond the words on my certificate."

WIDOWED AND DIVORCED CONVERTS

Converts who converted for the sake of marriage and find themselves no longer with their spouse, because of either death or divorce, may be in for a period that tests their commitment to Judaism. The convert may never have felt fully accepted by or assimilated into the Jewish family or community. Depending on how long ago one converted and how active a Jewish life one led, the convert may not have acquired much Jewish knowledge or a catalogue of Jewish memories from which to draw inspiration and strength to face the immediate challenges of mourning and separation and the longer-term challenge of rebuilding a life. The level of acculturation and commitment achieved by the convert prior to a life transition often determines whether the Jewish connection continues.

Some converts also face the possibility that Christian families will try to use a death or divorce to tempt the convert back to Christianity. Their motivation may be sincere as they try to provide religious comfort for their loved one in crisis. Or they may never have accepted the conversion and will use the fact that the born Jewish partner is gone to lure the "lost" family member, as well as his or her children, back to their former faith.

In times of crisis, the Jewish family and the community must provide the support necessary to show the convert that he or she still matters as a Jew. Many converts have told me that they were tempted back to Christianity only when their need for love, caring, and acceptance was not met. Converts who never felt accepted among Jews will feel that they have little reason to continue living as Jews. People in times of crisis and pain are seeking not a religion but, rather, the comfort that the religion provides. Solace can often be provided by those who represent a faith. A rabbi's words can provide comfort to a widow as a mother-in-law can provide care for the widow's young child. A Jewish friend can provide support when self-esteem has been diminished by divorce. That these support givers happen to be Jewish is a message to the convert who finds himself or herself alone.

Ginger Klayman was devastated by the death of her husband, Ian. She had relied on him for everything—from financial matters to taking the lead in religious observances. "I think Ian felt a little guilty that I'd had to convert, so he took full responsibility for Judaism in our home," she says. "The only blessing I knew was for lighting the Shabbes candles. His family came to stay with us right after his death, but two weeks later they were gone, and I was alone with my two children. Strangely enough, anything Jewish began to comfort me because it reminded me of Ian and his profound love for Judaism. I resolved to provide as much Jewish education as I could for the children. Even though I was grateful for his legacy, there were times when I cursed him because he hadn't insisted I learn the prayers or the rituals. I tried to bless the children on Shabbes the way he had, but I invariably messed up the order or the tunes. I was too embarrassed to invite another Jewish family to share our Shabbes, and no one thought to invite us. I tried to continue to attend synagogue functions, but it wasn't the same.

"Eventually our synagogue membership expired, and I didn't have the money to renew. I was embarrassed to ask for a reduced rate. We gradually slipped away from organized Jewish activities, although we continued to be observant at home. I was very lonely. One day my daughter begged me to attend a Purim party at the Jewish Y. I reluctantly gave in and found myself pleasantly surprised to meet a few friendly people, as well as a few other single parents. I realized that I needed to bring the family back into the community. Thanks to my daughter's urging, we reestablished the connection."

Gary Bass, a 42-year-old widower, says he almost found himself slipping away from Judaism when his wife died after a painful two-year bout with cancer. "In my traumatized state, no one could reach me. As a recent convert, I was unfamiliar with all the Jewish practices surrounding death. We barely touched on the subject during conversion class. No one even raised a question about it. Maybe because death seems so remote when you are young. I mechanically went through the funeral arrangements that Jennifer's family helped with. I felt guilty that, when alone at night, I found myself reciting Christian prayers from memory. My own family knew that I had converted more out of deference to Jennifer's wishes than because of true conviction. They began to steer me back toward Catholicism. If it had not been for our two sons and my in-laws' overriding love for Judaism, I think that I could very easily have become Catholic again. I went to our rabbi, a wise and compassionate man. He recognized my need for acceptance within the Jewish community and my family's need for nurturance and friendship. He put me in touch with other single parents. It was a tremendous boon knowing that they were there for me when I finally emerged from my self-imposed shell."

Tasha Richman was not so fortunate. "Even after I converted, I was not considered Jewish by Dan's family. His grandmother constantly referred to me as a 'shiksa.' She said it especially loudly when I was around. For Dan's sake and at the urging of my rabbi I became an exemplary Jew. I learned Hebrew and Yiddish and kept an observant home. Nothing I did helped. Dan was protective of me and ashamed of his family's behavior. When Dan was killed in a tragic car accident, I was five months pregnant with our first child, Daniel. Because of Dan's family's attitude, I decided to give up my Jewish observances. Why should I bother to be a practicing Jew when nothing I did would gain me acceptance by Dan's family? Little Daniel will be 3 years old soon. I suppose I must decide what kind of identity and religious affiliation I want to give him. I've maintained a kosher home out of force of habit, but nothing else I do says I'm Jewish. Right now, I'm too tired, angry, hurt, and confused to think about it. Dan's parents moved to Arizona. They never write or call. They have seen Daniel only once. Last Christmas my mother invited me to midnight Mass. I went. The next day I went to synagogue. Right now I don't feel as if I belong anywhere. I know more about Judaism than I know about Catholicism. But I just don't know what I will do."

After listening to Tasha's heart-rending story, as well as to Gary's and other similar ones, I am convinced that people in these difficult situations can easily be persuaded toward one religion or another simply by a demonstration of love, compassion, and sincere acceptance. Normally in the course of my interviews I make it a rule not to get involved in a direct way. In Tasha's case, I had to make an exception. I argued for the practice of Judaism for the sake of her young son and for the sake of the memory of her husband. Perhaps my strongest reason was a selfish one: as a convert, I felt deep, personal hurt. I also feel anger at Jewish parents who can so easily abandon a Jewish grandchild and a Jewish daughter-in-law. Tasha's in-laws are not the only ones to be blamed. The Jewish community as a whole bears part of the responsibility as well for not having worked harder to educate and sensitize born Jews to the needs and concerns of converts. If little Daniel is not raised as a Jew, we all share some of the blame.

Marriages that end in divorce after one of the spouses has converted have their own set of problems. Relations with Jewish in-laws who may have been important Jewish role models may become strained, draining from the family one of its most important Jewish resources. Will the convert feel secure enough to continue as a Jew? Did the convert ever feel it was something he or she really wanted in the first place?

Alice Robertson, the mother of four preteens, is one of those who held on, but with difficulty. "When Alan moved out, I was overwhelmed, anxious, and resentful. I had converted for him because his family wanted us to get married in a synagogue. During our marriage I became the leader for everything Jewish in our household. Alan just went along to keep the peace. He was much more of a cultural Jew than anything else. I was not surprised when I learned that he had left me for a Gentile woman.

"When he left, I didn't know what to do. I didn't like celebrating the holidays alone. I begged him to help me teach the children more about Judaism, but he responded only halfheartedly. We are having financial difficulties, and Alan refuses to pay for what he calls 'excess Jewish religious lessons.' I was unable to give my two older kids a party for their bar and bat mitzvahs. I am always exhausted after working full time and taking care of the house and kids. The children help me prepare for our simple Shabbat dinner. Going to services has become a sacrifice. The synagogue is a half-hour away. Sleeping late on Shabbat is such a luxury, but when I do sleep late, I feel so guilty."

If the conversion was coerced, there can be real problems, especially if the divorce is a nasty one in which one spouse might use religion and children as a way to get back at the other. After all, it is very easy to get rid of something you never really owned. One of the byproducts of an increasing rate of intermarriage, conversion, and divorce is the problem over who will have "spiritual custody" of the children. Several cases have already gone to court, including that of Babette Horsely. "I converted just to please my husband," she says. "He was only Jewish when it was convenient. I never saw any great commitment on his part. As for me, I missed my old religious celebrations. After the divorce, I won custody of our two children, and Bruce was furious. Soon I decided that it didn't make sense for me to continue to pretend to be Jewish. I returned to the Catholic Church, and, naturally, I took my children with me. Bruce took me to court. The judge ruled in his favor, claiming that since the children had known only Judaism, they would be confused if they began practicing a new faith. I argued that their knowledge was limited because their Jewish father was not observant, but the judge didn't listen. Now I, as a practicing Catholic, am supposed to raise my kids Jewish? It's ridiculous. We had to rework the kids' visiting schedule to their father so that they're with him on the Jewish holidays."

Albert Citronella had a similar problem, but his was reversed. Albert had converted to Judaism out of conviction prior to his marriage to Debra Barman, a nonpracticing Jew from an Orthodox background. After their marriage Albert became increasingly observant, much to his wife's dismay. She criticized him for being a fanatic. Divorce seemed to be the only thing they could agree upon. For a while things were civil between them because they shared equal custody of the children. But when Debra was remarried to a Catholic man, major problems ensued.

Albert explains: "I was furious with Debra for permitting Christmas trees and Easter egg hunts when the children were with her. My in-laws, who had been disappointed when my passion for Judaism didn't rub off on her, were also very angry at their daughter. But she just laughed in our faces. Our 6-year-old daughter seemed to enjoy the new diversions and additional gifts, but my 10-year-old son became very depressed and refused to visit his mother. Naturally she assumed I was influencing his decision. I tried to seek family therapy, but Debra refused to attend. After two years of harsh bickering, I refused to allow the children to go back to their mother and it became a legal issue. In my opinion, the judge completely mishandled the case. He let the children choose with whom to live, thereby dividing the family.

My daughter chose to live with her mother, my son with me. I couldn't afford any more legal fees, so I didn't appeal the decision, but I feel so bitter."

It is extremely upsetting when children are used as pawns in a bad relationship between husband and wife. Such cases underscore the need, prior to marriage and conversion, for partners to openly and honestly assess their feelings about their religion and the role it will play in their future lives.

Remarriage can also present problems for converts who would like to remain Jewish after a divorce or the death of a spouse but may have trouble meeting another Jewish partner. Older men and women, the primary candidates for second marriages, often know very little about conversion and may be hesitant to marry a convert out of either ignorance or prejudice. Bensen Kula, a 56-year-old widower, was surprised when his girlfriend ended their eighteen-month relationship after she discovered that he was a convert. He says, "I converted at the age of twenty-four and have remained a committed and observant Jew. I've been Jewish so long that the word 'convert' was no longer in my vocabulary. I wasn't trying to hide my past; it just wasn't an issue. Rhona, my girlfriend, told me she wished I had never told her because she has reservations about converts as authentic Jews."

Jan Mallen was divorced from her husband because he refused to get help for his alcoholism, but everyone assumed that it was her conversion that was somehow responsible for the dissolution of her marriage. "When I found myself dating again at the age of 35, many Jewish men tried to link my divorce with my conversion or my Irish background," she says. "Most of the men I'm dating now are Christian, and they'll most likely flee when I suggest that they will have to consider converting to Judaism in order to marry me."

Greta Bergman voiced another concern, that of children from a previous marriage: "A single adult can always consider conversion, but most men I meet at my age have also been married before and have kids. It is certainly not fair to expect his children from a previous marriage to convert. I would be aghast at the thought of someone even asking my children to convert. But the challenge of blending two faiths in one household while simultaneously trying to learn how to deal with stepparenting can certainly be overwhelming."

A ROLE FOR THE COMMUNITY

Synagogues and Jewish communal organizations tend to serve the needs of traditional families while ignoring the needs of singles in general as well as single-parent families. In Judaism, the family is a central institution for defining and transmitting Jewish identity. But the growth in the number of nontraditional family structures in American society (which, of course, includes the two-career family in addition to those we have discussed) compels the Jewish community to adapt to the new needs of its constituents. It is time the Jewish community began actively reaching out to these nontraditional Jewish families. The growth in the number of single-parent families is directly related to an increase in the divorce rate as well as to the growing numbers of single women and men who choose to have or adopt children without a partner. The community must address these needs, which reflect changes that are occurring among the entire Jewish population. Many argue that there is no need to invest much time, effort, or resources in helping single-parent families because they will eventually remarry. Even if this were true, what they often fail to realize is that the children in these families spend their formative years with one parent and often without any connection to the Jewish community. A divorced mother who derives no personal benefit from the synagogue may decide it is not worth joining even if it means her children will not receive a Jewish education.

For converts, these services are particularly essential because they may provide the only ongoing link with Judaism and may in fact determine whether they and their children continue to live as Jews. The approach used to reach out to these people must be comprehensive, considering the Jewish, social, economic, emo-tional, and educational needs involved.

The following are some of the suggestions offered by single parents regarding how the Jewish community can help address their needs: holiday and Shabbat programs that focus on prepa-ration as well as celebration; communal celebrations; workshops and seminars geared to single parents; workshops for children of single parents, including special ones focusing on divorce or los-ing a parent; Shabbaton weekend retreats with activities for both children and adults; car pooling or bus service for religious school (lists can be distributed); social events for single parents; informal home-study groups; a telephone resource line for infor-mation, emotional support, baby-sitting services, and profes-sional referrals; assistance in bar and bat mitzvah planning; peri-odic special single-parent family Shabbat services at a synagogue, Y, communal agency, or even private home.

Once the need for such programs in a particular community is established, concerned Jews must be willing to help organize the activities and support them. The leadership can come from both those who will derive benefit from the programs and others who understand the importance of encouraging, nurturing, and supporting all Jews in our midst—no matter what their marital status or background. The Jewish community is too small to shut out anyone who seeks to enter—least of all the person who chooses Judaism purely for reasons of personal conviction.

Daily reminders for the Jew by choice

1. To see each new day as an exciting opportunity to practice one's Judaism.

2. To approach each area of Jewish life with a healthy curiosity.

3. To identify with the positive, rather than the negative, characteristics of other Jews.

4. To respond to criticism of conversion with genuine humility, patience, and tolerance, rather than anger and revenge.

5. To see the fulfillment of *mitzvot* (religious observances) as a privilege, and to practice them with joy.

6. To use prayer as a time for closeness to the Almighty and as a time for self-evaluation and self-expression.

7. To grow spiritually by taking every opportunity to learn Torah.

8. To develop a set of Jewish values and a lifestyle that are meaningful to oneself and one's family.

9. To realize that no one else has the power to make you feel un-Jewish without your consent.

10. To relish the victory in overcoming a temptation or habit, and to use this feeling of triumph to motivate future growth (i.e., giving up favored non-kosher foods, Saturday morning golf, etc.).

11. To realize that you cannot control other people or situations, but you can always control your own attitudes.

12. To realize that change does not come easily. Appreciate small victories. You will reap great benefits through awareness, consistency, effort, and determination.

13. To share your intellectual and emotional zeal for Judaism with other converts and to help them in any way possible.

Basic Jewish vocabulary

Afikomen   The final piece of matzah that is eaten after the conclusion of the Passover Seder meal.

Aliyah   Literally, "going up, ascending": (1) the honor of being called up to the Torah to recite a blessing before the reading of Torah portion; (2) immigration to Israel.

Amidah, or **Shemoneh Esrei**   The principal prayer of each of the daily services, recited silently while standing.

Aron Kodesh   The place in the synagogue containing the Torah scrolls.

Ashkenazim   Jews whose ancestors settled in Eastern Europe.

Aufruf   Traditionally, the bridegroom's aliyah to the Torah on the Sabbath prior to his wedding. In non-orthodox synagogues today, the bride often has an aliyah as well.

Aveil   A mourner; one who observes the Jewish laws of mourning for a deceased family member.

Ayshet Hayil   Literally, "woman of valor," a phrase from the Book of Proverbs that describes the perfect wife.

Baal Tefillah   Leader of a prayer service.

Baal Teshuvah   A Jew who returns to observance of the commandments.

Bar Mitzvah   Age thirteen years and one day; age of maturity; when a boy is of legal age for performance of the commandments.

Bat Mitzvah   Age twelve, at which a Jewish girl attains maturity and undertakes adult responsibilities.

Beth Din Three-person religious rabbinic court, guided by principles of halakhah.

Bimah (1) The front platform of the synagogue where the ark containing the Torah stands; (2) the platform that contains the Torah reading table.

Birkat HaMazon Grace after meals, recited after eating bread or after a meal in which bread is eaten; also called "benschen" (blessing) in Yiddish.

Brachah Blessing, benediction.

Brit Milah (Bris) The covenant of circumcision, first practiced by Abraham. All Jews have their sons' foreskins removed on the eighth day after birth, with naming and blessings for the future.

Candlelighting Performed before the start of the Sabbath and festivals.

Challah Braided ceremonial loaves eaten on Shabbat or Yom Tov; the piece of dough or bread that is removed and burned before or after baking.

Cholent A long-simmering stew, begun before sundown on Friday and served hot for Shabbat lunch.

Chutzpah Affrontery, nerve.

Davening Praying.

Diaspora The dispersion of the Jewish people from their homeland; the places Jews live outside Israel.

Dreidel A spinning top used for a Hanukkah game.

Eruv The general term for several types of rabbinic enactments intended to promote the sanctity of the Sabbath; for example, the symbolic boundary around a town that encloses and transforms it into a private domain, thereby permitting one to carry objects within the circumference on the Sabbath.

Etrog A citron, one of the four species used ritually on Sukkot.

Gelt Coins given to children on Hanukkah.

Ger tzedek A righteous proselyte, a convert who has chosen to become Jewish purely out of religious conviction.

Get A writ of Jewish divorce.

Grogger A noisemaker used on Purim.

Haggadah The book used by Ashkenazic Jews during the Passover Seder to tell the story of the Exodus. Sephardic Jews call the entire ceremony of the first night of the Passover celebration *the haggadah* (literally, "telling").

Halakhah   The Talmudic code; a generic term for the whole legal system of Judaism, encompassing all the laws and observances.

Hallel   Psalms of praise (Psalms 113–118), recited on festive days.

Hameitz   Leaven; food prohibited on Passover.

Hamentaschen   Triangular cakes or cookies, eaten on the holiday of Purim.

HaMotzi   The blessing recited before eating bread.

Hanukkah   An eight-day celebration, commemorating the triumph of Judah the Maccabee over the Syrian Greek King, Antiochus, and the subsequent rededication of the Temple in Jerusalem.

Hanukkiyah   A nine-cupped candle holder or oil holder used on Hanukkah.

Haroset   A mixture of chopped fruits, wine, and spices eaten during the Passover Seder; it symbolizes the mortar and bricks that the Israelites made in Egypt.

Hashem   A name for God, used by those who do not wish to take God's Hebrew name "in vain."

Hatafat dam   To draw a drop of blood.

Hatan   A bridegroom.

Havdalah   The ritual service marking the end of the Sabbath or a holy day, to distinguish the sacred from the everyday.

Havurah   Literally, "community"; the contemporary havurah is a group organized informally for prayer, study, and celebration.

Hazzan   The professional cantor or prayer leader of the synagogue or service.

Huppah   Marriage canopy.

Kabbalat Shabbat   The opening section of the Friday evening service, welcoming the Sabbath.

Kaddish   A prayer of praise for God recited by the mourners during their period of bereavement after the death of a close relative.

Kallah   A bride.

Karpas   Parsley, lettuce, onions, or even potatoes, used as the symbol of the coming of spring and dipped in salt water during the Passover Seder.

Kashrut   The Jewish dietary laws.

Kavannah   Awareness and intent in preparing for and performing rituals; also, concentration in prayer.

Ketubbah   The Jewish marriage contract.

Kiddush   The blessing over wine on Shabbat and Yom Tov.

Kippah   A skullcap worn as a head covering for religious reasons; also *yarmulke.*

Klal Yisrael   The Jewish people.

Kohen   A member of the priestly tribe; a direct descendant of the high priest Aaron.

Kol Nidrei   The opening prayer recited on the night of Yom Kippur.

Kosher   Prepared in accordance with Jewish law, most often referring to food.

Lashon hara   Speaking evil of someone when he or she is not present.

Latke   A fried potato pancake, traditionally eaten during Hanukkah.

Levi   The tribe that assisted the priests in the Temple as well as all descendants thereof.

Lulav   A palm branch used on Sukkot.

Maariv   The daily evening prayer service.

Machzor   A special prayer book containing the prayers for the High Holy Days, Rosh Hashannah, and Yom Kippur.

Magen David   The six-pointed star of David.

Maror   The bitter herbs eaten during the Passover Seder.

Matzah   Unleavened bread used on Passover.

Mechitzah   The barrier in an Orthodox synagogue that separates men and women.

Megillah   Usually refers to Megillat Esther, read during the holiday of Purim. It is one of the five scrolls of the Bible.

Melaveh Malkah   A festive meal or gathering after the end of the Sabbath.

Menorah   The seven-branched candelabrum of the Temple in Jerusalem; also used synonymously with Hanukkiyah, which has nine branches.

Meshebeyrach   A prayer recited in synagogue to bless an individual called to the Torah or a sick friend or relative.

Mezuzzah   A parchment scroll inscribed with the first two paragraphs of the Shema and affixed to the doorposts of a Jewish home.

Mikvah   A ritual bath used for purification purposes by married women after menstruation, by brides before nuptials, and by converts at the culmination of the conversion ceremony.

Minchah   The daily afternoon prayer service.

Minyan   A quorum of ten adult Jews for purposes of public prayer.

Mishloach Manot   Sending gifts of fruit, candy, and cookies on Purim.

Mishnah The collection of rabbinic law compiled in 200 C.E. by Rabbi Judah HaNasi that forms the basis of the Talmud.

Mitzvah A commandment, positive or negative; one of the 613 Torah-given precepts or one of the rabbinic commandments added later; also loosely refers to a "good deed."

Mohel A person who performs a circumcision.

Musaf An additional service that follows *shacharit* on the Sabbath, Festivals, and Rosh Hodesh.

Oneg Shabbat A Shabbat evening gathering, usually with light refreshments served.

Parashah The weekly portion of the Torah, which is divided into fifty-four portions.

Parve Food that is neither "fleishig" (meat) nor "milchig" (dairy) and, therefore, can be eaten with either meat or dairy foods.

Pesach (Passover) The eight-day spring festival commemorating the Exodus of the Jews from Egypt. (See Sukkot.)

Pidyon Haben The redemption of the first-born child (if male and if not a Kohen or a Levi) on the thirty-first day after birth.

Purim A holiday celebrating the victory of the Jews over the Persian enemies in the time of Esther and Mordecai.

Pushkeh A Yiddish word meaning coin box, used for depositing money for charity (*tsedakah*).

Rav Rabbi

Rebbe Teacher

Rebbitzen Rabbi's wife

Rosh Hashannah The Jewish New Year.

Rosh Hodesh The head, or beginning, of the Jewish (lunar) month; a minor holiday, observed for one day when the preceding month has twenty-nine days and for two days when the previous month has thirty days.

Sandek The person who is given the honor of holding the baby during the circumcision ritual.

Sefirat HaOmer The ritual of counting the days from Passover to Shavuot.

Selichot The penitential prayers recited on the days preceding Rosh Hashannah and during the Ten Days of Penitence between Rosh Hashannah and Yom Kippur.

Sephardim Of or pertaining to the Jews whose ancestors settled in Spain or Portugal.

Shabbat, Sabbath, Shabbes   The day of rest; the seventh day of the week. Begins at sundown on Friday and ends at sundown on Saturday.

Shacharit   Morning service.

Shammes   (1) The sexton, the man in charge of the synagogue building; (2) the "helper" candle used to light the other eight candles of the Hanukkiyah.

Shavuot   (Pentecost, the Festival of Weeks) Celebrates the giving of the Torah at Mount Sinai. (See Sukkot.)

Shechita   The act of ritual slaughter; also, the laws pertaining to the manner and method of sanitary and humane slaughtering of animals for food.

Shema   The prayer that is the central creed of Judaism: the affirmation of faith and belief in one God.

Shivah   The first seven days of mourning.

Shochet   One who is trained in the laws and performance of ritual slaughter.

Shofar   The ram's horn that is sounded on Rosh Hashannah and at the close of Yom Kippur.

Shomer Shabbat   One who is observant of Shabbat.

Siddur   A prayer book.

Simcha   A joyous occasion.

Simhat Bat   A ceremony celebrating the birth of a daughter.

Simhat Torah   The holiday marking the completion in the synagogue of the annual cycle of reading the Torah and the beginning of a new cycle.

Sufganiyot   An Israeli Hanukkah specialty equivalent to doughnuts.

Sukkah   An outdoor temporary hut or booth, used during the Festival of Sukkot.

Sukkot   (Feast of Tabernacles) One of the three ancient harvest and pilgrimage festivals (with Pesach and Shavuot); the Thanksgiving and harvest holiday that occurs five days after Yom Kippur.

Synagogue, Shul   House of worship.

Taharat Hamishpachah   The laws of ritual purity observed between husband and wife.

Tallit   A prayer shawl.

Talmud   A compilation of Rabbinic teachings, comprising the Mishnah and the Gemara, which expands on the Mishnah.

Tashlich   A ceremony in which pieces of bread (representing sins) are tossed into an ocean or stream on the afternoon of the first day of Rosh Hashannah.

Tefillah   Prayer or worship.

Tefillin   Phylacteries; leather cubes that are strapped to the arm and head by observant Jews during daily morning prayers; each contains quotations from the Bible.

Teshuvah   The act of repentance.

Tevilah   Immersion in a *mikvah*.

Tisha B'Av   The fast on the ninth of Av, commemorating the anniversary of the destruction of both the First and the Second Temples.

Torah   (1) The Five Books of Moses; (2) the sacred texts of Judaism.

Tref   Non-kosher, forbidden food.

Tsadik   A saintly person.

Tsedakah   Charity.

Tsitsit   Fringes (woolen threads) applied to corners of four-cornered garments worn by men and boys throughout the day and also to the corners of shawls (*tallitot*) worn by adults during the recitation of prayers.

Yahrzeit   The anniversary of the date of a death.

Yeshiva   An academy for the study of Torah.

Yizkor   The memorial prayer for deceased relatives, recited on the Festivals (last day of Passover, Shavuot, Shemini Atzeret) and on Yom Kippur.

Yom Ha'atzmaut   Israel's Independence Day, celebrated on the fifth of Iyar, commemorating the day that Israel became an independent state—May 14, 1948.

Yom Hashoah   Holocaust remembrance day.

Yom Kippur   (Day of Atonement) The holiest day of the Jewish religious year, the last day of the Ten Days of Penitence. A fast day, during which the Jew seeks forgiveness for sins.

Yom Tov   A festival or holiday.

Zemirot   Shabbat songs.

Suggested reading

The following selections are recommendations given most often by converts to Judaism.

General

Donin, Hayim Halevy. *To Be A Jew: A Guide to Jewish Observance in Contemporary Life.* Basic Books, 1972.
> Excellent general guide book for the couple who want to learn the basics of running a Jewish household.

Klagsburn, Francine. *Voices of Wisdom: Jewish Ideals and Ethics for Everyday Living.* Pantheon, 1980.
> Sensitively and beautifully written presentation of Jewish values for living Jewishly in the modern world.

Kolatch, Alfred J. *The Jewish Book of Why.* Jonathan David, 1981.
> Clear and unbiased answers to hundreds of fundamental questions about Jewish life. Excellent for Christian parents who want to understand Jewish practices.

Kolatch, Alfred J. *The Second Jewish Book of Why.* Jonathan David, 1985.
> Deals with complex and controversial topics such as bio-ethics, Christian-Jewish relations, intermarriage, and many other issues.

Prager, Dennis, and Telushkin, Joseph. *Eight Questions People Ask About Judaism.* Tze Ulman, 1985.

Provocative and challenging discussion about philosophical and moral concerns encountered in fundamental Judaism. Recommended for Jews and Christians.

Steinberg, Milton. *Basic Judaism.* Harcourt Brace Jovanovich, 1947.

Clear presentation of the fundamentals of Judaism for the Jew and Gentile.

Jewish Practice

Goodman, Phillip. *The Hanukkah Anthology.* Jewish Publication Society, 1976.

Goodman, Phillip. *The Passover Anthology.* Jewish Publication Society, 1961.

Goodman, Phillip. *The Purim Anthology.* Jewish Publication Society, 1949.

Goodman, Phillip. *The Rosh Hashanah Anthology.* Jewish Publication Society, 1970.

Goodman, Phillip. *The Shavuot Anthology.* Jewish Publication Society, 1975.

Goodman, Phillip. *The Sukkot and Simchat Torah Anthology.* Jewish Publication Society, 1973.

Goodman, Phillip. *The Yom Kippur Anthology.* Jewish Publication Society, 1971.

The JPS anthologies are most popular with converts because they offer general guidelines for the celebration of Jewish festivals. Contain sections on history, ancient and modern rituals, art, music, recipes, and poetry.

Kitov, Eliyahu. *The Jew and His Home.* Shengold, 1974.

Excellent resource for the Orthodox convert to Judaism. Conveys the joyous holiness of the ideal Jewish family as projected in Jewish tradition.

Klein, Isaac. *A Guide to Jewish Religious Practice.* The Jewish Theological Seminary of America, 1979.

Comprehensive discussion of why and how of Kashrut, marriage, divorce, conversion, adoption as well as bio-ethical concerns. Practically every subject is treated in detail.

Lamm, Maurice. *The Jewish Way in Death and Mourning*. Jonathan David, 1972.

Informative guide to Jewish practices concerning the death and mourning processes.

Reimer, Jack. *Jewish Reflections on Death*. Schocken Books, 1974.

Presentation of the historical development and current status of the Jewish way of death, through sensitively chosen articles written by outstanding Jewish thinkers.

Strassfeld, Michael, Strassfeld, Sharon, and Siegel, Richard. *The Jewish Catalogue: A Do-It-Yourself Kit*. Jewish Publication Society, 1973.

Clear, easy reading. Informal style. Provides information on kashrut, Jewish calendar, holidays, and the arts.

Strassfeld, Michael, and Strassfeld, Sharon. *The Second Jewish Catalog: Sources and Resources*. Jewish Publication Society, 1976.

Logical continuation of *The First Jewish Catalog*, with information on education, prayer, life-cycle events, and crafts.

Strassfeld, Michael, and Strassfeld, Sharon. *The Third Jewish Catalog: Creating Community*. Jewish Publication Society, 1980.

Indispensable source book about organizations, Soviet Jewry, tsedakah, Yiddish, social action, and Israel. Contains a brief discussion on conversion and intermarriage.

Prayer

Donin, Hayim Halevy. *To Pray As A Jew*. Basic Books, 1980.

Deals with dynamics of Jewish worship in modern times. Helps the new Jew to be more comfortable with synagogue rituals and prayers.

Millgram, Abraham. *Jewish Worship*. Jewish Publication Society, 1971.

For the Jew who wants to expand his or her knowledge of the organization and content of the Siddur and for the non-Jew who is seeking an understanding of the rites, symbols, and ceremonies of Jewish worship.

Petuchowski, Jacob. *Understanding Jewish Prayer.* Ktav, 1972.

Deals with evolution of Jewish worship from the biblical period through modern times. Includes an anthology of essays on Jewish prayer by outstanding contemporary scholars.

Marriage

Diamant, Anita. *The New Jewish Wedding.* Summit Books, 1985.

Creative options for those who want a personalized wedding that combines spirituality, traditions, and their own input. Has many examples of invitation styles, poems, and ketubbot.

Faux, Marian. *Childless by Choice: Choosing Childlessness in the Eighties.* Anchor Press, 1984.

Offers a candid discussion of the attitudes and misconceptions concerning those who wish to remain childless. Useful for the parents of the childless couple.

Feldman, David M. *Marital Relations, Birth Control and Abortion in Jewish Law.* Schocken Books, 1968.

Analysis of bio-ethics and traditional Judaism. An understanding of Jewish law is helpful.

Gittelsohn, Roland B. *Love, Sex and Marriage: A Jewish View.* Union of American Hebrew Congregations, 1980.

Candid discussion of Jewish sexual ethics in modern times.

Gold, Michael. *And Hannah Wept: Infertility, Adoption and the Jewish Couple.* Jewish Publication Society, 1988.

Rabbinic and practical guide for infertile couples and would-be adoptive parents. Compassionate and highly informative.

Gordis, Robert. *Love and Sex. A Modern Jewish Perspective.* Farrar, Straus, and Giroux, 1978.

An analysis of contemporary issues affecting Jewish family life, such as divorce, homosexuality, premarital and extramarital relations, intermarriage, and many other related issues.

Greenberg, Blu. *How to Run a Traditional Jewish Household.* Simon & Schuster, 1983.

Describes the functioning of the modern Orthodox Jewish household. Personal, well-organized guide for the traditional convert.

Greenberg, Blu. *On Women and Judaism: A View from Tradition.* Jewish Publication Society, 1981.

A critical look at the contemporary issues confronting the dedicated Orthodox Jewish woman in relation to the feminist movement. Challenging and thought-provoking.

Lamm, Maurice. *The Jewish Way in Love and Marriage.* Harper & Row, 1980.

Authoritative presentation of Jewish teaching in light of the traditions and laws of the Bible.

Latner, Helen. *The Book of Modern Jewish Etiquette.* Schocken Books, 1981.

Excellent for Jews and non-Jews who are unsure of the proper way to plan a Jewish wedding. Reassuring reference for the Christian family.

Waxman, Chaim I. *Single Parent Families: A Challenge to the Jewish Community.* Institute of Human Relations, American Jewish Committee, 1980.

Well-documented report on single parenting problems and concerns and suggestions for helping to alleviate them.

Parenting

Bial, Morrison D. *Your Jewish Child.* Union of American Hebrew Congregations, 1978.

A handbook to help parents create a home that promotes Jewish identity. Covers topics such as baby-naming, discussing God, death, and afterlife.

Blidstein, Gerald. *Honor Thy Father and Mother.* Ktav, 1975.

Warm, loving guide on how to be an effective Jewish parent.

Donin, Hayim Halevy. *To Raise a Jewish Child: A Guide for Parents.* Basic Books, 1977.

Excellent guide on how to raise and educate a Jewish child and how to deal with secular influences that impact upon the Jewish family.

Cohen, J. Simcha. *Intermarriage and Conversion: A Halakhic Solution.* Ktav, 1987.

> Provides halakhic insights into the issues of conversion and interfaith marriages as well as a discussion on women, marriage, and parenting in Judaism today.

Cowan, Paul. *An Orphan In History*. Doubleday, 1982.

> Traces the family roots of the author through a personal, religious, and cultural quest for a Jewish identity that culminates in a deeply moving conversion by his wife.

Cowan, Paul, with Cowan, Rachel. *Mixed Blessings: Marriage Between Jews and Christians*. Doubleday, 1987.

> Well-written presentation, based on work done with couples who attended various support groups that were run by the Cowans. To be read prior to marriage.

Kaye, Evelyn. *Crosscurrents: Children, Families and Religion*. Clarkson N. Potter, 1980.

> A selection of interviews with interfaith and conversionary couples. Quite insightful.

Kukoff, Lydia. *Choosing Judaism: A Guide for Jews by Choice*. Union of American Hebrew Congregations, 1982.

> Warm, personal account of questions and concerns that the author experienced during conversion. Includes practical, basic information for the potential convert.

Lester, Julius. *Love Song: Becoming a Jew*. Henry Holt, 1988.

> Compelling personal account of author's life from boyhood as the son of a black Methodist minister in the South to his conversion to Judaism.

Mayer, Egon. *Love and Tradition. Marriage Between Jews and Christians*. Plenum, 1985.

> Sociological exploration of the issues encountered by couples who marry out of their faith. Clear and insightful reading for Jews and non-Jews.

Schneider, Susan Weidman. *Intermarriage: The Challenge of Living with*

Differences. Free Press, 1989.

Surveys a wide range of issues through interviews with interfaith couples.

Seltzer, Sanford. *Jews and Non-Jews Falling in Love.* Union of American Hebrew Congregations, 1976.

Informal guide to interfaith marriage, written by a rabbi who sometimes performs them.

Stern, Arlene L. *International Mikvah Directory.* Armis, 1981.

Good resource for locating a mikvah for conversion, ritual purity, or adoption purposes.

Wigoder, Devorah. *Hope Is My House.* Prentice Hall, 1966.

Beautifully written autobiography of an Irish Catholic woman's personal triumph and tribulations as she immerses herself in Judaism and, finally, converts.

Israel

Eban, Abba. *My Country: The Story of Modern Israel.* Random House, 1972.

Begins with the formation of the state of Israel in 1948 and provides a visual account of the history and life of the Israeli people.

Grosse, Peter. *Israel in the Mind of America.* Knopf, 1983.

An historical analysis of America's connection to Jews and Israel from colonial times through the creation of the State.

Sachar, Howard M. *A History of Israel: From the Rise of Zionism to Our Time.* Knopf, 1979.

Excellent, well-written, comprehensive history of Israel for Jew and non-Jew.

Schoenbrun, David, with Lucy and Robert Szelely. *The New Israelis.* Atheneum, 1973.

Focuses on young Israelis during the early 1970s. Intensely moving book that helps a new Jew understand the Israeli in daily life. Puts today's events in perspective.

History

Bamberger, Bernard J. *The Story of Judaism*. Schocken Books, 1964.

Complete social, political, cultural history of the Jewish people in a single, readable volume.

Grayzel, Solomon. *A History of the Jews*. Jewish Publication Society, 1968.

Interpretive history, from the Babylonian exile to the end of World War II.

Roth, Cecil. *A History of the Jews*. Schocken Books, 1970.

Traces social, religious, and cultural development of Jewish people from biblical times to the present.

Sachar, Howard M. *The Course of Modern Jewish History*. Dell, 1958.

Comprehensive history of the Jew from the French Revolution to the present day. Discusses Jewish and non-Jewish social and cultural influences.

Sacher, Abram. *History of the Jews*. Knopf, 1967.

Comprehensive account of over 3,000 years of Jewish existence. Includes religious and philosophical development.

Holocaust

Davidowicz, Lucy S. *The War Against the Jews: 1933–1945*. Bantam, 1976.

Powerful study of the Holocaust. Comprehensive and scholarly.

Epstein, Helen. *Children of the Holocaust: Conversations with Sons and Daughters of Survivors*. Putnam, 1979.

Memorable stories of children of survivors of the Holocaust as well as their personal accounts and reactions to their parents' past.

Frank, Anne. *Anne Frank: The Diary of a Young Girl*. Doubleday, 1967.

Unforgettable diary of a girl's thoughts during her two years in hiding from the Nazis.

Levi, Primo. *If Not Now, When?* Summit Books, 1985.

A gripping novel by the eminent survivor about Jews who fought back during the Holocaust. For readers with prior background on the subject.

Levin, Nora. *The Holocaust: The Destruction of European Jewry 1933–1945.* Schocken Books, 1973.

Comprehensive, scholarly account of the Third Reich's program for the extermination of world Jewry. Written with clarity and well documented. For Jews and non-Jews.

Morse, Arthur D. *While Six Million Died: Chronicle of American Apathy.* Hart, 1975.

Discussion of U.S. indifference and world apathy during the Holocaust. Treatment may be too sensitive for some non-Jews.

Volakova, Hana. *I Never Saw Another Butterfly: Children's Drawings and Poems from Terezin Concentration Camp, 1942–1944.* Schocken Books, 1978.

Moving collection of pictures and poems by children in the Terezin concentration camp.

Wiesel, Elie. *Night.* Avon, 1972.

Unforgettable, powerful autobiographical account of the author's experiences and impressions during the Holocaust.

Gay and Lesbian

Baetz, Ruth. *Lesbian Crossroads: Personal Stories of Lesbian Struggles.* William Morrow, 1980.

Compelling stories that help to educate and sensitize people to the feelings and concerns of lesbians and gays.

Balka, Christie and Rose, Andy (eds.). *Twice Blessed: On Being Lesbian, Gay, and Jewish.* Beacon Press, 1989.

A collection of essays by and about gays and lesbians who are maintaining their ties to Judaism.

Beck, Evelyn Torton (ed.). *Nice Jewish Girls: A Lesbian Anthology.* Beacon Press, 1989.

Writings by women of all ages about what it means to be Jewish and lesbian.

Epstein, Louis M. *Sex Laws and Customs in Judaism.* Ktav, 1967.

Biblical and halakhic explanations for the current Jewish views on lesbianism and homosexuality.

Silverstein, Charles. *A Family Matter: A Parent's Guide to Homosexuality.* McGraw-Hill, 1977.

Wonderful, informative, and supportive book for the parents of gays and lesbians. Helpful resources listed.

In addition to these books, it is recommended that every Jewish home have a set of *The Encyclopedia Judaica* (Jerusalem: Keter, 1972).

Movement guidelines for conversion

REFORM GUIDELINES

These guidelines were prepared under the chairmanship of Joseph A. Edelheit by the Committee on Gerut of the Central Conference of American Rabbis (CCAR) in 1980; they were endorsed for circulation by the Executive Board in April, 1981. This revised version incorporates the final report of the Committee on the Status of Children of Mixed Marriages as it was adopted by the CCAR National Convention, March, 1983.

DIVRE GERUT
GUIDELINES CONCERNING PROSELYTISM

Introduction
The Central Conference of American Rabbis represents a diversity of views on theology and ritual observance; thus, these guidelines and suggested procedures seek to establish a working consensus of practice within the Reform Rabbinate rather than a set of standardized requirements in matters concerning *gerim*.[1] The Conference publishes these guidelines as a reaffirmation of its long-standing position on the full acceptance as Jews of those individuals who, of their own free will, wish to accept the joys and responsibilities of the Jewish faith and people. This document underscores the inherent freedom of Reform Judaism and draws from the vast literature of the tradition in confronting an issue fundamental to *Am Yisrael*.

The Status and Acceptance of Gerim

The status of those individuals who become Jews through formal *giur* has long been established in Judaism as fully equal to those born as Jews. The *Tanach* and rabbinic literature are replete with statements regarding the meritorious status, respectively, of the *Ger* and the *Ger Zedek*, the righteous stranger who chooses to become a member of the Jewish people and faith. Thus, it is incumbent upon our colleagues and congregations to accept fully, as equals, in all areas of participation, those who complete *giur*. To that end, we emphasize that once an individual has gone through the requirements of *giur*, he/she is fully Jewish. The warmth and vigor with which we accept these Jews and integrate them into our communities and activities are among our highest priorities and obligations.

Chaveirut

The entire issue of the status of those born as Jews who may have become estranged from Judaism and wish to reaffirm their Jewish identities must be dealt with on an individual basis. A process or ceremony of *chaveirut* (affiliation) would be appropriate in actualizing such a reaffirmation. The CCAR Committee on Gerut has prepared such a ceremony.

Marriage and Giur

We are aware that each individual has his/her own unique and complex motivation in making the final decision to become a Jew. We recognize the issue of mixed marriage as a critical area of concern. The CCAR has long held the position that the initial motivation of marriage is a wholesome and appropriate stimulus in seeking Jewish identity.[2] Thus, as the problem of mixed marriage continues to concern the Jewish community, the Conference once again reaffirms its stand: The individual who seeks Judaism because of his/her desire to establish a Jewish marriage, Jewish home and *shelom bayit* is to be encouraged in all matters of *giur*. Further, the Conference urges its members to implement more actively point two of the third paragraph of its 1973 Resolution on mixed marriage: "To provide (for those already in a mixed marriage) the opportunity for *giur* of the non-Jewish spouse."

An individual involved in *giur* should be sensitized to the fact that the gravity of any decision and the necessary exposure to Judaism have higher priority than the social pressures of a wedding date. The rabbi,

whenever possible, should work closely with the potential *ger/gioret* and
the mate or future mate as well as the respective families. It is important
whenever possible that the mate or future mate be encouraged to attend
the classes in Judaism with the *ger/gioret*. The rabbi, congregation, and
community should provide these individuals with opportunities to
share the experiences, learning, and feelings attendant to *giur* with Jews
who came to Judaism through *gerut*.

Children and Giur
The CCAR reaffirms its current practices and standards regarding children and the question of *giur*. Such cases involve: (a) an adopted child,
(b) a child born of a mixed marriage.[3]

For the adopted child, the practices of Reform Judaism that pertain
to any natural child are recognized as appropriate. (See Solomon B.
Freehof, *CCAR Yearbook*, vol. LXV, 1956, pp. 107–110; *Gates of Mitzvah*, CCAR, p. 18.)

The current position of the Reform Movement regarding the status
of a child born of a mixed marriage was established in 1983:

> The Central Conference of American Rabbis declares that the child
> of one Jewish parent is under the presumption of Jewish descent.
> This presumption of the Jewish status of the offspring of any mixed
> marriage is to be established through appropriate and timely pub-
> lic and formal acts of identification with the Jewish faith and peo-
> ple. The performance of these mitzvot serves to commit those who
> participate in them, both parent and child, to Jewish life.

> Depending on circumstances, mitzvot leading toward a positive
> and exclusive Jewish identity will include entry into the covenant,
> acquisition of a Hebrew name, Torah study, bar/bat mitzvah and
> Kabbalat Torah (Confirmation).[4] For those beyond childhood
> claiming Jewish identity, other public acts or declarations may be
> added or substituted after consultation with the rabbi.

The above-mentioned position may be found in the new edition of *The
Rabbi's Manual*.

GERUT: THE PROCESS OF BECOMING A JEW

Gerut involves a complex set of variables for each individual. Each person brings his/her own emotional, familial, spiritual, and intellectual
needs and background into *gerut*. It is beyond the scope of these guide-

lines to define any specifics regarding how long each process should take or the course of study for it. We offer a consensus of opinion and practice, knowing that the rabbi and prospective *ger/gioret* will ultimately have to define such terms within each given situation. The time required for *giur* will vary, depending upon the rabbi and the community's educational program, whether it is a group course or private tutorial, and the prospective *ger/gioret* and his/her specific background in Judaism. With all of these variables considered, the least amount of time recommended for *gerut* should be four months, with an average of six to nine months and some situations extended to a full year.

The fundamentals of Judaism that should be taught encompass ritual observances of Shabbat, holy days, festivals, and life cycle *mitzvot* in the home and the synagogue; basic theology and values; Jewish history; liturgy, and Hebrew language. These areas provide the basis of the educational process of *gerut*. The particulars of any course are relative to the community and rabbi. It should be carefully indicated to the *ger/gioret* that any course of study is by definition only an introduction to Judaism. Rabbinic involvement in *gerut* beyond an educational level is essential; mere sponsorship in a community course without regular tutorials and meetings is not appropriate. Individuals will undoubtedly require advice, counseling, and encouragement during and *after* their decision-making process.

Since *gerut* involves more than just cognitive learning, the *ger/gioret* should be encouraged to experience Jewish life by attending Sabbath services regularly and participating in holy day and festival observances and other Jewish communal activities. Opportunities for exposure to Jewish home observance of the Sabbath and festivals should be made available. Finally, the importance of synagogue affiliation and a Jew's communal responsibility should be discussed and emphasized so that the *giur* will be a statement of communal as well as religious commitment.

Giur: The Ceremony of Welcoming

The CCAR requires that the *ger/gioret* declare acceptance of the Jewish faith and people before three adult witnesses made up of no less than one rabbi and two associates or lay people. Such a group might be considered, for those so inclined, as a *bet din* and function in such a capacity. Some suggest that the use of the *witnesses/bet din* as a part of *giur* is also of great value, for it provides the opportunity to discuss and evaluate with the *ger/gioret* the process of becoming a Jew. This should not take on a critical or defensive tone, for the rabbi should already be aware of the *ger/gioret's* level of knowledge and commitment.

The traditional *halachic* ritual requirements of *berit milah, hatafat dam-berit,* and *tevilah,* have not been required practices by most Reform rabbis. There is a long-standing CCAR position that obviates the necessity for these traditional *halachic* prescriptions.[5] Today, the spectrum of belief, interpretation, and practice within Reform Judaism is broad and diverse. Thus, many members of the Conference now ". . . recognize that there are social, psychological, and religious values associated with the traditional rituals, and it is recommended that the rabbi acquaint prospective *gerim* with the *halachic* background and rationale for *berit milah, hatafat dam-berit* and *tevilah* and offer them the opportunity, if they so desire, to observe these additional rites."[6]

The actual ceremony leading to *gerut* may vary in place, time, and format, depending on the rabbi, community, and *ger/gioret.* However, any ceremony should include the rabbi's asking the *ger/gioret* the following six questions,[7] or using the affirmation that follows them.

1. Do you choose to enter the eternal covenant between God and the people Israel and to become a Jew of your own free will?

2. Do you accept Judaism to the exclusion of all other religious faiths and practices?

3. Do you pledge your loyalty to Judaism and to the Jewish people under all circumstances?

4. Do you promise to establish a Jewish home and to participate actively in the life of the synagogue and of the Jewish community?

5. Do you commit yourself to the pursuit of Torah and Jewish knowledge?

6. If you should be blessed with children, do you promise to rear them as Jews?

> *Affirmation:* I make this affirmation as I enter the eternal covenant between God and the people of Israel: I choose to become a Jew of my own free will. I accept Judaism to the exclusion of all other religions, faiths and practices and now pledge my loyalty to Judaism and the Jewish people under all circumstances. I promise to establish a Jewish home and participate actively in the life of the synagogue and the Jewish community. I commit myself to the pursuit of Torah and Jewish knowledge. If I am blessed with children, I will rear them as Jews.

The ceremony may include appropriate liturgical passages as well as readings dealing with *gerut*, such as Ruth 1:16–17. The rabbi may then choose to speak to the *ger/gioret* welcoming him/her into *Am Yisrael*. As a symbol of the newly acquired Jewish identity, the *ger/gioret* is given a Hebrew name. The Hebrew name should be chosen by the proselyte, and is added to the traditional phrase *ben/bet Avraham Avinu Ve-Sarah Imeinu*.[8] After conferring the name, the ceremony concludes with the *Birkat Kohanim*.

A certificate, *te-udat gerut*, is presented to the *ger/gioret*, with the appropriate signatures of the rabbi and other witnesses. Three additional copies of the *te-udat gerut* should be kept, one for the synagogue's archives, one for the rabbi's records, and the other for the American Jewish Archives in Cincinnati, Ohio.

Whenever possible and appropriate, one should take into consideration the *ger/gioret's* family and friends. Their presence at the *giur* can be very positive and supportive. The rabbi might take the opportunity before or after the ceremony to speak with them to further their understanding and clarify their questions. The relationship developed with the rabbi and *ger/gioret* should continue beyond the ceremony of *giur*.

Notes

1. This document uses the Hebrew terms: *ger/gioret/gerim* (male/female proselytes); *gerut* (the process of becoming a Jew); *giur* (the actual ceremony through which one formalizes the acceptance of the *ger/gioret* as a Jew). These terms are found to be more appropriate and less potentially stigmatizing than the use of such intrinsically non-Jewish terms as convert and conversion.

2. *CCAR Yearbook*, 1947, p. 158ff, Solomon Freehof's Report on Mixed Marriage.

3. In reference to the above-stated practice in Reform Judaism, it is essential to explain carefully to parents the variations practiced by other branches of Judaism. This is suggested in order to insure a fully sensitized understanding by the parents and, when appropriate, the child.

4. A full description of these and other *mitzvot* can be found in *Gates of Mitzvah* (CCAR, 1979).

5. See *Rabbi's Manual*, 1928 ed., pp. 153–154; *CCAR Yearbook*, vol. I (1891–1892), p. 36.

6. Statement of the CCAR Committee on *Gerut*, 1978, published in *Gates of Mitzvah*, CCAR, pp. 146–147.

7. These questions have been incorporated in the new edition of the *Rabbi's Manual*.

8. While the traditional phrase is only *Avraham Avinu*, it is well within the mood of the Movement to be more broadly inclusive. *Berachot* 16b provides us with the generalized terms of patriarch and matriarch:

"*Ein korin avot ela leshelosha ve-ein korin imahot ela le-arba.*" "The term 'patriarchs' is applied only to three and the term 'matriarchs' only to four." Therefore, references to both patriarchal and matriarchal names are appropriate.

CONTACT: CCAR Committee on Gerut
Central Conference of American Rabbis
192 Lexington Avenue
New York, NY 10016
(212) 684-4990

ORTHODOX GUIDELINES

DRAFTED BY THE COMMISSION ON GERUT OF THE RABBINICAL COUNCIL OF AMERICA

The Interview
A. Three Steps
    1. Discussion covering the following areas:
       a. Religious and educational background
       b. Familial relationships
       c. Motivations, e.g., marriage, friends, search for spiritual meaning
       d. Economic and occupational situation
    2. General outlines of Jewish concepts and practices
       a. Concept and role of G-d
       b. Shabbat, Kashrut, Tefillah, Taharat hamishpacha
       c. Ethical values
       d. Bible and Talmud: sources of Halakha
    3. Outlining a program of studies and religious and cultural experiences
B. One preliminary interview will most likely be inadequate. The interviewing rabbi requires additional time for probing and for digesting both the information and the impressions made by the candidate. Furthermore, the prospective candidate may not be relaxed during the first session, and in order to do him or her justice, more than one session would be in order. It may also be necessary for the in-

terviewing rabbi to consult a colleague, Bet Din or a special committee for their Chavas Daas. This point will be taken up later in these guidelines.

Required Schedule of Studies and Religious Experiences

A. The candidate must undertake a formal program of studies. He/she should enroll in the synagogue's adult education program, and if it is inadequate or unavailable, he/she should enroll in an institute of Jewish studies.

   1. In areas where such formal studies are nonexistent, a private tutor should be engaged.

   2. Should the sponsoring rabbi be the tutor in an area where other options for formal instruction are available? Most members of the commission are of the opinion that it is preferable for the rabbi to undertake the task. In this way, the rabbi becomes the spiritual mentor of the candidate and the relationship will continue after the conversion process is completed, since the convert will require continued guidance and encouragement until he/she is fully acclimated to the new situation.

      The other view is that the sponsoring rabbi should not be the private tutor. The two roles, namely, that of a formal tutor and that of a spiritual mentor, should not be confused. The rabbi should, however, schedule periodic meetings, at which time he will assess the candidate's progress, discuss any questions he or she may have, and clarify points in an informal atmosphere. The spiritual relationship can be forged by the rabbi in the same manner as with congregants in general.

B. The following is a minimum schedule of skills and topics to be covered:

   1. Hebrew reading—a moderate fluency is required

   2. Basic Tefillot, e.g., Shema, Shemonei Esrai, Berachot, Birkat Hamazon, Kiddush

   3. Selections from the Torah, e.g., Parashat Hashavua with commentary, Nach—a bird's-eye view in the vernacular

   4. Fundamental Halakhot—Shabbat, Kashrut, Taharat Hamishpacha, Tzedakah, Yomim Tovim, Mitzvot Bein Adam L'Chavero

   5. A cursory reading on Jewish history

C. Outline of religious concepts

   1. Nature of G-d

2. Reward and punishment
3. Mashiach
4. Torah Min Hashamayim
5. Torah She B'Al Peh
6. Ethical and moral principles
7. Peoplehood of Israel
8. Eretz Israel

D. The following experiences are recommended
   1. Weekly Shabbat morning shul attendance and weekday morning shul attendance (at least once a week)
   2. Monthly invitation for a Shabbat at a religious home
   3. Three Yom Tov invitations

E. A minimum of one year of study and experiences are recommended
   1. At mid-point the candidate should meet with a committee of three rabbanim to determine the level of knowledge and the seriousness of the motivation. It may also be necessary to decide whether additional requirements are advisable.

Procedures for the Conversion Act

A. A Bet Din of three rabbanim should make a thorough investigation of the attitudes of the candidate and the materials studied. A written list of questions should be prepared in advance of the meeting.

B. Commitments should be made regarding the following:

Shabbat, Kashrut, Taharat Hamishpachah, Tefillah, Tzedakah, Yeshiva education for the candidate's children and future children
   1. Additional commitments: Membership in an orthodox shul, and residing within walking distance of a shul
   2. Both an oral and a written commitment should be made.

Bet Din and Other Considerations

A. The Rabbinic Council of America (RCA) Bet Din or a specially appointed commission on Gerut procedures should serve as the formal consultation body for Halakhic questions on Gerut for RCA members.

B. It is recommended that the already existing Batei Din in the several cities across the country shall be asked to serve as regional Batei Din. In those regions where formal Batei Din are absent, regional Batei Din shall be established under the guidance of the national office.
   1. The function of these regional Batei Din shall be twofold:

a. They or their designees shall supervise conversion procedures.

b. They shall advise the regional rabbanim on Halakha, and L'Fi R'os Eyney Ha Bet Din guide them in cases requiring special Halakhic application.

C. The conversion Bet Din should consist solely of rabbanim.

D. The commission recommends that fees should not be received for conversions.

E. If one adopting parent is non-Jewish and is not intending to convert, the adopted child should not be converted.

F. Minimum Halakhic standards for RCA acceptance of conversion of adopted children should be as follows:

1. Kashrut
2. Encourage Shabbat observance
3. Membership in an Orthodox shul within walking distance
4. Yeshiva education for the child

It is suggested that the parents be urged to accept Shmirat Shabbat.

Purpose of Guidelines

The approval of the Guidelines is an important step in establishing minimum Halakhic guidelines for Gerut. The Guidelines incorporate both Halakhic positions and supplementary conditions to enhance and strengthen the meaning and procedure of Gerut. In special situations the national or regional bodies will rule in accordance to the principle of L'Fi R'os Eyney Ha Bet Din. Conversions that conform to the Guidelines will receive the imprimatur of the national office.

CONTACT: RCA Commission on Gerut
Rabbinical Council of America
275 Seventh Avenue
New York, NY 10001
(212) 807-7888

RECONSTRUCTIONIST GUIDELINES

The following Guidelines on Conversion are the fruit of study and debate by the Commission on Gerut, under the chairmanship of Rabbi Dennis C. Sasso, during three Annual Conventions of the Reconstructionist Rabbinical Association (RRA). They were finally approved in General Assembly at the Annual Convention held in Philadelphia on January 15–17, 1979/Tevet 16–18, 5739.

These guidelines approach the issue of conversion to Judaism as an important area of concern in the agenda of modern Judaism. On theoretical and practical grounds they set forth directives that seek to strike a balance between the spiritual needs of the group and those of the individual.

The Jewish community today must take cognizance of the potential for strength and enrichment that Jews by choice can provide and proudly offer to those who search the vast spiritual values and cultural resources of our tradition.

Sincerest thanks are offered to all the rabbis in the Reconstructionist Rabbinical Association who during those three years took the time and had the interest to write extensively or to communicate orally with Rabbi Sasso on the subject of conversion in all its ramifications. A special expression of respect and appreciation goes to all the rabbis who during the three conventions participated in the lengthy, often heated, but always warm and friendly debates.

These guidelines, which represent the consensus of the Reconstructionist Rabbinical Association membership, are offered not in the sense of prescriptive Halakha but in the hope that they will provide guidance in the task of transmitting the beauty of Judaism.

RECONSTRUCTIONIST RABBINICAL ASSOCIATION GUIDELINES ON CONVERSION

Introduction

We understand conversion to be a process, the goal of which is a wholehearted and informed acceptance of Judaism for its own sake. We consider the formal adoption of Judaism by a person who has been born a non-Jew to be a decision that is to be accorded respect and a process to be invested with seriousness of purpose and dignity.

The preparation, counseling, and final ceremonies should give expression to the fact that even though conversion to Judaism is primarily a religious act, its dimensions and consequences are more encompassing. A person seeking to become a Jew should be sensitized to the realization and manifest an awareness that there is involved also an act of incorporation into a people whose civilizational values are now entrusted to him/her to internalize and express in attitude and practice.

We deem it the responsibility of Jewish congregations and of the Jewish community at large to welcome warmly into their midst, and involve in all their activities, persons who have converted to Judaism.

Conversion for the Sake of Marriage

We recognize that the decision to convert is in each case unique and involves a multitude of feelings, influences, motivations, and purposes. We deem marriage to a Jewish partner to be a justifiable and commendable initial reason for conversion. It must be, of course, evident that the candidate, after proper instruction and counselling, freely chooses to become a Jew. Conversions for the sake of marriage may serve to strengthen the marital relationship (*Sh'lom Bayit*) and can also serve to enrich Judaism and enlarge the Jewish people. A significant number of converts through marriage have become truly dedicated Jews (*Gerei Tzedek*).

Outreach to Converts

Every possible outreach effort should be made to incorporate warmly into the Jewish community those people interested in conversion to Judaism, especially non-Jewish spouses of Jews.

Process of Preparation

1. The duration of the process of preparing a candidate for conversion will be at the sponsoring rabbi's discretion. It is suggested that it last between six months and a year, affording the candidate the opportunity of both theoretical Jewish learning and the personal experience of a major portion of the Jewish calendar cycle.

2. The learning process should include both group instruction (where possible) and individual tutorials and counseling. Additional participation in adult education programs should be encouraged, as well as attendance at services and participation in other areas of Jewish communal, religious, and cultural life.

3. When the prospective convert is married to or contemplating marriage to a Jew, the Jewish partner should also participate in the preparation process.

4. The role of the rabbi in the conversion process should not be limited to the transmission of information, but should take into account the varied emotional needs on the part of the convert and his/her Jewish spouse or friend and their respective family relations.

Procedural Guidelines

1. We endorse *T'vilah* (ritual immersion) as an initiatory rite, for both men and women proselytes.

2. Non-circumcised male proselytes should be circumcised *L'ot B'rit* if there is no extraordinary physical or emotional hazard.

3. The practice of *Hatafat Dam B'rit* (symbolic circumcision on already circumcised males) will be at the discretion of the sponsoring rabbi.

4. The proselyte should be encouraged to make a *tzedakah* offering to a Jewish cause, in keeping with an ancient Jewish custom (cf. *Gerim* 2:5).

5. The *Beit Din* should consist of three adult Jews, of which at least one should be a rabbi. Male and female alike may serve in a Reconstructionist Beit Din.

6. The function of the *Beit Din* will not be primarily to put the candidate through a "dissertation defense" type of examination, but to elicit from him/her thoughts and feelings, discuss areas of concern and interest, offer encouragement and counsel, and reiterate the responsibilities of involvement with the Jewish people and Judaism. The *Beit Din* experience should be warm and memorable.

7. A religious ceremony of acceptance of Judaism should be celebrated following the completion of ritual requirements and the *Beit Din* session. These have been usually private ceremonies, but some may wish to consider a group and/or public ceremony of conversion. Such a religious service would emphasize the covenantal link established mutually between the convert and the Jewish people, and it would have the additional positive function of sensitizing the community to the need to welcome and support the convert (*Hakhnasat Hager*). Certain holidays, such as Hanukkah, Shavuot, and Simhat Torah lend themselves particularly to such a ceremony.

8. The ceremony should include a "declaration of acceptance of

Judaism" on the part of the convert. The ritual may be enriched with appropriate selections from classic or contemporary Jewish sources. The rabbi or a member of the congregation may wish to address the candidate, who, in turn, might want to make a personal statement.

9. A Hebrew name is to be selected by the convert, followed by the expression: *"ben/bat Avraham avinu v'Sarah imenu."*

10. A document, signed by the three members of the *Beit Din*, officially certifying the conversion, should be given to the convert, and copies kept in congregational and the Movement's records. It is suggested that copies be also kept in the personal records of the rabbi.

General Remarks

1. The convert is to be considered a full Jew, with all the privileges and responsibilities this identity entails.

2. Since Reconstructionism does not consider applicable the division of Jews into the categories of Kohen, Levi, and Yisrael, laws pertaining to prohibited marriages between converts and the priestly class are not binding.

3. In the spirit of *K'lal Yisrael*, the Reconstructionist Movement recognizes conversions performed under the sponsorship of bona fide rabbis or movements within the Jewish community, whether or not similar conditions as those upheld by the Reconstructionist rabbi or Movement were required.

4. If one parent is Jewish, either mother or father, the offspring is to be regarded as Jewish and should undergo the rites prescribed by our tradition (*B'rit Milah* for boys, or a covenantal naming ceremony for girls); but no special conversion procedure is required.

IS JEWISH BIRTH THE BASIC QUALIFICATION FOR BEING A JEW?

No. Being born a Jew is doubtless the most natural condition that results in one's being a Jew, but it is not the most basic qualification. Many persons born Jewish have become renegades and have often evinced the greatest hostility to Judaism. On the other hand, many converts to Judaism have been distinguished by their understanding of Judaism and their devotion to it.

The basic qualifications for being a Jew are (1) the identification of oneself as a Jew, i.e., the acceptance of the Jewish People with its past, its present, and its future as one's own People; (2) belief in the spiritual values of the Jewish tradition, i.e., the conviction that the Jewish spiritual heritage affords inspiration for living and constitutes a worthy contribution to the totality of man's spiritual wisdom; and (3) participation in Jewish life, i.e., sharing in those activities that help to insure the perpetuation of the Jewish People and the advancement of its civilization.

These qualifications, and not Jewish parentage, have been stressed in the bulk of our tradition. Jews were enjoined to qualify themselves for the study of Torah (i.e., Judaism) "because it is not subject to inheritance." Converts, on the other hand, were told to address God in worship in the same terms as born Jews, as "our God and God of our fathers, God of Abraham, God of Isaac, and God of Jacob," because converts are regarded as authentic Jews (*na-asu ikkar k'yisrael*).

from *Questions Jews Ask*
by Rabbi Mordecai M. Kaplan

CONTACT: RRA Commission on Gerut
Reconstructionist Rabbinical Association
Church Road and Greenwood Avenue
Wyncote, PA 19095
(215) 576-0800, extension 45

ADDENDUM

Resolution on the Children of Mixed Marriages, Jews by Choice, and Proselytism

Approved at the Reconstructionist Rabbinical Association Annual Convention at Philadelphia, Pennsylvania, January 20–23, 1980/ 2–5 Shevat 5740

As Reconstructionist Jews, we welcome the recent proposals concerning the Jewishness of a child, either of whose parents is Jewish. We are pleased to note that such a recommendation was adopted already by the Reconstructionist Movement two decades ago at a joint convention of rabbis and laity and later reaffirmed by the Reconstructionist Rabbinical Association in its *Guidelines on Conversion* (adopted at the 1980 convention, and containing the deliberations of a 3-year working committee, 1976–79), to wit:

> "If one parent is Jewish, either the mother or the father, the offspring is to be regarded as Jewish and should undergo the rites prescribed by our tradition (*b'rit milah* for boys, or a covenantal naming ceremony for girls) but no special conversion procedures are required." (*Guidelines on Conversion*, VI:4)

In addition, it was affirmed:

> "We deem it the responsibility of Jewish congregations and of the Jewish community at large to welcome warmly into their midst and involve in all their activities persons who have converted to Judaism." (*Guidelines on Conversion*, I)

> "Every possible outreach effort should be made to incorporate warmly into the Jewish community those people interested in conversion to Judaism, especially non-Jewish spouses of Jews." (*Guidelines on Conversion*, III)

We call upon Reconstructionist Rabbis and congregations to join efforts with like-minded colleagues and groups in developing activities that will strengthen the Jewish people quantitatively and qualitatively through the mitzvah that our Guidelines have labeled "*Hakhnasat Hager*" (welcoming Jews by choice).

We are, however, averse to developing any active method of proselytizing for Judaism. While every effort should be made to make the non-Jew, as well as the Jewish community, aware of the fact that Judaism is open to and welcomes those wishing formally to join our religious civilization and peoplehood, it is our grave concern that any programmatic missionary activity, no matter how restrained, dignified, and decorous in the beginning, might snowball in directions that might later be regrettable.

It is our opinion that active missionizing of any kind will be self-defeating, in that it can hurt the Jewish community more than it can help, as it might stimulate counter efforts that would, considering our small number, affect us significantly. Moreover, any efforts on our part to proselytize, even among the unchurched, might lead to the deterioration of the good relations that have existed between the Jewish community and responsible Christian leadership and church entities. Just as we would not appreciate, and have indeed resented and spoken against the fact that there have been Christian missionary efforts di-

rected at the unaffiliated Jew, let us be sensitive to the fact that an unchurched Christian might still be claimed by his community as a Christian by the mere fact of his birth, family ties, and initiation into that
fellowship.

Let us ever be aware, particularly as Reconstructionist Jews, that
Judaism does not operate on the assumption that "salvation" is limited
to Jews. Wary of fundamentalism and militant fanaticism that are prev-
alent in our day, let us not participate in any effort that might promote
the slightest impression that ours, too, is a triumphalist religion.

While we respect the integrity and good intentions of those who
have so far called for some form of programmatic missionizing, we
hereby express our disapproval and disagreement in this matter. Even
as we recognize the fact that there is a history of missionary activity in
Judaism, let us be aware that times and conditions have changed. Let
our Judaism convince others by example rather than through persuasion. Let us, in accordance with the counsel of our tradition, as voiced
recently by Elie Wiesel, not attempt to make the world Jewish but to
make it more human.

CONSERVATIVE GUIDELINES

Conversion to Judaism is a serious matter, never to be undertaken
lightly. It is more than a change of religion; it is a new birth, involving
many changes and adjustments on the part of the convert and, very
often, on the part of the convert's family.

When an individual comes to speak with a Conservative rabbi about
the possibility of conversion, he or she should not expect an immediate
statement of agreement on the part of the rabbi. Far more likely, the
rabbi will begin by asking questions about matters of family background and degree of religious commitment and involvement. Should
the individual be considering marriage to a Jew, the rabbi will want to
speak to the couple to probe the extent to which they understand the
new orientation that will be required of them and the degree to which
that orientation will affect their daily lives.

If the rabbi finds the initial meeting promising, it is likely that an
offer will be made to begin training the non-Jew toward conversion. No
commitment will be made at this point to complete the process, during

the course of which either the prospective convert or the rabbi might discover that conversion is not appropriate. As one Conservative rabbi who heads an institute for conversion put it: "Conversion to Judaism is a serious process. It requires the ability to sever without guilt any link to one's past religion. It requires the steadfast courage to accept Judaism despite the awareness of the role of anti-Semitism in Western history. While every individual's synthesis of Jewish values and practices will be unique, one who elects Judaism must affirm its basic beliefs, must live its traditional patterns, and must identify with the dreams and destiny of the Jewish people." If either the prospective convert or the rabbi finds any of these requirements unable to be fulfilled, the conversion probably will not take place.

Conversion for the sake of marriage to a Jew has not been looked upon with great enthusiasm by Jewish law and traditions. Conservative rabbis will agree to begin the process in such a situation, with the anticipation that the original motivation will be deepened as the process proceeds. In the final analysis, the conversion will be completed only when both prospective convert and rabbi are convinced that a deep and sincere appreciation of Judaism has been reached.

The actual conversion process will begin with an extended period of instruction. The actual length of time will vary between six months and a year. The prospective convert, and the Jewish partner, will be expected to attend the classes regularly; they will be expected to study and prepare for them.

The classes can be in large, formally organized, groups; in smaller groups; or even private lessons. Such decisions are often dependent on the availability of resources as well as on a joint decision of the prospective convert and the rabbi.

Although details of the curriculum may vary from rabbi to rabbi, prospective converts and their partners can expect to learn Hebrew reading, some Jewish history, fundamentals of Jewish belief and practice, liturgical skills, and basic theology. They should also expect to begin slowly adopting the types of practices that will be expected of both of them after the conversion has been completed: regular attendance at Sabbath services, beginning the observance of the dietary laws, observance of the holidays.

When the period of instruction has come to an end and the rabbi is satisfied that the conversion may be completed, the rituals of conversion will be performed. Uncircumcised males will have to have a circumcision. The rabbi will arrange for this to be done in accordance with the dictates of Jewish law. If the male has already been circumcised medically, the ritual performed is called *hatafat dam brit*. In this ritual, a small drop of blood is let from the penis as a symbolic act of ritual (as opposed to medical) circumcision.

The two final ceremonies pertain to both men and women; they are immersion in a ritual bath, and the acceptance of the obligations of Jewish tradition and law before a Jewish court. The rabbi will make all of the arrangements for the court and for the use of the ritual bath. Very often (although not always) the court will interview the candidate at the *mikvah* (the ritual bath). The candidate will then immerse in the *mikvah* immediately after the interview.

In the case of a male who has had to undergo an actual circumcision, the final two steps will await healing. Where only *hatafat dam brit* is required, it will often take place at the *mikvah* itself, so that all three of the rituals will be accomplished at the same time.

Following the convert's immersion, he or she is officially inducted into the Jewish people, usually in the presence of the court, and given a Hebrew name. This formal induction may take place at the *mikvah*, but more often is likely to take place at a synagogue.

Following the completion of the conversion ceremony, the convert is considered a Jew for all matters, and the conversion is considered irrevocable in Jewish law. It is not contingent on the marriage of the convert to his/her intended spouse. Even if the marriage fails to take place, the conversion remains valid and binding. If the marriage takes place and is terminated through divorce, this conversion remains valid and binding. Once completed, a conversion is forever.

Among the most difficult of the issues that will have to be worked out carefully before completing the conversion is the matter of the nature of the on-going relationship with the non-Jewish parents of the convert to Judaism. Clearly, the bonds of love and blood that existed before the conversion cannot be severed, nor should they be; but, since the conversion marks a new spiritual birth and the adoption of a new and different religion from that of the non-Jewish parents, certain types of interaction may be inadvisable. These issues must be addressed forthrightly by the couple, the rabbi, and the families. This difficult element of conversion was recognized by the *midrash* which asserts: "The Holy One, blessed be He, loves proselytes exceedingly. We likewise should show favor to the proselyte who left his family, his ancestral house, his people, and all the gentile peoples of the world, and came to us. He therefore deserves special protection."

CONTACT: Committee on Jewish Law and Standards
Rabbinical Assembly of America
3080 Broadway
New York, New York 10027
(212) 678–8060

Contact your local board of rabbis, or the Rabbinical Assembly, for the names of Conservative rabbis in your area.